The Limits to Union

Law, Meaning, and Violence

The scope of Law, Meaning, and Violence is defined by the wide-ranging scholarly debates signaled by each of the words in the title. Those debates have taken place among and between lawyers, anthropologists, political theorists, sociologists, and historians, as well as literary and cultural critics. This series is intended to recognize the importance of such ongoing conversations about law, meaning, and violence as well as to encourage and further them.

Series Editors: Martha Minow, Harvard Law School
                       Elaine Scarry, Harvard University
                       Austin Sarat, Amherst College

Narrative, Violence, and the Law: The Essays of Robert Cover,
edited by Martha Minow, Michael Ryan, and Austin Sarat

Narrative, Authority, and Law, by Robin West

The Possibility of Popular Justice: A Case Study of Community Mediation in the United States, edited by Sally Engle Merry and Neal Milner

Legal Modernism, by David Luban

Surveillance, Privacy, and the Law: Employee Drug Testing and the Politics of Social Control, by John Gilliom

Lives of Lawyers: Journeys in the Organizations of Practice, by Michael J. Kelly

Unleashing Rights: Law, Meaning, and the Animal Rights Movement, by Helena Silverstein

Law Stories, edited by Gary Bellow and Martha Minow

The Powers That Punish: Prison and Politics in the Era of the "Big House," 1920–1955, by Charles Bright

Law and the Postmodern Mind: Essays on Psychoanalysis and Jurisprudence, edited by Peter Goodrich and David Gray Carlson

Russia's Legal Fictions, by Harriet Murav

Strangers to the Law: Gay People on Trial, by Lisa Keen and Suzanne B. Goldberg

Butterfly, the Bride: Essays on Law, Narrative, and the Family, by Carol Weisbrod

The Politics of Community Policing: Rearranging the Power to Punish, by William Lyons

Laws of the Postcolonial, edited by Eve Darian-Smith and Peter Fitzpatrick

Whispered Consolations: Law and Narrative in African American Life, by Jon-Christian Suggs

Bad Boys: Public Schools in the Making of Black Masculinity, by Ann Arnett Ferguson

Pain, Death, and the Law, edited by Austin Sarat

The Limits to Union: Same-Sex Marriage and the Politics of Civil Rights, by Jonathan Goldberg-Hiller

The Limits to Union

Same-Sex Marriage and the
Politics of Civil Rights

JONATHAN GOLDBERG-HILLER

Ann Arbor

THE UNIVERSITY OF MICHIGAN PRESS

2005   2004   2003   2002   4   3   2   1

A CIP catalog record for this book is available from the British Library.

Library of Congress Cataloging-in-Publication Data

Goldberg-Hiller, Jonathan, 1958–
    The limits to union : same-sex marriage and the politics of civil
rights / Jonathan Goldberg-Hiller.
       p.   cm. — (Law, meaning, and violence)
    Includes bibliographical references and index.
    ISBN 0-472-11223-6 (cloth : acid-free paper)
    1. Same-sex marriage—United States.   2. Same-sex marriage—Law
and legislation—United States.   3. Gay rights—United States.
4. United States—Politics and government—1993–2001.   5. United
States—Social policy—1993–   I. Title.   II. Series.

HQ1034.U5 G65   2002
306.84'8—dc21   2001004251

For Sandy

Contents

Acknowledgments

I have gained many worthwhile debts as this book has been written. Repayment must begin with some public acknowledgment and sincere thanks. My appreciation is extended to the many activists who gave me their time, sitting for interviews and helping me understand their fears, hopes, and expectations. Their names are too numerous to list here, but they can be found in the footnotes. Particular mention needs to be given to David Smith of the Human Rights Campaign, to Linda Rosehill, and to Barbara Ankersmit for their kind permission to examine polling data and public relations materials that guided the campaign for same-sex marriage in Hawai'i.

I am also grateful to the many scholars who have read earlier drafts and chapters of this book and given me invaluable counsel. In order of the alphabet, I wish to thank Julia Adams, Kathy Ferguson, Alexandra French, Shelley Gavigan, Manfred Henningsen, Didi Herman, Kaleikoa Ka'eo, S. Krishna, Neal Milner, Shane Phelan, Sandy Schram, Mike Shapiro, Noenoe Silva, Nevzat Soguk, Carl Stychin, Phyllis Turnbull, and several anonymous readers. Their suggestions have been important to the shape of this book, although as author I take full responsibility for what it says. A special acknowledgment and thank-you goes to Austin Sarat, whose own enthusiasm for my project was a frequent inspiration. My gratitude is also due Jeremy Shine and Charles Myers, who have been unparalleled editors.

Previous aspects of this research have been published in *Social and Legal Studies;* in *Studies in Law, Politics, and Society;* in *Sexuality in the Legal Arena,* edited by Didi Herman and Carl Stychin (London: Athlone Press, 2000); in *Laboring for Rights: A Global Perspective on Union Response to Sexual Diversity,* edited by Gerald Hunt (Philadelphia: Temple University Press, 1999); and in *Tales of the State,* edited by Sanford F. Schram and Philip T. Neisser (Lanham, Md.: Rowman and Littlefield,

1997). I thank these publishers and editors for permission to use this material in this book.

Finally, I wish to acknowledge the University of Hawai'i Department of Political Science and its inspirational faculty, graduate students, and staff. As a home in which to study critical theories, to teach, and to write, no ka oi.

Chapter 1

A Trip to the "Alter"

In November 1998, 69 percent of the voters in Hawai'i approved an amendment to the state constitution to permit the legislature "to reserve marriage to opposite-sex couples." Coming five years after the Hawai'i Supreme Court, in *Baehr v. Lewin*,[1] held for the first time that same-sex marriage was a matter of equal protection law, and two years after the state lost its legal defense of "traditional marriage" on remand, the hard-fought vote capped a political uprising against same-sex marriage that tore through the nation and reverberated around the world. Although not one legally recognized marriage between two men or two women existed, the prospect of same-sex marriage—and gay rights more generally—has antagonized electorates and legislatures in all fifty states, fueled constitutional amendments to remove civil rights protections, and provoked the federal Defense of Marriage Act,[2] which authorizes the nonrecognition of same-sex matrimony. This movement and countermovement has reworked fundamental American ideals about law, democracy, and citizenship. This politics of the rights of gays and lesbians is only tangentially about the gay body and gay practice; by implicating the place of courts and the limits of legal discourse, same-sex marriage operates as a transformative metonym for the body politic. The manner in which civil rights have been challenged by this reaction and the means by which they inform and reform the mentalities of American governance is the terrain investigated by this book.

Disputing about Courts

The 1998 amendment to the Hawai'i constitution overshadowed another that was passed in Alaska on the same day by an identical lopsided margin.[3] Both votes were local referenda on the extension of civil rights protection to lesbians and gays, but it was the Hawai'i case with its sinuous and protracted struggles that mobilized the concern and interest of national civil rights and religious organizations, and politicians of all stars and stripes. The Hawai'i case began in 1990 when two lesbian couples and one gay couple[4] applied for marriage licenses from the department of health. Although these six people acted on their own initiative, similar uncoordinated, dispersed efforts to challenge marriage laws were taking place in other states, with a golden national payoff: the first state to grant rights would open the door for lesbians and gays throughout the United States, who could rely upon constitutional guarantees that contracts in one state would be given "full faith and credit"[5] in any other.

Similar efforts in other states had been rebuffed as early as the 1970s.[6] There were, thus, dashed hopes but little surprise when the Hawai'i attorney general, secure in these earlier precedents, denied the applications for marriage licenses.

Joined by Dan Foley, a local civil rights attorney, the three couples sued in state circuit court, alleging violations of their rights of privacy and equal protection. At trial in 1991, the court case was dismissed by Judge Robert Klein, who ruled, after considering equal protection arguments, that same-sex couples did not enjoy a right to marry. Foley appealed, and in May 1993, the state supreme court in *Baehr* made the first national ruling that rejection of these marriage applications was unconstitutional gender discrimination absent a showing of compelling state interest. The state immediately filed a motion for reconsideration, citing the public interest in restricting marriage to opposite-sex couples as a means to uphold moral values and protect children, but the supreme court rejected the motion and remanded the case for a trial in the circuit court to determine whether such an interest could be adequately asserted.

The aftershock of the supreme court's decision trembled throughout Hawai'i and headed for the mainland like a slowly building tidal wave. Rightly believing the standard of a compelling state interest could not be met, legislators concerned about the potential fiscal, political, moral, and social impacts of the ruling sought to mold public opinion into opposition to same-sex marriage and resistance to the role of courts in extending civil rights protections and social policy. In a series of hearings held in the fall of 1993, just months after the *Baehr* ruling, testimony from hundreds of citizens on all islands was heard by a circuit-riding house Judiciary Committee in anticipation of legislative action to derail the case. Although the passionate testimony was mixed in its support for, and opposition to, court-sanctioned same-sex marriage, the house leadership was firmly opposed and produced legislation in the spring of 1994 declaring procreation to be the basis of the marriage laws (a position purged from the law books by the same body in 1984 as prejudicial against the handicapped, the elderly, and others). The new legislation declared "that Hawai'i's marriage licensing laws were originally and are presently intended to apply only to male-female couples, not same-sex couples." In addition, the law, signed by the governor, declared the supreme court's decision "essentially one of policy, thereby rendering it inappropriate for judicial response."[7] In exchange for the support of the more progressive senate for the legislation, a constitutional amendment reinforcing this position was not brought up for a vote.

Uncertain of the effect of the new statutory language and spurred on by conservative religious groups who were aroused by the first significant opportunity for political mobilization by conservatives in the state's history, the legislature created a Commission on Sexual Orientation and the Law to advise it on public policy, mandating two seats for Mormon and Catholic representatives. The makeup of the commission was successfully challenged in court on First Amendment grounds, and a newly constituted board purged of its official religious representatives began to take testimony in the fall of 1995. With two conservatives dissenting, the commission ultimately recommended five-to-two that no further interference with the *Baehr* case be contemplated and that, as an alternative, a comprehensive domestic partnership statute be created to give same-sex couples most of the benefits of marriage. Conservatives reacted vigorously against the commission report, agitating for a political end to the case before the court trial—scheduled for the fall of 1996—would place another legal support in the foundation for same-sex marriage. Again, conservatives demanded a constitutional amendment to limit marriage to opposite-sex couples. Emotional hearings on an amendment were held by the senate (where support for it was uncertain), which again drew hundreds of citizens testifying for and against same-sex marriages. Amid heavy lobbying by groups for all sides, the senate remained deadlocked, rejecting a midnight attempt to revive the amendment on the last day of the session.

When the circuit court trial finally began in September 1996, marriage law remained substantially unchanged since the *Baehr* decision. The judge, Kevin Chang, would ultimately disappoint opponents of same-sex marriage with his ruling that rejected every argument made by the state in behalf of restricting access to marriage. But before the trial began, Congress had moved quickly to forestall unwanted national ramifications of the Hawai'i decision. The Defense of Marriage Act was passed in four months from the time it was introduced in the House—in spite of the summer recess. Final approval by the Senate was timed to coincide with the opening day of the Hawai'i trial, September 10. DOMA was signed by President Clinton days later, three months before the Hawai'i judge handed down his ruling.

Despite the unequivocal nature of the Hawai'i trial court's decision, which legalized same-sex marriage, Judge Chang allowed the state's motion for a stay pending another appeal to the same supreme court, which had issued the original *Baehr* ruling. As the ultimate judicial outcome was no longer in doubt, opponents doubled their efforts to stop the case. With public focus high, several longtime legislators, marked (sometimes unfoundedly) as supporters of same-sex marriage by their challengers, were thrown out of office in the November 1996 elections. Fearful of more electoral carnage, legislators held hearings again in 1997, and once more hundreds of people presented oral and written testimony. Added into the legislative mix for the first time were conservative groups that brought together religious and lay activists and many citizens who had never before been involved in social politics and were wary of both legislative and judicial handling of same-sex marriage. This grassroots campaign was kicked off by a five-thousand-person rally at the state capitol in January 1997, the largest political rally Hawai'i had seen since statehood. No longer able to resist the ferment of opposition, the senate finally agreed to amendment language in exchange for the house's support for the country's most comprehensive domestic partnership legislation. Bowing to concerns that the political process was no longer working in the interest of popular forces and the desires by some activists to have a second bite at the marriage issue, the legislature also authorized a ballot measure calling for a constitutional convention. The siren song of same-sex marriage saturated Hawai'i politics—including media time and fund-raising—throughout 1997 and 1998 until the November election.

What is true for Hawai'i—social iconoclasm and independence, a history of political stability, and insularity—is also true of Alaska. In 1994, inspired by the *Baehr* decision, two Alaska men filed for a marriage license in their home state. Although Alaska authorities rejected the demand on the authority of a previous ruling that Alaska's statutory scheme did not contemplate same-sex marriage, a court in February 1998 ruled that Jay Brause and his partner were entitled to a marriage license unless the state could show compelling reasons at trial to deny equal protection.[8] In an opinion that seemed to consciously search for a judicial antidote to the anticourt politics attendant on the *Baehr* decision in Hawai'i, circuit court judge Peter Michalski strove to justify same-sex marriage as an inevitable consequence of the individual right to choose one's life partner. Within months, the Alaska legislature proposed an amendment for the fall ballot similar in wording to the Hawai'i amendment designed to limit court jurisdiction.[9]

Also inspired by the Hawai'i case, three same-sex couples in Vermont who had been denied marriage licenses sued for relief in the summer of 1997. The trial judge, Linda Levitt, agreed with the state's arguments that the language of "bride" and "groom" in the statutes was evidence of legislative intent to limit marriage to couples of the opposite sex, and she dismissed the case.[10] The plaintiffs appealed. Ten days after the Hawai'i Supreme Court issued its final ruling in *Baehr* that the 1998 amendment had removed its jurisdiction over marriage and further signaled its unwillingness to resurrect the constitutional equal protection principles it had enunciated in 1993,[11] the Vermont Supreme Court revived the *Baehr* template and ruled that same-sex couples are entitled to "the common benefit, protection, and security that Vermont law provides opposite-sex married couples."[12] Whether common benefit requires marriage or some other "equivalent" legal status was a question left by the court to the legislature in cognizance of the popular reaction against judicial activism in Hawai'i and Alaska, as well as the "political caldron"[13] stirred by the marriage rulings that have led thirty-three states to ban same-sex marriage since 1995.[14] The Vermont legislature ultimately opted, in the early months of 2000, for the creation of a "civil union" for lesbians and gays. Signed into law on April 26 by Governor Howard Dean, the legislation went further than any other state law in recognizing same-sex partnerships.

But seven years after the Hawai'i court had ruled that marriage was a matter of equal protection, civil union stands as an ambiguous sign for the progress of civil rights. Unlike marriage, civil union lacks portability outside of Vermont and is unlikely to affect federal rights and duties. As a sign of equality, civil union thus appears in some light as an atavism, a throwback to the separate-but-equal status rejected in

Brown v. Board of Education (1954). Many commentators agree with
Andrew Sullivan (2000) that civil union for gays and lesbians "is an act
of pure stigmatization." Yet, in its recognition of the cloyingly divisive
political atmosphere that has targeted courts for their support for gay
and lesbian rights, it is a thoroughly contemporary decision, marking
the denouement of civil rights.

Why have the idea of same-sex marriage and the struggles over its
legalization in Hawai'i antagonized so many so quickly? And how has
this politics produced a willingness on the part of courts in Hawai'i and
Vermont to retreat from a post-*Brown* commitment to equality without
separate legal status? Popular opposition to same-sex marriage has
been variously voiced as a compelling matter of tradition, religious
teaching, and natural law. For the Mormon Church, which has spent
millions of dollars to thwart same-sex marriage, "This issue has nothing to do with civil rights. For men to marry men, or women to marry
women, is a moral wrong."[15] For others, it "is not about civil rights. It is
about the survival of a civilization."[16] Despite these protestations
against the significance of civil rights to the same-sex marriage issue,
rights seem to have everything to do with it.

Indeed, it is surprising from the various sources of authority
invoked by the guardians of traditional marriage that marriage policy
itself is not more fully on trial. One activist in Hawai'i complained
against this oddity by pointing out that "The CONVICTED felons in our
State penitentiary are able to marry and receive ALL the benefits of marriage, even while they are still in prison. Why am I, a law-abiding and
taxpaying citizen, not able to have the rights that a convicted felon
has?"[17] The line drawn at same-sex marriage seems especially curious
considering the degree of toleration acceded the right to marry. As
M. D. A. Freeman has noted,

> We allow murderers and rapists (even those who have murdered
> or raped previous spouses) to marry; we allow pedophiles and
> child molesters to marry. We do not stop child abusers or . . . "dead
> beat dads" . . . from marrying. Sadists, masochists and fetishists
> may marry and are not obliged to choose partners with similar
> inclinations. People who are HIV-infected or suffer from AIDS are
> allowed to marry. There is special legislation to facilitate death-bed
> marriages. Transvestites may marry (that the groom is wearing a
> bridal dress is no impediment to marriage). And transsexuals may

marry [in some states] so long as they marry someone of the other gender from that which they themselves were born in: two "women" may thus marry if one of them was born a man. Indeed, two transsexuals may marry, provided one was born a boy, the other a girl. . . . [T]here are furthermore no laws requiring persons wishing to marry to prove that they are heterosexual: homosexual men may marry women and lesbian women may marry men (and, indeed, do). (1999, 1)

Public acquiescence to these potentially objectionable unions tacitly sanctions the Supreme Court's recognition in 1967 of the liberty to marry as "essential to the orderly pursuit of happiness" and "one of the 'basic civil rights of man.'"[18] The recognition of marriage as a vital civil right, alongside the declining tendency to criminalize sodomy[19] and the growing tolerance for diverse living arrangements, makes the public rejection of same-sex marriage seem all the more a significant limit in need of explanation and comprehension.

I argue in this book that the political majorities aligned against same-sex marriage should be understood as a consequence of two interlocking movements that together reveal the changing character of rights discourse. The first is a reaction against the fast-growing visibility of gays and lesbians and the forms of knowledge and political presentation of the self under which the demand for civil rights has been made. This has created a responsive set of political strategies that use lesbian and gay identities and political claims as an "alter" against which majorities have realized their opposing interests. If the challenge by lesbians and gays for recognition and legal protection is the underlying motivation for these majorities, it is not in itself sufficient to account for such an energetic reaction against same-sex marriage. I explore a second, related reason for the vitality of this politics. The rhetorical tactics used to retain the privilege of marriage for nongays have combined formerly diverse, contradictory, and sometimes dormant American discourses into mutual coherence, amplifying their effects. This hybrid political language has sampled from liberal and nonliberal political ideologies, neoliberal economic notions, nationalist ideas of political space, religious morality, themes of civilization, and even—indeed, especially—from the discourse of civil rights. Cobbled together, these discourses aid the constitution of new identities capable of building majorities and driving them to the polls in opposition to courts and rights-based movements. The organization of political power that is focused through the lens of opposition to same-sex marriage, more than just defensive of traditional hierarchies and privileges challenged by sexual minorities, has projected a new and compelling American sovereignty with important consequences for our understanding of law and civil rights.

While an emphasis on the same-sex marriage debates as public culture will tend to miss much of the private vitriol and religious vilification that have underscored recent opposition to lesbian and gay rights in the United States (see Herman 1997), it provides a chance to explore the political forces that bowdlerize these debates, the character of, and opportunities opened by, rights talk amid massive public opposition, and the political field of alliance and majority formation, all tasks that this book takes up. Understanding the ways civil rights have been deployed in these public debates does not necessitate a choice between the moral good or utilitarian ill of same-sex marriage, nor need it lead to a normative argument about how liberalism can best be saved from its emerging illiberal counterparts, issues that have likewise been removed to the background of this narrative. Nevertheless, my interest in this study remains critical. As Foucault reminds us, one "does not [have] to be 'for' or 'against' the Enlightenment" (1984, 43) in the interest of discovering where the possibilities of freedom remain to be found today. In order to trace the opportunities revealed and foreclosed in the same-sex marriage controversy, I study public discourses about rights and assess their consequence for the identities and tactics of the social movements involved in the same-sex marriage debates that have taken place in Hawai'i and elsewhere. As a national and local politics linking marriage for some to the status of citizenship, this is a multifaceted study of the limits to union.

A New American Sovereignty

The reaction against same-sex marriage and other rights for lesbians and gays has been depicted as a long-simmering culture war with three broad fronts: attacks on state programs aiding group empowerment, restaffing of the judiciary with personnel less supportive of minority rights, and direct referenda asserting the interest of the "people" above the civil rights of minorities.[20] Imagined severally as a

moral crusade, reassertion of the traditional, standing up for civilization, or defending and reinforcing domestic and international security,
the inchoate culture war is nonetheless confronted with a singular
problematic: the constitution of a majoritarian political identity committed to social, political, cultural, and economic change. Facilitating
the creation of common cause among religious conservatives, neolib-
erals, and the generally intolerant and socially disgruntled has been a
language of sovereign right and entitlement. Sovereignty long pre-
dates this political coalition but has morphed along with it. In democratic political discourse, sovereignty is often seen to contour the shad-
ows of more animating modern political inventions: the nation-state,
the rule of law, the autonomous and rationally self-interested individual, the historical career of civilization. What is novel today is that sovereignty is increasingly articulated as an autonomous discourse able to
realign democratic institutions, remake social commitments, anneal
political memories, and unify new majority identities. Lesbian and gay
demands for civil rights have increasingly bumped up against the language of sovereignty.

Democratic sovereignty has usually been thought synonymous, or
at least coterminous, with the rule of law and the state. This modern
genealogy derives from the defeat of the divine right of kings (Morgan
1988, 24ff.), orienting us toward the sanctity of autonomous individuals, the will of political majorities, and a singular and exclusive source
of political power—a diversity within unity represented by a constitution—to which both political and legal spheres must ultimately answer.
This sovereign logic is enshrined in one form of celebrated contemporary constitutional culture: "Beginning with the words, 'We the People,' the Constitution is a collective representation because it signifies
the unified body of the nation, fusing that nation into a single text in
which all members can find themselves represented" (Levin 1999, 2).
Nonetheless, the very form of this representation—especially the
abstractions of individual autonomy and the assumptions of unity supporting a constitutional nation—tends to work against new demands
for inclusion by particular claimants, making prominent an alternative
form of American constitutional culture: the spectacle of popular limitations to the universal (see Smith 1997).

The same-sex marriage debates draw their energy from this alternative model made possible by the political dissociation of sovereignty,
law, state, and nation. The defense of sovereignty raised against the

intrusion of civil rights for same-sex partnerships is projected by political majorities as one means of realizing that security that state and
government are expected to provide, as well as defining the meaning of
rule that law and civil rights are understood to enforce. Pulled loose
from its moorings in the state and delaminated from the rule of law, the
articulation of sovereignty can be used to create new identities, redirect
state actors, instruct judges, and frustrate those asking for acknowledgment of their full rights of citizenship.

Distinguishing sovereignty from its common association with
state, nation, and law helps make sense of several historical and philosophical problems. The first is that citizenship has long been an unfin-
ished category. In the United States, this incompleteness is recognized
in the constitutional impediments to democratic participation of slaves
and later people of color, women, workers, the indigenous, and resident aliens. Despite the common progressive narratives of expansion of
political opportunities, many today—such as lesbians and gays—assert
identities that are not fully recognized in the law, limiting democratic
participation.

If citizenship is a limited category, so, too, is the nation that
famously has been given problematic status by Anderson as an "imagined political community . . . imagined as both inherently limited and
sovereign" (1983, 15). What limits the nation is, in part, that which con-
tributes to the power of this imagination, and the potential dissociation
of national boundary and sovereign authority asserts a powerful ideological force in this regard. As Stychin has argued, "The boundaries of
nations and nation states are rarely identical, but the belief that they
should be has conveniently served as the basis for dominance by some
national groups at the expense of others and for the construction of
minorities as outside of the nation *and* the nation state" (1998, 3). In the
case of America, this general problem of fixing boundaries is exaggerated by the weakness of the usual categories of national history. Without a strong tradition of class conflict, or a common origin of the settler
community, lacking a full accounting of indigenous sovereignty and a
bounded space unperturbed by an expanding frontier, there is no foundational referent for "America." As Campbell has argued, "if all states
are 'imagined communities,' devoid of ontological being apart from the
many and varied practices which constitute their reality, then America
is the imagined community *par excellence*" (1992, 105).

The imaginary and sovereign boundaries of nation-states as much as nations-as-peoples continue to be flexed and tested by geopolitical and economic changes long after the frontiers have been closed and historical memories have been fixed. International markets have given rise to powerful global corporations and significant transnational flows of capital rivaling the economic resources of many smaller countries. While rivals in size, these same markets have also revalued the meanings of national security around which sovereign borders have been drawn. Tourism, for example, has enabled border crossing to shift meaning from a danger to state security to the enhancement of economic well-being of the commodified state. This holds important implications for internal threats to security, as once-dominated cultural minorities are increasingly marketed as exotic attractions or economically desirable customers (Alexander 1994; Evans 1993; Hennessy 1995). At the same time, globalization has accelerated social change, altering on the one hand the forms of self-identification, social aspiration, and demands for inclusion that some excluded groups, such as indigenous peoples and social movements, can make, and, on the other hand, forcing migrants and refugees to cross borders and challenge national imaginaries (Soguk 1999). Economic changes have also established new forms of political authority that, in the case of the European Union, create multinational opportunities for reasserting legal rights, identities, and international imaginaries that confront traditional notions of state sovereignty (Darian-Smith 1995, 1999; Stychin 1999). All these factors have tended to dissociate the representational strategies around which nation, state, and sovereignty are imagined and articulated.

What, then, is unique about the representation of sovereignty? Marx observed in *The Eighteenth Brumaire* that the origins of modern democratic sovereignty and the consolidation of bourgeois power in nineteenth-century France were yoked to a hierarchical dichotomy separating *security,* voiced in the recurrent theme of "property, family, religion, order," from *anarchy,* understood primarily as socialism and communism (Marx 1963). Property signifies the realm of the sovereign individual whose self-ownership justifies the ownership of things (Locke 1963) or whose things guarantee self-possession and subjectivity (Hegel 1967), secured within wider institutions of society, government, thought, and order, demonstrating the essential linkage—if not overlap—between sovereignty writ small and democratic, political sovereignty. Today, the dangers of anarchy that Marx noted are represented less by the body of the proletariat that took aim at property and bourgeois individuality, than in the accelerating political and social dynamics of modern capitalism, and the bodies representing these threats to economic and political order. Nevertheless, both the particularities of the construction of sovereignty and the rhetorical form of the dichotomy between sovereignty and anarchy suggest a remarkable consistency.

Consider the case of the family that in the same-sex marriage debates has once again become a significant rallying cry for political order. The conservative politics of family values entails a particular forgetting of the wild diversity of forms in which familial relations have been lived and sanctioned in the past in order to create the image of a stable, naturalized, and timeless social institution (see Brown 1995a, 206ff.; Nicholson 1997; Shapiro 2001). What remains historically constant, as McClintock (1995) reminds us, is that the family has served as a handy naturalizing metaphor for hierarchy, generalizing the subordination of woman to man and child to adult into the ordering of social difference—what she calls a naturalized "hierarchy within unity" (45). As she and other postcolonial theorists have remarked, family rhetoric and the sovereign imagination that it upholds have particular affinities to the discourses of civilization and Christianity that promise security, progress, and salvation on the renunciation of savage sexual customs, and the institutionalization of monogamy and patriarchy (see Merry 1998, 2000). Imagining sovereignty in the terms of the family legitimates a form of order in which social differences have their place.

The latent tensions of a "hierarchy within unity" in the family prevent a sovereign politics of family values from reaching any definitive closure. Feminists have argued that patriarchal power is not entirely contained by profamily political rhetoric. De Beauvoir (1953), for example, argued for the importance of autonomy within the private sphere, what she called a "precarious sovereignty" enjoyed by women despite the identification of sovereignty with male privilege. As Hoffman (1998, 65ff.) has noted, this idea of a precarious sovereignty endorses the notion of the sovereignty of self-control within the private realm that lies alongside a hierarchical notion of state sovereignty. Minow has shown how women used the social and legal assumption of their caregiving roles adhering to this private realm to establish a "shadow government" based on imputed feminine norms that later permitted the exercise of power within the public sphere (1985, 837ff.). In like manner, gays and lesbians, disadvantaged by heterosexual family rhetoric, have been setting up same-sex marriages, increasingly solemnized by churches and synagogues and informally recognized by some employers, without recourse to state sanction. Their attempts to move out from this shadow government into public acceptance have obviously hit a sore public nerve, suggesting the importance of boundaries between the sovereignty of private autonomy and its universal form.

Boundary maintenance is challenged by more than shadow governments. Evolving economic relations such as the extermination of the family wage, the advent of flexible production, and the commodification of domestic work have encouraged the family to be reimagined away from the nuclear forms associated with industrial capitalism and now articulated in the conservative rhetoric of family values (see Casey 1995; D'Emilio 1983; Gramsci 1971, 296ff.; Stacey 1996). Seemingly agent-less mechanisms of social change, economic processes have proved to be poorer political targets than social movements and the culture industries that embrace social difference. Identifying new familial forms with more visible targets permits inchoate concerns over economic uncertainty, the meaning of progress, and even civilization to reinforce dominant norms by sharpening lines of social cleavage.

Nietzsche's notion of *ressentiment* as an affect of suffering that blames particular groups in order to assuage the hurt of poor fortune seems particularly apt to explain this dynamic. Connolly observes that, fueled by *ressentiment*, identity increasingly "requires difference in order to be and converts difference into otherness in order to secure its own self-certainty" (1991, 64). In an important sense, the political identity of citizenship that assumes this logic emerges as gendered and sexualized: "citizenship is about virility, that is, active defense of that which is threatened, rather than being the victim of threat" (Phelan 1999, 73). Herman (1997) and Patton (1995, 1997, 1998) have demonstrated that the Christian Right has increasingly become focused on gays, and to a lesser extent lesbians, as an alter against which it has clarified its message of Christian identity, cultural cleansing, and national renewal. Stychin (1998) has furthered this exploration of sexuality as a normalizing discourse and demonstrated the implications of family rhetoric for nationalism. Across numerous case studies he has shown that the homosexual body has become a marker in terms often applied to the feminine: as weakness unbefitting nationhood, and as a lack of control and subversion threatening order and security (see also Moran

1991). The demands for marriage and for recognition are a powerful combination that, for many, makes homosexuality a significant threat to political sovereignty.

If sovereignty is still imagined on the terrain of family, property, religion, and order, it also has maintained a consistent rhetorical form. This form, understood as the dichotomy between sovereignty and anarchy, has been shown by scholars critical of the unreflective traditions of international relations to require the discursive production of "insecurity" as much as the security supposedly guaranteed by sovereign states (e.g., Ashley 1988; Campbell 1992; Weldes et al. 1999). I argue in this book that the primary site for this articulation is not necessarily the state as is commonly presumed, but is often also the "people" differentiating itself from state procedures and institutions, particularly the rules of law. What distinguishes sovereignty from the state is a particular form of subjectivity and rationality with no essential connection to the legitimated violence of the state or the justice guaranteed by law. As Ashley sees it,

> The sign of "sovereignty" betokens a rational identity: a homogeneous and continuous presence that is hierarchically ordered, that has a unique centre of decision presiding over a coherent "self," and that is demarcated from, and in opposition to, an external domain of difference and change that resists assimilation to its identical being. . . . The sign of "anarchy" betokens this residual external domain: an aleatory domain characterised by difference and discontinuity, contingency and ambiguity, that can be known only for its lack of the coherent truth and meaning expressed by a sovereign presence. [Sovereignty is invoked] as an originary voice, a foundational source of truth and meaning . . . that makes it possible to discipline the understanding of ambiguous events and impose a distinction . . . between what can be represented as rational and meaningful (because it can be assimilated to a sovereign principle of interpretation) and what must count as external, dangerous, and anarchic. (1988, 230)

From this perspective, the discourse of sovereignty draws attention to its grounded epistemology, opposing itself to legal logic, state procedure, and minority political demands through claims that each violates the bulwark of common sense and natural hierarchy. As a unifying form of interpretation, sovereignty stands against anarchy in the guise of the body politic, an organic whole threatened by dissociation, plural meaning, and practice. "The trope of the body politic works powerfully to transform contests within society into attacks on society" (Phelan 1999, 73).

The image of the body politic has important implications for the public sphere in which the sovereign voice is articulated (Habermas 1989). Warner has suggested that the body politic is persuasive to the extent that it enacts a "utopian universality" in which "what you say will carry force not because of who you are but despite who you are" (1992, 382). For this reason, sectarian religious sentiments that have exercised some recent antirights activism are nonetheless publicly suppressed in favor of more universalist positions. Nonetheless, this does not mean that all differences are restrained. Women, gays, people of color—all those who are figured as passionate more than rational—are marked with a "surplus corporeality" (Berlant 1997) that softens sovereign boundaries through excess or weakness, making them vulnerable to penetration (Bordo 1993; Butler 1990; Phelan 1999). As Warner argues,

> The ability to abstract oneself in public discussion has always been an unequally available resource. Individuals have to have specific rhetorics of disincorporation; they are not simply rendered bodiless by exercising reason. . . . The subject who could master this rhetoric in the bourgeois public sphere was implicitly, even explicitly, white, male, literate, and propertied. These traits could go unmarked, even grammatically, while other features of bodies could only be acknowledged in discourse as the humiliating positivity of the particular. (1992, 382)

One consequent logic of the public sphere has been silence, not just about those whose positivity is marked by difference, but also as a privilege of those whose unmarked presence can go without saying. The enforcement of silence in this latter form, as I show in the chapters that follow, is one paradoxical aspect of the public articulation of sovereignty in the debates over same-sex marriage. Of course, the democratic sovereign, recognizing itself as political majority, is necessarily more inclusive than the unmarked bodies protected by this silence. Thus, some "particular" bodies are symbolically remarked as valuable through commodification, or integrable due to sanctioned political

memory, acceptable lifestyle, or protected legal status, and conceptually united through common consumption of public symbols and figures (celebrity), as well as antipathy and anxiety toward those—especially lesbians and gays—whose bodies and practices are not permitted
to conform to the markings of publicity and the naturalized hierarchies
of sovereignty.

I have argued that sovereignty takes the rhetorical and representational form of rationality and publicity with a logic incidental to that of
the state. I have also suggested that the substantive concerns and forms
of sovereignty have an enduring history, but I do not want to treat sovereignty in this book in the same timeless, ahistorical fashion in which
it is often articulated by its partisans. My interest in this concept is not
designed to abstract sovereignty from its history, but, contrariwise, to
show how it is modulated by subtle shifts in economic reason and the
political dynamics of group demands, how as a trope it reinforces political rule and also dissolves extant forms of rule in favor of other types
of authority. Perhaps nowhere has the dissociation between state and
sovereign become so visible in recent years as in contemporary political
conflicts pitting electorates against civil rights.[21] The classical liberal
contractarian theorists saw law and rights as coterminous with state
authority since, in their narrative, it was a collectivity of self-sovereign
individuals who first banded together in the interest of security for
their persons and their property to create a government.[22] Civil rights
for women, people of color, and others have become one set of markers
for those whose inclusion in this original compact was incomplete or
disregarded, and whose later struggles for inclusion have been deemed
worthy and compatible with collective well-being.

In a logic similar to that of the modern public sphere, civil rights
operate as a sign of inclusion only to the extent that they continue to
mark particular bodies as capable of generality, of remaining, in Marx's
words, "an imaginary participant in an imaginary sovereignty . . . filled
with an unreal universality" (1977b, 46). Wendy Brown sees this paradox as inherent in liberalism.

> [T]he latent conflict in liberalism between universal representation
> and individualism remains latent, remains unpoliticized, as long
> as differential powers in civil society remain naturalized, as long
> as the "I" remains politically unarticulated, as long as it is willing
> to have its freedom represented abstractly, in effect, to subordinate

> its "I-ness" to the abstract "we" represented by the universal com-
> munity. (1995b, 203; see also Danielsen and Engle 1995, xiv ff.)

Where the imagination or naturalization of generality fails, or where this is not allowed to occur, the claims of civil rights as a marker for inclusion become a palpable threat to sovereign authority. To no small degree, this threat is magnified by rights claims because of the power of courts to command speech and demand the defense of privilege, thereby breaking the sovereign entitlement of silence while threatening to mark the abstract self as the particular. One need only recall the marriage trial that occurred in Hawai'i in 1996, in which the state lost every argument on behalf of "traditional" marriage, to see how dangerous the compulsion of speech can be. Faced with this threat, *ressentiment* reemerges as a triple achievement: Brown notes that "it produces an affect (rage, righteousness) which overwhelms the hurt; it produces a culprit responsible for the hurt; and it produces a site of revenge to displace the hurt" (1995b, 214).

That site of revenge has increasingly become the law in an attempt to pry courts and legal doctrine loose from the demands of lesbians and gays and from the sovereign imaginary across a broad spectrum of issues. Service in the military, criminal regulation of same-sex conduct, employment protections against discriminatory treatment and same-sex harassment, public speech and the right to parade, domestic partnership and same-sex marriage have all been sites of intense anti–gay rights politics. Of course, this anxiety over rights is not without precedent. Arguments about civil rights protections as "special rights" that have been used to position gays and lesbians as "strangers to the law" (Keen and Goldberg 1998; see also Gerstmann 1999; Goldberg 1994) were voiced against the 1964 Civil Rights Act (Marcosson 1995), and recent initiatives to forestall legal enforcement of civil rights for gays in Colorado, Oregon, Alaska, Hawai'i, and elsewhere were previewed in California and Akron in 1964.[23] Despite similarities to the past, significant differences reflecting the defense of sovereignty abound. For one thing, as Gamble (1997, 257ff.) has observed, gays and lesbians have seen their rights put to popular vote more often than any other minority group; in forty-three incidents between the years 1977 and 1993, 79 percent of these ballot measures were passed by what Madison would have called "tyrannical" majorities opposed to civil rights for lesbians and gays. In addition, the assertion of majority power opposed to judicial acknowledgment of the rights to same-sex marriage and other civil rights for gays and lesbians has taken new and paradoxical forms. For instance, the 1964 mobilizations against rights for African Americans prodded a national state applying federalist prerogatives to end racial segregation, whereas federal sovereignty in response to antigay mobilization is limited by lack of political will and formally barred by the Defense of Marriage Act.[24] It is now the rise of popular (and perhaps populist) majorities who make the claim of political sovereignty, one bound to an image of the state whose guarantee of public and individual security is promoted by doing less, rather than more, on behalf of civil rights. In self-conscious parody, civil rights themselves have been put on political trial.

Empirical studies of political attitudes suggest the depth and breadth of this concern over civil rights, especially for gays and lesbians. Research into public opinion since the civil rights movement of the 1950s and 1960s has shown that support for and faith in rights exists inconsistently, more in the abstract than the concrete (McClosky and Brill 1983; Prothro and Grigg 1960; Sarat 1977). For instance, early surveys uncovered strong support for the Bill of Rights and for such ideals as free speech with particular exceptions for communists, atheists, and socialists. More recently—but prior to the recent mobilization against gay rights—these studies reveal what one theorist has called a "pluralistic intolerance" (Sullivan et al. 1982; see also Grossman and Epp 1991), denoting the broad diversity of targets denied support for their civil rights. Recent concerns over the free speech rights of flag burners and hate-mongers, welfare rights of immigrants, the right to bear automatic arms, the right of women to have abortions and their opponents to protest, and the rights of the homeless to housing remind us of the diverse anxieties that civil rights provoke. However ill-focused these anxieties have been in the past, there is growing reason to speculate that this equal-opportunity intolerance has found a fresh coherence coalescing around a new social outcast. Alan Wolfe's recent study of American attitudes reveals the deep unease over the place of gays and lesbians in American politics and society. Despite finding many diffuse antipathies, gays and lesbians emerge in his study as "the ultimate test of American tolerance: the line separating gay America from straight America is a line that an unusually large number of middle class Americans are unwilling to cross" (1998, 77; see also Button, Rienzo, and Wald 1997; Herman 1997; Yang 1999).[25]

The manner in which civil rights have been promoted and opposed to rigidify this line is a concern of this book. I argue that the separation of rights from the sovereign imagination fueling the opposition to same-sex marriage and gay rights generally is a complex and somewhat paradoxical division. Sovereignty—governed by ideas of individual autonomy, rationality, and universalism—competes with alternative discourses that bypass a sovereign logic, yet also promise collective and individual security. Concerns for economic value and the viability of postindustrial markets, the maintenance of social status, and the requirements of knowledge about and control over the self ground security in normalizing disciplinary modes of authority. These are all concerns that Foucault, in his narrative of modernity, has called a resurgence of the *social:* discourses comprising what he has termed a governmentality inclusive of, but extending beyond, the boundaries of political sovereignty. "Government not only has to deal with a territory, with a domain, and with its subjects, but . . . also with a complex and independent reality that has its own laws and mechanisms of disturbance" (Foucault 1989, 261). Governing the social involves promoting self-regulating domains as small as the family and as large as the political economy.[26]

The relationship between sovereignty and alternative discourses and practices of security comprising the social is complex. "Sovereignty [is] democratized through the constitution of a public right articulated upon collective sovereignty, while at the same time this democratization of sovereignty [is] fundamentally determined by and grounded in mechanisms of disciplinary coercion" (Foucault 1980b, 105). This does not imply, against my arguments here, that sovereignty is a mere patina disguising bureaucratic power and objective knowledge, or that rights cease to have important meaning in contemporary governmentality (see also Constable 1993; Dillon 1995; Fitzpatrick 1999). Rather, Foucault has urged us to "see things not in terms of the replacement of a society of sovereignty by a disciplinary society by a society of government; in reality one has a triangle, sovereignty-discipline-government" (1991, 102).[27] This triangular relationship suggests that autonomy, rationality, and the like are frequently evaluated not as ends in themselves, but as specific values promoting identifiable social interests. It is for this reason that the ability of civil rights law to mark the appropriate generality associated with citizenship and inclusion in the sovereign community is never far removed from the specific social rationales for inclusion. This conceptual proximity permits disruption of the sovereign/social relationship with important implications for the ability of courts and civil rights to regulate citizenship demands. I further elucidate this point below in a discussion of equal protection law, especially as it has affected lesbians and gays.

Equal Protection at the End of Civil Rights

Equal protection law has one of its justifications in what Ely (1980) has called "representational reinforcement," or the constitutional imperative to protect "discrete and insular"[28] minorities who would otherwise remain at the mercy of political majorities. This interpretation of the Fourteenth Amendment's equal protection clause is inherently countermajoritarian and cognizant of the limits of the passive Madisonian political solution to American antagonism in which multiple political factions make it "less probable that a majority of the whole will have a common motive to invade the rights of other citizens" (Hamilton, Madison, and Jay 1961, 83, no. 10).

The universalist impulses behind equal protection law—that is, its goal of integrating excluded minorities and re-creating the democratic sovereign—ironically has been seen to depend upon the acknowledgment of difference in the form of "suspect" and "quasi-suspect" classes that raise the governmental threshold for differential treatment. Thus, in federal equal protection law, race is treated as a suspect class, and gender as a quasi-suspect class requiring a lesser, though still "heightened," level of scrutiny or suspicion of official discrimination; any other target of discrimination need be defended as merely "rationally" related to a legitimate governmental interest. However, as Gerstmann has cogently argued, this three-tiered framework was created not to further antidiscrimination policy but "to sharply limit the scope of the equal protection clause in the wake of the Warren Court's and early Burger Court's adventurous expansion of equal protection doctrine" (1999, 5).

Indeed, nearly commensurate with the creation of the doctrine was a judicial unwillingness to expand suspect or quasi-suspect class status beyond race, gender, illegitimacy, ethnic identity, and alienage to other groups demanding protection from official discrimination; despite countless demands by gays and lesbians, poor people, and the elderly in federal litigation, no additional protections have been forthcoming since 1977.[29] Gays have faced difficulty even gaining minimal protection under the rational-basis threshold of the bottom tier. Indeed, much in the manner that the rights of Communist and socialist pamphleteers were held unprotected earlier in this century, since their advocacy was seen to contribute nothing to rational and democratic discourse, gays and lesbians have been historically banned in the legal imagination from participating in the rational polity, making discriminatory policies hard to legally restrict.

Bowers v. Hardwick (1986) made this exclusion explicit. Coming after more than a decade of increased lesbian and gay activism, the case was developed as a test of a Georgia antisodomy statute that was used to justify the arrest of a man observed by a police officer making love with another man in his own bedroom. Although decided under the due process clause that avoided raising equal protection questions,[30] *Hardwick* nonetheless set out the parameters under which gays could be denied privacy rights and their sexual expression subjected to the criminal law. The majority opinion by Justice White and concurring opinions marshaled a phalanx of historical, ethical, biblical, and natural authorities in their repugnance toward homosexuality.[31] As volumes of subsequent analysis have made clear, "to the lower courts, *Bowers v. Hardwick* was not a case about the implied right to privacy, but a case about lesbians and gay men" (Matthew 1997, 1357). As such, the case stands as justification for further public as well as private discrimination based on the "tendency or desire"[32] of gays for homosexual relations (Koppelman 1988; Schacter 1997a; Tymkovich, Daily, and Farley 1997, 309). *Hardwick's* legacy has been that sexual orientation should be seen as a matter of legal status, lacking analogy to the "discrete and insular" character of other civil rights subjects, a legal exclusion with deep resonance to *Plessy v. Ferguson* (1896)[33] and *Dred Scott v. Sandford* (1856),[34] which refused to recognize the legal subjectivity of blacks or slaves.

Hardwick's genealogy in these pre–civil rights cases[35] emphasizes exclusion by what I want to call the delimitations of the social. By failing to recognize gays and lesbians as legitimate legal subjects able to claim rights under the constitution, and by emphasizing their difference via reference to their sexual behavior or desires, the opinion reveals a particular epistemological assumption about the ends of government. The Court's failure to authenticate the distinction between public and private spaces in which autonomy for homosexual desire

can survive allows state power to extend broadly over both by enchain-
ing liberal categories not to a jurisprudence of contractarian theory or
natural law, but to social ends. The private sphere, White argues in
Hardwick, is protected as a matter for "family, marriage, or procreation"
that has no imaginable link to "homosexual activity."[36] Although the
private sphere is defined within law and distinguished from political
life, it is nonetheless permeable to social regulation for a given end.
This expectation of social regulation has no proper site of enunciation
in this opinion; judgments of majorities, religious and other moralities,
the weight of tradition, as well as authentic families are all legitimate
guardians of public power applied in the interest of social well-being. It
is this connection between common purpose broadly realized and collective security that constrains this social moment while estranging
gays and lesbians.

Interpreted from the perspective of the social, *Hardwick* reveals
some of the liberal mentalities of rule (govern*mentality*) that render
reality thinkable. These mentalities can be seen to constitute the conditions under which particular forms of power are "assembled into com-
plexes that connect up forces and institutions deemed 'political' with
apparatuses that shape and manage individual and collective conduct
in relation to norms and objectives . . . constituted as 'non-political'"
(Rose 1996, 37–38). As rights based on gay and lesbian identity are not
judicially thinkable, those epistemologies, moral forms, and modes of
reasoning that oppose these rights and open the door to sovereign
authority reinforce the former "regime of invisibility" (Schacter 1997a)
that has kept activist gays and lesbians in a legal closet.

While *Hardwick* is not overruled in fact, the entitlement to hostility[37] toward gays and lesbians for which it stands has been superseded
by two significant legal developments. The first is *Romer v. Evans*
(1996), which struck down Colorado's Amendment 2, which would
have eliminated local antidiscrimination ordinances protecting gays,
lesbians, and bisexuals. The *Romer* Court argued that there was no
rational basis for excluding gays and lesbians from antidiscrimination
protections. Although the lower Colorado courts had called for a more
fundamental right not to be politically excluded, the *Romer* majority
rejected this line of reasoning, merely interrogating the banning of local
antidiscrimination statutes for their tight relationship between permissible means and ends. This ultimately substituted the Court's "rela-

tively adventurous" (Sunstein 1994b, 269) moral judgment about the propriety of discrimination for that of the Colorado legislature. If the issue of suspect class standing was sidestepped by the opinion, so, significantly, was the *Hardwick* case, which was never once mentioned by the majority, an omission that Janet Halley wryly observes to "take the sex out of homosexual" (Halley 1997, 433). Behind this desexing lies the rather dubious assumption that while Colorado's majority was wrongly passionate in its rejection of antidiscrimination protection for gays and lesbians, its action as a rational democratic body could only take place through the partial erasure of lesbian and gay identity.

The protection of and appeal to public rationality that lies behind *Romer*'s murky reasoning provides gays and lesbians at most with what one observer has called "thin gay rights" (Massaro 1996). Gays and lesbians "can win [but] only by appealing to judicial sympathy and intuitions about fairness rather than by invoking any coherent legal principle" (Gerstmann 1999, 8). The weak protection that this provides can be seen in the courts' wandering directions, upholding the "Don't ask, don't tell" military policy,[38] ordering the protection of a gay student,[39] prohibiting homosexuals from immigrating,[40] and the like. Public reaction to court-enforced protection policies has been intense, suggesting to some that "hate, vituperation, and personal insult have been let out of their [legal] boxes and probably cannot be entirely pushed back into them" (Halley 1997, 437).

The legal policy of thin gay rights articulated by the *Romer* court also has meaning for the types of identities articulated within the law. Antidiscrimination complaints have often been personally costly in terms of the need to identify as a victim and have courts accept the claim that one is representative of a socially and politically powerless group (Bumiller 1988). Without clear recognition of a history of oppression, or a long-term visibility as a discrete minority, gays have been forced to assert and assume identities with an uncertain democratic and legal status. As Gerstmann understands this, "rather than framing their arguments in terms of equality, gays and lesbians must frame their arguments in terms of oppression and difference. This renders gays and lesbians vulnerable to charges that they are seeking special rights rather than equal rights" (Gerstmann 1999, 39). In light of *Hardwick*'s claim that behavior *is* identity, gays and lesbians are also vulnerable to popular dismissal based on the assumed behavioral—and thus voluntary—markers of their identity, forcing an adverse surface comparison of their claims with blacks or women whose identity seems much more naturalized.[41]

Despite these serious limitations of *Romer,* the opinion is voiced in a much different tone than *Hardwick.* Where the earlier case articulates the *social* as a means of reasserting the barriers to gay and lesbian integration, *Romer* emphasizes what I will call here the *sovereign* moment with its attention to the comportment of democratic majorities and the forms of rationality made on behalf of public policy. To the extent that this rationality remains general and disembodied, the unity to which it aspires permits rights to be imagined as expansive and flexible entitlements entailing no undue burden on others and having no necessary connection to the goals and aims of collective security. Nonetheless, *Romer* does not guarantee inclusion through appeal to the sovereign, for it still leaves lesbians and gays unmarked and, so, unentitled to the protections of the universal.

The meaning of civil rights is contested between the social and sovereign discursive frameworks that characterize *Hardwick* and *Romer,* but they are not fully discrete in the legal imagination. This is evident in the second line of cases that have modified the *Hardwick* holding, the marriage cases. Like *Romer, Baehr v. Lewin* (1993) failed to find gays and lesbians a suspect class. Rather, the Hawai'i court argued that gender discrimination—a quasi-suspect class under federal law but a declared suspect class in Hawai'i due to that state's equal rights amendment— was the basis for concluding that a denial of marriage licenses to same-sex couples was impermissible without compelling justification.[42] *Baehr* depends upon the sovereign imagination to conjure the power of what might be called deep analogy. Rather than simply identify gays as discrete minorities like women or blacks, the court argued that denial of marriage licenses to same-sex couples was *exactly* like the Supreme Court's refusal to abide the denial of marriage licenses to interracial couples in *Loving v. Virginia* (1967).[43] In so doing, the court defeated arguments of symmetry that were used to deny racial discrimination in the miscegenation case.[44] The court also separated itself from prior decisions that had defeated attempts to secure same-sex marriage by claiming that marriages were, by definition, strictly between a man and a woman (and, by implication, solely determined by a higher authority beyond the power of courts and legislatures to redefine).[45] A vast outpouring of scholarly support for the analogy between antimiscegenation statutes and prohibitions against same-sex marriage supports the Hawai'i court's arguments by analyzing oppression against gays and lesbians as a consequence of the reproduction of gender inequality: women's subordination is seen to be furthered by constricting the appropriate expression of partner choice in the same manner that antimiscegenation statutes reproduced white supremacy by separating the races in the name of racial purity, thereby perpetuating attitudes about racial difference, social hierarchy, and limited social roles for particular races (Koppelman 1988, 1994; Sunstein 1994a, 1994b; Valdes 1995, 198ff.). Additionally, some feminist and queer theorists have shown the strong linkages between rigid gender roles and heterosexism (Butler 1990; Okin 1996; Richards 1998). And the Supreme Court has recently unanimously ruled that, at least when it comes to sexual harassment under Title VII, same-sex harassment *is* discrimination on account of sex.[46]

Whether the scholarly and juristic recognition of this analogy will translate into increased popular support for gay rights is an open question, one I pursue further in chapter 6. One problem is that deep analogies of this type tend to efface analysis of the particularities of gay and lesbian oppression; in an effort to promote an appropriate marker for inclusion they hide the sex under a cloak of race. The invitation to analogy is also an invitation to comparison, and here, both from the perspective of rights detractors and from gays and lesbians whose social identities stress difference, gays who lack a clear legal identity reemerge as a particular whose sovereign claims on the universal are open to challenge through arguments about their social contribution to security and community. For some gay and lesbian advocates, the analogy model is actually a reason to *question* the marriage goal. As Lehr has recently argued, "It is not at all clear . . . that *Loving* played a significant role in furthering either a decline in racial discrimination or an increase in interracial interaction, since systems of domination are maintained in part by private relationships, but even more by structural constraints" (1999, 39). As these concerns make clear, the Hawai'i marriage case has left lesbian and gay rights vulnerable to challenge.

Both the Vermont case, *Baker v. Vermont* (1999), and the Alaska marriage decision, *Brause v. Bureau of Vital Statistics* (1998), attempted to skirt the analogy issue and ground same-sex marriage rights in a more strictly sovereign framework. The Vermont plaintiffs appealed a superior court decision that upheld the state's argument that its interest in procreation provided a rational basis for denying marriage licenses to same-sex couples. The plaintiffs asked the supreme court to find against the state under the Vermont constitution's common benefits clause, which reads as follows.

> That government is, or ought to be, instituted for the common benefit, protection and security of the people, nation, or community, and not for the particular emolument or advantage of any single person, family, or set of persons, who are a part only of that community. (Vt. Cons., chap. 1, art. 7)

The expectation was that the sovereign language of "people, nation, or community" would compel not only heightened scrutiny for discrimination against gays and lesbians, but also a legal command to "an equal share in the fruits of the common enterprise"[47] that would encompass marriage. Despite accepting the plaintiffs' arguments that the common benefits clause controlled the case and required equal protection for same-sex couples, the Vermont Supreme Court could not agree that marriage was the necessary remedy.

If the Vermont case suggests that sovereign strategies will not compel same-sex marriage, the Alaska same-sex marriage case demonstrated that analogies to other civil rights subjects often hide submerged beneath the legal surface. The Alaska court that heard the demands of Brause and his partner for a marriage license sidestepped the *Baehr* court's argument-by-analogy to find a strict scrutiny protection for same-sex marriage in the constitutional protection for privacy (an argument that was advanced, but not accepted, in *Baehr* as well). The trial judge who heard the case wrote that the Hawai'i court began its reasoning with the wrong questions.

> The relevant question is not whether same-sex marriage is so rooted in our traditions that it is a fundamental right, but whether the freedom to choose one's own life partner is so rooted in our traditions. . . . Here the court finds that the choice of a life partner is personal, intimate, and subject to the protection of the right to privacy.[48]

Perhaps correctly sensing the weak popular appeal of such reasoning, the judge also alluded to the *Loving* analogy in obiter dicta, suggesting,

"In some parts of our nation mere acceptance of the familiar would have left segregation in place."

The legal recourse to the antimiscegenation analogy demonstrates the ironic incompleteness of civil rights for gays and lesbians seeking constitutional and community integration through marriage law. Bereft of clear legal identities and dependent upon assumptions that do not resonate deeply even within gay and lesbian communities, the legal supports for equal protection have remained an attractive target for opponents of further development of civil rights. If this politics is emblematic of what Schacter (1997b) has evocatively called the "post–civil rights era," it is not because civil rights are eclipsed as much as because they are paradoxically deployed in new ways and given new meanings.

The mix of sovereign and social discourses in the marriage cases demonstrates the potential polarities in the contemporary legal space, but it also offers a clue as to why civil rights seem to provide neither a boundary against gay and lesbian demands (for those worried about same-sex marriage), nor a simple exposition of citizenship (for its supporters). The failure of equal protection doctrine to provide identities adequate for gays and lesbians to mobilize the law against discrimination has left the sovereign claims linking civil rights with citizenship vulnerable to the social claims articulating rights with the well-being of community and economy. This ambiguity has forced advocates of same-sex marriage to argue not just for the right to marriage as a sign of citizenship but also for the economic and social value of diverse family relationships as the basis for social welfare and community security. In like manner, the weak specification of adequate public rationality associated with sovereign majorities encourages opponents of same-sex marriage to articulate their political will as representatives of the sovereign community as much from antipathy toward meddling courts as from economic dangers imagined to inhere in gay rights.

In the examination of the boundaries separating these cross-cutting discursive frameworks, I pay particular attention to how the changing dynamics of the political economy that underlie the conception of social value have altered the ability of groups to successfully mobilize the law. Much as the discourse of sovereignty divides political space in order to exclude some from access to the commons, the emerging neoliberal political economy today bars many—including large segments of the middle class—from sharing the spoils of economic growth and exposes many more to increased economic risk due to rapid changes in production and a rotting safety net. This is also an economy no longer dominated by labor unions that traditionally valorized rights and the rule of law. How these material changes have influenced collective identity and social movement strategies around rights organizes many of the central questions of this research.

Social Movements, Sovereign Movements

The politics of sovereignty has been magnified by the limitations of equal protection law for lesbians and gays and the social movement strategies that have been pursued. Many of the organizational and representational novelties of lesbian and gay politics can be traced back to the dynamics of union organizing in the United States. The civil rights movement (advancing the interest of African Americans) and the women's movement were partially impelled by the failure of the American labor movement to significantly spread workers' gains beyond the population of white males and to subsequently recognize group identity and demands for political equality that were fast replacing class interest as the lingua franca of political mobilization (Boris 1994; Draper 1994; Fraser 1997; Gabin 1990; Goldfield 1997).[49] The rise of legal and administrative departments and discourses designed to enforce civil rights for these groups implicitly acknowledged the failure of workers' rights to express universal interests, while they also changed the political logic of social space from an "immigrant" model based on incorporation into a universal body politic to an "integrationist" model in which wrongly excluded groups comprised a divided, pluralist space (Patton 1997, 8; W. Brown 1995b). The democratic fiction that pluralist spaces were infinitely flexible and did not materially overlap was threatened by union decline in the mid-1970s, which tumbled the progressive, civil rights wing of the Democratic party at the same time that it raised economic tensions between downwardly mobile workers and identity groups (Edsall and Edsall 1991).

The implications of these dynamics for gay and lesbian politics cannot be downplayed. Once sexual minorities successfully challenged the stigma of a medical psychopathology in the early 1970s, many of the public rationales for isolating and restricting gays from immigration, public service, housing, and everyday life by which they previously had been socially "contained" (Fortin 1995) were dissolved.

Freed from a malignant classification and broadly mobilized, lesbians and gays began to develop distinctive social and political identities and divergent strategies around these postpluralist conceptions of public space.

Lesbian and gay social movement strategies have bifurcated roughly along what has been called an ethnic/essentialist and a deconstructive (or queer) model (Gamson 1996; Seidman 1993, 1997; Sinfield 1996). Each faces particular difficulties in light of civil rights law and the transformations of the political economy. The ethnic/essentialist model projects gay and lesbian identity as a quasi ethnicity, one

> complete with its own political and cultural institutions, festivals, neighborhoods, even its own flag. Underlying that ethnicity is typically the notion that what gays and lesbians share—the anchor of minority status and minority rights claims—is the same fixed, natural essence, a self with same-sex desires. The shared oppression, these movements have forcefully claimed, is the denial of the freedoms and opportunities to actualize this self. In this *ethnic/essentialist* politic, clear categories of collective identity are necessary for successful resistance and political gain. (Gamson 1996, 396)

The maintenance of distinctive social and cultural categories that enhance self-actualization is undermined by law that has refused to recognize sexual orientation as the basis for heightened scrutiny. As a consequence, lesbian and gay rights activists have been forced to assert and defend analogies to other ethnic groups whose more naturalized identities make gays vulnerable to the claims that they are seeking rights for deceptive reasons. The power of analogy is weakened by the problems of mutual understanding and common cause among progressive social movements exacerbated by the growing material consequences that flow from official recognition (Valdes 1997a; Brandt 1999; Butler, 1996, 40; Hutchinson 1999). Absent an assimilable marking that could accommodate an integrationist pluralism, ethnic/essentialist gay politics faces a particularly difficult hurdle with a rights strategy. Because "male and female homosexualities [are] still fuzzily defined, undercoded, or discursively dependent on more established forms" (De Lauretis quoted in Weeks 1995, 109), it is not accidental that this politics privileges "coming out" (Blasius 1992; Stychin 1995b, 143ff.)— not coming across boundaries, but emerging already—from within

suburban and urban life, family and workplace, church and organization. For some queer theorists and activists, this has been a conscious
"project of cultural pedagogy aimed at exposing the range and variety
of bounded spaces upon which heterosexual supremacy depends, [to]
see and conquer places that present the danger of *violence* to gays and
lesbians, to reterritorialize them" (Berlant and Freeman 1993, 205). The
love that once dared to speak its name has now spoken, but in borrowed languages and reclaimed spaces. This tactical bricolage has pro-
foundly unsettled the sovereign practices and tacit understandings
around which status and personal security have been seen to cohere, "a
kind of ultimate heresy or treason against essential moral values"
(Richards 1999, 90). As Sinfield has observed, this treason against sovereign privilege is a complex war of maneuver.

> [Even] the phrase "coming out" . . . is not special to us. It is a
> hybrid appropriation, alluding parodically to what debutantes do;
> the joke is that they emerge, through balls, garden parties, and the
> court pages of the *Times*, into centrality, whereas we come out into
> the marginal spaces of discos, cruising grounds and Lesbian and
> Gay Studies. This implication in the heterosexism that others us
> has advantages. It allows us to know what people say when they
> think we aren't around. And at least we can't be told to go back to
> where we came from, as happens to racial minorities. . . . Con-
> versely though, it makes us the perfect subversive implants, the
> quintessential enemy within. (1996, 281)

The uncertain legal status of lesbians and gays who have argued
for inclusion into a pluralist polity, and the threats to sovereign understandings posed by a "subversive" queer politics have allowed and
even encouraged new conservative movements in the 1990s to operate
on similar but countervailing notions of political space. As Patton has
argued,

> The New Right and queer activists each . . . in contrast to liberal
> pluralism . . . [believe] that that space is deeply material and non-
> partitionable, and the presence of any group necessarily presses on
> every other group. . . . The New Right views dissident bodies—
> homosexuals, women who seek abortion, Afrocentric blacks—as
> intrusions of evil into space, intrusions encouraged by liberal plu-

ralism's mismanagement and fragmentation of space. "Queer" politics stepped into this gap and attempted to produce a politics of presence that did not rely on the dispossession strategy held in common by lesbian and gay rights and black civil rights groups. In this logic, space is a matrix of surges and flows in which queerness precedes any attempt to balkanize bodies that represent points of density in a continuous, gridlike space. . . . New Right and queer activist logics of space may be more similar to each other than either is to liberal pluralist conceptions. (1997, 10, 11)

On the terrain of nonpartitionable space, political stakes and sovereign demands are both conceptually magnified.

These spatial ideas also have important consequences for the ways in which the demand for equal marriage rights is articulated, even by nondeconstructionists. For some neoconservatives unhappy to embrace the full panoply of gay cultural politics, the normalizing effects of marriage are likely to lead to greater acceptance of gays and lesbians by ensconcing the dangers of sexuality in the traditional republican space of the domestic sphere (Bawer 1993; Eskridge 1996). For Andrew Sullivan, marriage rights burden the state less than antidiscrimination statutes, whose intrusion into private freedoms he opposes on grounds of liberal philosophy and efficiency: legalizing gay marriage would accomplish "ninety percent of the political work necessary to achieve gay and lesbian equality. . . . [Marriage is] ultimately the only reform that truly matters" (1996, 185; see also Epstein 1994).

Some liberal supporters of same-sex marriage are less concerned with disturbing boundaries between public and private. Wolfson sees the attainment of marriage by same-sex couples as "conservatively subversive" (1994, 580). "Winning marriage rights would alter society's understanding of, and attitude toward, gay people and same-sex love generally—the rising tide that raises all boats" (604). This buoyant subversion even appeals to some radical theorists who are fundamentally skeptical of the rights-based and culturally mainstream marriage project. As Patton has argued,

No matter how disgustingly suburban I found the Ideal Lesbian moms who appeared in a 1993 *Newsweek,* they were a radically different image of neonatalistic Mommism to the majority of even the most liberal readers. They both reaffirmed a conservative ideal and shattered the image of the family; they both aligned with and reformed the project represented in the Contract with America. (1997, 22)

Understood from these varied perspectives, marriage retains the potential for a more insistent politics of difference by loosening not only its gendered form, but also its very sign of privilege, permitting greater social acceptance of alternative and emergent forms of sexuality and gay culture (Butler 1998; Donovan, Heaphy, and Weeks 1999; Herman 1994; Law 1988; Okin 1996). As Catharine MacKinnon—a cultural feminist who is ambivalent about marriage—has noted, "I do think it might do something amazing to the entire institution of marriage to recognize the unity of two 'persons' between whom no superiority or inferiority could be presumed on the basis of gender" (1987, 27).[50]

How the political arguments for and against equal marriage rights affect the success and strategies of lesbian and gay, and right-wing social movements is one concern that this book takes up. I pay particular attention to how the discursive field of sovereignty has altered the meaning of civil rights and the tactics used by social movements. Of particular interest in this regard is how these discourses have influenced coalitions and alliances among defenders of equal rights to marriage, unions and nationalist groups on the one hand, and conservative groups and their electoral supporters on the other.

Legal Mobilization and Legal Demobilization

Much has been written from the standpoint of keeping the law in our lives. Sociolegal studies have oriented a legion of scholars toward the constitutive character of law that has eroded the conceptual dualisms of law *and* society and questioned assumptions about the autonomy of self from social and legal discourse. As Ewick and Silbey express this methodological perspective:

Law does not simply work on social life (to define and to shape it). Legality also operates through social life as persons and groups deliberately interpret and invoke law's language, authority, and procedures to organize their lives and manage their relationships. In short, the commonplace operation of law in daily life makes us all legal agents insofar as we actively make law, even when no formal legal agent is involved. (1998, 20; see also Merry 1990; Trubeck and Esser 1989)

Constitutive analyses examine culture, consciousness, and social action in order to gain a "bottom-up" picture of the law and rights in their everyday manifestations (Bumiller 1988). From this perspective, law "shapes society from the inside out, by providing the principal categories that make social life seem natural, normal, cohesive, and coherent" (Sarat and Kearns, quoted in Silverstein 1996). At the same time, this perspective acknowledges that "social life is a vast web of overlapping and reinforcing regulation" (Galanter 1983, 129) in which law comprises only part of social ordering.

The ubiquity of law from this perspective ironically raises particular questions about the efficacy of law for social transformation (Scheingold 1974). Studies of "legal mobilization" critically examine the reproduction and successes of rights advocacy with the understanding that "legal norms and discourses derive their meaning primarily through the practical forms of activity in which they are developed and expressed" (McCann 1994, 261–62), a contemporary echo of Marx's argument that law is one of the "ideological forms in which men become conscious of . . . conflict and fight it out" (1977b, 390; see also Bourdieu 1987; Ewick and Silbey 1992; Thompson 1975, 267). Mobilization theory suggests that rights are conducive to social alliance, and hence, facilitative of group conflict (McCann 1994; Milner 1986; Scheingold 1974; Silverstein 1996; Zemans 1983). Legal meaning is therefore not precise and definitive, but rather contingently mapped onto wider social textures and dependent on divergent experiences with and beliefs about rights (Herman 1994; Milner 1986) as well as the "inclinations, tactical skills, and resources of the contending parties who mobilize judicial endowments" (McCann 1994, 170). This diversity of belief and engagement with the law reveals legal consciousness to be "variable, volatile, complex and contradictory" (McCann 1994, 8).

In efforts to fix meanings, agents exploit this pluralistic environment, extending conflict to legal norms and institutions in novel contexts and in social spaces beyond the primary arena. Herman (1994) has explored the ways in which litigation on behalf of gays and lesbians can advantageously destabilize legal and social categories by challenging gender expectations in various settings, and how, when legal and nonlegal discourses mix, gays and lesbians are sometimes harmed. Legal mobilization studies have also revealed that law retains a powerful source of meaning for social groups even where favorable opportunities and adequate resources for legal action are few. In McCann's study of the pay equity movement in the 1980s, law and legal rights were shown to be an enduring force even after litigation had failed and the rights sought were never vindicated in court. These studies reveal the ways in which the social imagination is vividly constructed through legal meaning.

The vast majority of these studies have approached law from an implicit civil rights model in which law's utility for social action is evaluated from the standpoint of progressive groups seeking fundamental political and social reform. The same-sex marriage controversy raises interesting questions rarely asked in these studies, however. Primary among these is how some social movements mobilize *against* the law and seek to transform discourses about rights—particularly civil rights—into exclusionary limits. An important ancillary issue, too often forgotten, is how rights discourses and legal strategies may fail to provide the glue of common interest and a social imaginary shared between groups advancing civil rights strategies. Legal mobilization theory does suggest, I believe, many of the correct starting points for an analysis of the politics of same-sex marriage. Law's articulation with other political and economic languages, the interconnection between local strategies and more global legal consciousness, and an assessment of how well law serves social movements are all integrated into the present study.

But while mobilization studies are exemplary for building a phenomenology of law by getting into the heads of legal actors, they can also trade off two related issues of importance for the present study. The first is large-scale changes in social and economic structure—the contours of governmentality—that have a diffuse and indirect bearing on legal mobilization. Mobilization studies have addressed the impact of resources including beliefs about the law, social movements, rules of legal standing, and the like. But the emphasis on ground-level struggle to make the law work for disadvantaged groups often overshadows the broader structural changes with relevance for understanding the social context in which law is mobilized. An example can be found in McCann's study of pay equity, which reveals that materially dominant social groups do not retain every advantage, in part because they are susceptible to rights talk and because workers can mobilize within unions providing sanctuary, momentum, and solidarity. Nonetheless, McCann misses one of the most important structural and hegemonic changes occurring in American labor politics at the time these pay equity struggles were taking place: union membership declined drastically, and the place that unions had struggled so hard to get and maintain was threatened as it had not been since before the New Deal. With union density decline in the 1980s, emblematically captured by the demise of Professional Air Traffic Controllers Organization at the hands of President Reagan, came a period of diminished political power, decreased activism and solidarity, and increasing fragmentation. This loss of momentum provides an alternative interpretation to that propounded by McCann in his observation that the events in Philadelphia in 1986 were a turning point for the pay equity movement. McCann argues that it was Philadelphia's "belief that the union could not win in court which most sustained official resistance to large-scale wage restructuring during the 1980s" (1994, 186). However, this conclusion might have followed from a gestalt of the tide running against the entire labor movement.

The transparency of structural concerns points up one of the weaknesses of the phenomenological perspective where structure is not ignored but instead reduced in solidity. A second concern is that this very emphasis on the fluidity of legal mobilization tends to see more law than its social and discursive limits. One tactic advanced by some mobilization theorists (Herman 1994; Milner 1986) and students of legal consciousness is to examine the discursive structures of law in order to attend to the social spaces into which law rarely intrudes, or to the contradictions through which law enunciates its own applicable limits. Ewick and Silbey have examined these discursive limits in their elicitation and analysis of stories that people tell about their encounters with the law. Three types of narratives emerge in their analysis: stories about law as a separate sphere in which objectivity is seen as the normative ideal, stories about law as a game in which interested representation is idealized, and stories about law as a product of power. "Woven together . . . the three stories collectively constitute the lived experience of legality as a struggle between desire and the law, social structure and human agency" (Ewick and Silbey 1998, 29).

Legal consciousness appears to be a contradictory amalgam of various types of narratives in this account. For Ewick and Silbey, the constitution of law as both normative ideal and practical knowledge is the source of its appeal. They show that since these various images are dependent on each other for their very potency and meaning, these divergent and ambivalent beliefs about the law become an integral aspect of legal meaning. As structure, these contrasting images operate to divide the legal from the nonlegal.

> At the same time that legality is constructed as existing outside of everyday life, it must also be located securely within it. Legality is different and distinct from daily life, yet commonly present. Everyday life may be rendered irrelevant by a reified law, but the relevance of law to everyday life is affirmed by the gamelike image of law. In the gamelike threat of hegemonic legality, law is available as an aspect of social relations in which one can deploy the resources and experiences of everyday life to gain advantage through its special rules and techniques. (232)

Of course, these images of inside and outside the law are part of the ideological construction of law itself, for "with the constitutive theory, there can no longer be any inexorable mode or structure of connecting law to society" (Fitzpatrick 1992, 8). Yet this modern myth of law's transcendence, as Fitzpatrick calls it, offers its own hegemonic overlay to the stories of law. Modernity is constituted by the paradoxical myth that it has transcended myth, and in the wake of that story follows "not the destruction of myth but, rather, its perfection" (1992, 36).

With myth seeking to harmonize "mutual relations of opposition and support, of autonomy and dependence" (Fitzpatrick 1992, 146), the juxtaposition of various legal narratives and their potential for contradiction are enhanced and regulated. Among other antinomies, Fitzpatrick shows how modern law seeks to reconcile the particular (rights) with the general (justice), to reconcile order with illimitable sovereignty, the universality of the nation with the particularity of citizenship, the guarantee of progress with ordered legality, the autonomy of the subject with the power of the state. "Outside" of the law but within this mythical field, law is countered by other myths seeking a similar comprehensiveness, such as individuality and popular justice. These opposing myths reconcile the stories told about law's place and its absence, without problematizing its ontological status.

In my presentation of the debates over same-sex marriage, I emphasize the power of these competing discourses to solidify and dissolve the limits to law. Specifically, I strive to bring material discourses and practices into alignment with narratives told about gays and civil rights in order to explore the popular appeal for limiting the reach of law and courts.[51] Attending to antinomical tensions within the law and the relationship of law to alternative discourses of governance, I show how these debates over same-sex marriage are all about rights, and ironically all about their limits.

Plan of the Book

In this book, I elaborate on the public articulation and collective implications of sovereign and social discourses in order to show how they have framed the debates over same-sex marriage. The chapters that follow show that these two broad discourses have produced majorities willing to oppose rights granted to gays and lesbians by the courts, and to inhibit the formation of political allies—especially those of organized labor, ethnic groups, and indigenous nationalists—that gays and lesbians can use to defend their legal victories. At the same time that these discourses are deployed to inhibit civil rights, I conclude, they are sufficiently ambiguous and contradictory to provide novel forms of argumentation that could revivify public commitments to diversity and inclusion for gays and lesbians.

Using these discourses as guideposts, the story I tell about the same-sex marriage controversy forms less a linear narrative than a series of interlocking themes. These themes have emerged from my study of public testimony, legal briefs and arguments, public documents relating to same-sex marriage, and personal interviews with more than a hundred activists, lawyers, politicians, professional advisors, and religious and union leaders in Hawai'i and elsewhere who have been involved in the controversy. Most of the discussion in the pages that follow centers on the Hawai'i experience because of its legal importance. The *Baehr* case, despite its ultimately disappointing outcome, has secured the legitimacy of the legal category of same-sex marriage and, from the mid-1990s on, served to center Hawai'i in national political debates over this issue. However, the Hawai'i case also warrants this scrutiny for many other reasons. For one, as I have already discussed, the issue of same-sex marriage thoroughly saturated Hawai'i politics in the years after the 1993 ruling, and the subsequent maneuvering by political activists and professional politicians to have

a say in the court proceedings offers an opportunity to examine the intimate connection between legal rights and political anxieties. In order to
offer the reader a reference for these complex political interventions, I
have included a timetable at the end of this chapter that chronicles their
order and development.

Hawai'i is also an important venue for this study for its place in the
cultural imaginary. Hawai'i has long been identified in popular culture
as a paradise of "primitive" erotic desire to which honeymooning couples ritually retreat to secure their love and explore their sexuality. The
concern that Hawai'i might also have been the first of the world's governments to legalize same-sex marriage opens to scrutiny important
cultural and economic concerns about this legal change. In addition,
Hawai'i is a unique American cultural landscape lacking an ethnic or a
Christian majority and no recent organization of conservative forces.
As a one-party government, thoroughly dominated since statehood by
a Democratic party and the strong public labor unions that undergird
it, political authority has been premised on cultural and ethnic tolerance built over the layers of violence, segregation, and cultural destruction of its colonial past. Yet the memory of Hawai'i's precolonial past
that allows the marketing of this social tolerance as "aloha" is also
resplendent with acceptance for diverse forms of *sexual* expression. The
ways in which same-sex marriage has played upon this complex cultural and political terrain and the means used by conservative groups
to organize within this postcolonial space offer an important laboratory
for understanding the contemporary limits to union.

In chapter 2, I open a discussion of the social and sovereign discourses that have been deployed in debates over gay and lesbian rights,
including the demand for marriage rights. A common theme in these
debates has been the notion that lesbians and gays ask for "special
rights" above and beyond the equal rights that are their due. I show that
the argument for special rights has been supported by a neoliberal economic discourse that has borrowed from the idioms of global competition, the need for flexible production, and the premise of material
scarcity to picture civil rights (particularly gay rights) as excessive,
costly, inefficient, and antagonistic to private property interests. The
manner in which social hierarchies, sovereign rationality, and superma-
jorities are constructed to defend community security through the
exclusion of lesbian and gay civil rights provides the central concerns of
this chapter. I have sought to sink the roots of these discourses deeply

by drawing from the debates surrounding Colorado's Amendment 2 and the marriage controversies in Hawai'i, Alaska, and Vermont.

This discussion provides a springboard for later explorations. Chapter 3 examines the ways in which neoliberal ideas have amalgamated domestic partnership and same-sex marriage into fused concerns. I argue that this entanglement has confounded the progressive and modern expectation held by many lesbian and gay rights activists that domestic partnership might provide a back door to citizenship rights avoiding the agonistic politics of sovereign exclusion. Because the interplay of economic and sovereign demands is articulated on the very form of legal norms—mitigating the contrast between status and contract—domestic partnership is easily rhetorically projected as a surrogate for marriage, raising majority ire. The means by which neoliberalism has furthered this discursive dynamic in Hawai'i and elsewhere is a particular issue this chapter takes up.

Resistance to neoliberalism by labor unions—the quintessential Fordist institutions designed to advance worker rights and benefits within a local environment—made them a potentially promising ally in the same-sex marriage issue, yet one whose support never materialized. Chapter 4 looks at labor unions in order to assess and explain their mixed record working on behalf of civil rights. Again, my explanation of the difficulties faced by unions asked to form a coalition with other progressive social movements centers on the powerful effects of the economic and sovereign discourses that surrounded the case. Although unions see themselves as champions of the rights of workers, and have long committed themselves to increasing benefits for their members, same-sex marriage was resisted as an important union fight due to the perceived economic costs imposed on private and public employers as well as its challenge to the historical frameworks of union governance.

Chapter 5 asks whether and by what means another potential ally—Native Hawaiian nationalist groups who have a dramatically different argument about sovereignty than those opposed to same-sex marriage—have been able to change the nature of the debate. In particular, I examine the ways in which the arguments of tradition and civilization rallied in the name of sovereignty by antirights groups played themselves out among the poorly buried remnants of Hawai'i's colonial and precolonial past. Native Hawaiians emerged as much more than allies to civil rights advocates during the marriage debates. Because they were a constant reminder of the nineteenth-century history of violent imposition of Western rule, custom, and Christianity, Native Hawaiian demands for self-governance provoked a particular anxiety about tradition, progress, and sexuality that upset conservatives as much as they complicated common cause with rights activists.

Chapter 6 turns to the analogies that have run through same-sex marriage litigation and the public political campaigns designed to halt these legal cases. Lurking behind debates over the appropriateness of these analogies are two concerns. The first is the respect of other sovereigns, which I suggest is an essential element of sovereign discourse. The second is the fear of international competition that limits acceptance for novel legal developments. Both issues have made North American and European responses to the global demands for same-sex partnerships an inescapable issue for American courts and publics, and, I argue, have ultimately worked to modify the understanding and acceptability of the demand for equal rights. Finally, in chapter 7, I ask what alternative strategies can now emerge in the twilight of civil rights.

TIME LINE

1984	All statutory language regarding procreation as a basis for marriage is found by the Hawai'i legislature to be prejudicial against the handicapped, elderly, and others and is stricken from the law books.
17 December 1990	Two lesbian couples and one gay couple apply for marriage licenses from the Hawai'i Department of Health.
February 1991	Hawai'i attorney general denies these licenses on account of the sex of the applicants.
1 May 1991	Dan Foley, attorney for the three couples, files suit in circuit court alleging violations of plaintiffs' privacy and equal protection rights.
3 September 1991	Trial, *Baehr v. Lewin*. Circuit court judge Robert Klein rules that same-sex couples do not have a right to marry, but agrees to consider further equal protection arguments.

9 September 1991   Trial, *Baehr v. Lewin,* continued. Foley argues that gays and lesbians have historically been targets of discrimination, that sexual orientation is immutable, and that they are entitled to equal protection in this case. Judge Klein dismisses the case. Foley appeals.

5 May 1993   Hawai'i's Supreme Court rules that denying licenses to same-sex partners is under the state's equal rights amendment discriminatory absent a compelling state interest. Supreme Court remands case for trial in circuit court to determine whether such an interest can be adequately asserted.

Autumn 1993   Public hearings held by the House Judiciary Committee throughout Hawaii to elicit testimony on same-sex marriage.

April 1994   State legislature passes law declaring procreation to be the basis of the marriage laws and "finds that Hawai'i's marriage licensing laws were originally and are presently intended to apply only to male-female couples, not same-sex couples." Legislature rejects a constitutional amendment to stop same-sex marriage.

April 1994   Legislature creates a Commission on Sexual Orientation and the Law to advise it on same-sex marriage.

June 1994   Governor signs marriage statute limiting marriage to opposite-sex couples.

August 1994   Two Alaska men file for a marriage license, which is denied by the State Office of Vital Statistics on the basis that "marriage between two persons of the same sex is not contemplated by [Alaska's] statutory scheme."

September–December 1995   Commission on Sexual Orientation and the Law hears evidence. It issues a report

	in December recommending recognition of same-sex marriages and no legislative interference with *Baehr v. Lewin.* As a second alternative, the commission recommends a comprehensive domestic partnership statute.
September 1996	Circuit court judge Chang hears the trial of *Baehr v. Miike* (as the case is renamed) on remand from the supreme court.
September 1996	President Clinton signs the Defense of Marriage Act, which is designed to keep other states from having to recognize same-sex marriages made in Hawai'i and elsewhere.
3 December 1996	Judge Chang rules in *Baehr v. Miike,* ordering the state to stop discriminating against same-sex marriages. Same-sex marriage is legal in Hawai'i until the next morning, when Judge Chang stays his order pending final appeal to the Hawai'i Supreme Court.
January 1997	House Judiciary Committee holds public hearings on same-sex marriage and domestic partnership.
24 January 1997	5,000 protesters amass at state capitol to demand a legislative solution ending the same-sex marriage cases. This is the largest political rally since statehood.
29 April 1997	Legislature passes a bill putting a constitutional amendment before voters: "Shall the legislature have the power to reserve marriage to opposite sex couples?" Reciprocal Beneficiaries Act, the nation's most comprehensive domestic partnership legislation, is passed at the same time.
July 1997	Two lesbian and one gay couple sue Vermont after their applications for mar-

	riage licenses are turned down. *Baker v. Vermont* is dismissed in December. The appellants appeal in early 1998.
February 1998	Circuit court judge Peter Michalski rules that Alaska's constitutional right to privacy entitles same-sex couples to a trial to determine whether a compelling state interest can be shown for the ban on same-sex marriage found in the Alaska Marriage Code.
Spring 1998	Hawai'i's attorney general invalidates health benefits for reciprocal beneficiaries who are partners of state employees. State prepares to collect benefits already paid out under the program.
July–November 1998	Same-sex marriage dominates fall campaign in Hawai'i.
3 November 1998	Same-sex marriage amendment declaring in part, "No provisions of this constitution may be interpreted to require the state to recognize or permit marriage between individuals of the same sex" passes with 69% of the vote in Alaska.
3 November 1998	Amendment designed to give the legislature jurisdiction over marriage passes with 69% of the vote in Hawai'i.
November 1998	Arguments before the Vermont Supreme Court in *Baker v. Vermont.*
December 1998	Hawai'i Supreme Court calls for briefs from both sides in the *Baehr* case evaluating the constitutional effects of the new amendment.
10 December 1999	Hawai'i Supreme Court rules that the amendment took the Hawai'i marriage statutes "out of the ambit of the equal protection clause of the Hawai'i Constitution," making the plaintiffs' demands for a marriage license moot.

20 December 1999	Vermont Court rules in *Baker v. Vermont* that same-sex couples are entitled to equal protection. The court refuses to rule on a specific remedy and refers the issue to the legislature to consider whether comprehensive domestic partnership or marriage is the appropriate choice.
26 April 2000	Vermont enacts civil union legislation.

Chapter 2

Sovereign Rites, Civil Rights

How sad and undemocratic that a small but well-financed group of politically sophisticated activists—identifiable only by claimed sexual behaviors—came so close to bullying an entire nation into submitting to their forced redefinition of the institution of marriage.
—Robert Larrimore Jr., letter to the *Honolulu Advertiser*, 1997

For most legislators, this debate boiled down to one simple question: should we allow unelected judges to impose a radical redefinition of marriage on this state, or should we let the people of Alaska decide? Tonight, the answer was clear: the people will decide.
—Alaska senator Loren Lehman, 1998

I think what the Vermont Supreme Court did last week was in some ways worse than terrorism.
—Presidential candidate Gary Bauer,
reacting to *Baker v. Vermont*, 1999

The unassailable arrogance of the gay rights movement should be evident to all as now it boldly and frontally assaults America's cherished core founding principle—majority rule.
—advertisement by the Geopolitical Strategist, reacting
against Vermont's establishment of civil unions

Gay rights and gay activism have increasingly become the central axis for conservative claims of cultural and political implosion and the imperative of a politics of values (Herman 1997; Patton 1997). Stories about extensive gay and lesbian political agendas, outrageous queer direct action, poor hygiene and AIDS, pedophilia and the threat of youth "recruitment," and imminent economic and social collapse—a modern-day Sodom and Gomorrah—are commonly deployed to recapitulate the importance of "family," "civilization," and Christian values and to reinforce social hierarchies and devalue diversity. When these "perversions" are said to be protected by "special rights" that further impede the function and efficiency of democratic government and social institutions, a fusion of voters into an outraged majority has been driven to the polls in the quest for political purification and the restoration of political sovereignty.

This call for purification responds directly to the social politics of visibility of lesbians and gays and recent decisions in the courts advancing gay rights. In a mirror of their liminal social visibility, gays and lesbians have asserted civil rights to transform their subversive identities and bolster their hold over marginal spaces. Without official grounds for hostility due to the declining salience of *Hardwick,* nor allowable claims to protection on the basis of gay and lesbian social identities recognized under the rubric of suspect class status, opposition to the extension of civil rights protection has proceeded along two novel pathways. One has involved democratic moves to block courts from hearing these new rights demands. This is less a rejection of law than a de-emphasis of rights voiced severally by moderates and communitarians rejecting an excess of associated social identities (Currah 1997), and reemphasis by New Right groups struggling to peel "illegitimate" gay rights claims from those of African Americans and other communities they consider more deserving of civil rights, in order to broaden their antigay appeal (Patton 1995).

This partial valorization of the law by conservatives is compounded by the complex logic of formal legal instruments designed to prevent excessive civil rights claims. Restrictions preventing gay, lesbian, and bisexual identities from gaining standing before the law for purposes of equal protection litigation simultaneously recognize these same "orientation[s], conduct, practices or relationships"[1] as constitutive of the identity languages justice will remain blind to. This continues to make law the site at which some coding of identity is both enunciated and suppressed, keeping law available for mobilization (Bower 1994; McCann 1994; McClure 1993). Another approach attempts to thwart these insurgent identities and reduce the threat of these mobilizations by deploying new discourses of state security. Rather than increase state power to contain these threats, these new claims justify a broad conservation of state authority. I argue in this chapter that it has been these new discourses of sovereignty and the transformed values of rights compatible with them that have fueled this politics today.

Special Rights and Sovereign Silences

In response to arguments that antidiscrimination protection in general and marriage rights in particular are hallmarks of full citizenship for gays and lesbians, conservatives have responded that gays ask not for civil rights but special rights designed to protect their distinctive behavior (see Gerstmann 1999, 99ff.; Keen and Goldberg 1998, 133–57). Despite the recent lack of success of such arguments in courts, this discursive move has succeeded at the level of the popular imagination because it performs two stock and legitimating operations. First, it provides a cultural focus for policy language advocating political retreat. Rather than regulate sovereignty by strengthening national boundaries (as does immigration legislation), by invoking jurisdictional limits established by federalism, or by preserving the contours of social space—all of which demand an increase or valorization of governmental authority—majorities and state officials attuned to their electoral demands have asserted the need to withdraw from formerly acknowledged public commitments to universal equality and liberty. As I demonstrate in the next section of this chapter, these limits on governmental authority deeply resonate with other common discourses of scarcity and exclusivity endemic to American liberalism, confusing in the process civil rights based in the values of a free and democratic society with entitlements that have always been qualified by the level of economic development.

Second, where everyday constructions of sovereignty are institutionally challenged (e.g., by social movements and by courts), the sovereign individual privilege of silence is undone by the risky and unpracticed requirement to justify hierarchy, exclusion, and the control of state authority. As one person illustrated this concern in her testimony before the Hawai'i legislature, "I never thought in my lifetime, I would have to defend marriage. . . . Please let the meaning of 'FAMILY' live on One Father, One Mother and their Children."[2] No longer able to avoid the disciplinarity of discursivity (Brown 1998), speech reinstating privilege threatens to dissolve the "sovereign conceit" (Butler 1996) through exposure of illegitimate language games that make such speech intelligible.

Special rights arguments modulate speech and silence in the re-creation of sovereign privilege in two ways. Initially, they specify the commitments preserved as traditional and conservative, renaming the threatened but culturally valued institutions as the minority interests to be protected from civil rights advances (Patton 1993). This rhetorical position is glaringly evident in the title of the federal Defense of Marriage Act (1996), which permits states more latitude in denying recognition of same-sex marriages conducted in other states as though such unions were a direct imposition upon heterosexual marriage (incidentally exposing the national character of these sovereignty concerns). This rhetoric is also evident in the voiced concern that gay and lesbian demands victimize the majority through a straitjacket of hate speech. In a metaphor made increasingly common during the amendment campaign, one activist opposed to same-sex marriage imagines this as a form of public rape:

> I believe that a small minority of homosexual marriage advocates are trying to force their values down the throats of the people of Hawai'i. I do not think that they're evil. I think they have an agenda. . . . And anyone who disagrees with them is labeled a homophobe, or is labeled a gay basher.[3]

A newspaper advertisement placed by the Alliance for Traditional Marriage, which this activist heads, repeated the same concern (fig. 1).

The hortatory notion voiced in this ad that only "one word will set it straight" implicates the limits of any rhetorical riposte to the parry of rights demands. The prison house of civil rights language is ultimately seen to subvert the very foundations of liberal sense-making. Consider the following passage from a legal brief arguing against same-sex marriage in Vermont:

> [Appellants] hope to prevail because they understand that appearances can be deceiving. For this is *not* a straight-forward challenge to Vermont's marriage law. Though couched in the familiar language of our Western liberal tradition, the analytical framework the Appellants actually urge this Court to adopt in granting them relief . . . has extraordinarily drastic and dangerous implications for our constitutional democracy. This case involves far more than a traditional tug of war between legislative and judicial power. Rather, we believe that the entire discursive context in which the Appellants argue, and in which the state has been forced to offer its response, is inappropriate and deeply subversive both to the fun-

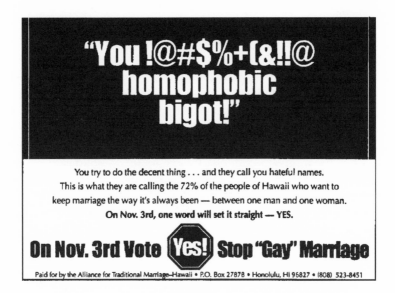

Fig. 1.   Advertisement in favor of amendment to Hawai'i's constitution giving legislature jurisdiction over marriage, placed by the Alliance for Traditional Marriage. (*Honolulu Star Bulletin*, 28 October 1998, A14.)

damental organizing principles of our society and to the political foundations on which our democracy rests.[4]

Democracy, in this view, is constrained by the sovereign discursive binary separating sense from anarchic nonsense, from which the state should be protected by the judiciary.

With the animus rhetorically reversed and socially located (Halley 1997, 437), hostility to the social demands of gays and lesbians is then rendered redundant as well as distasteful. One conservative observer unwittingly makes this point when he argues that refusing to associate with gays and lesbians may force those

> individuals and groups who wish to be left alone . . . to engage in the unhappy task of group defamation in order to achieve that rather simple end. The upshot is that the entire process sanctions a level of antigay and antilesbian rhetoric that is better left unspoken in public settings. (Epstein 1994, 2472)

As the phenomenologist Alfred Schutz generalizes this process,

> the in-group feels itself frequently misunderstood by the out-group; such failure to understand its ways of life, so the in-group feels, must be rooted in hostile prejudices or in bad faith, since the truths held by the in-group are "matters of course," self-evident and, therefore, understandable by any human being. This feeling may lead to a partial shift of the system of relevances prevailing within the in-group, namely, by originating a solidarity of resistance against outside criticism. The out-group is then looked at with repugnance, disgust, aversion, antipathy, hatred, or fear. (1970, 86)

Eliminating criticism therefore emerges as a natural means to protect in-group values while providing the rationale for projecting hostility on those who dare to mount an epistemological challenge.

Colorado's Amendment 2 seems to have been designed to enforce truth along these very grounds. Passed in 1992 by a majority of Colorado's voters, the amendment prohibited the state or any of its political subdivisions from enacting any

> statute, regulation, ordinance, or policy whereby homosexual, lesbian or bisexual orientation, conduct, practices or relationships shall constitute or otherwise be the basis of, or entitle any person or class of person to have or claim any minority status, quota preferences, protected status or claim of discrimination.[5]

Amendment 2 reinforced what Richards has called "the cultural pall of unspeakability" (1999, 177) about the intimate lives of gays and lesbians.

> Amendment 2 expressly made its reactionary point in terms of banning all laws that recognized antidiscrimination claims of gay and lesbian people; its target was specifically the claims to justice that constitute gay and lesbian identity. Its aim was decisively that advocates of gay and lesbian identity should be compelled to abandon their claims to personal and ethical legitimacy and either convert to the true view or return to the silence of their traditional unspeakability. (Richards 1999, 92)

Colorado's deputy solicitor who defended Amendment 2 made the same point in simpler language: "Amendment 2 [was meant to] ensure that at some point the shouting in the room ceases" (Tymkovich 1997, 315). Law can serve both to command speech and preserve the ontological comforts of silence, and both tactics seek to draw important distinctions between courts and publics, with significance both for sovereignty and for the formation and contestation of identities.

The ontological anxieties over the intrusions of discourse that have characterized debates over Amendment 2 and same-sex marriage have positioned courts as the guardians of majority interests through a critical rhetorical reversal inverting the notion of injury and the duty of protection. In Colorado, the state's effort to show the courts that Amendment 2 was not, itself, evidence of discrimination led to the argument that other, more worthy minoritarian interests were at stake. The language of antidiscrimination law was implicated in this reversal by arguments that gays, lesbians, and bisexuals could not be easily fit within equal protection doctrine. Because this "group" (given a legal identity, if not social coherence, by the antidiscrimination statutes that they had sought in Denver, Boulder, and Aspen) had disproved their powerlessness by their very success—despite being outspent 17 to 1 in the fight over Amendment 2 (Goldberg 1994, 1074)—the state claimed they could not be compared to those groups with a demonstrable history of prejudice. This argument minimizes the importance of social facts of discrimination at the same time as it establishes an impossible catch-22: any group able to protect itself through antidiscrimination statutes does not really need legal protection after all.

Bolstering this paradoxical reading, the state implied that local ordinances designed to protect jobs, housing, and the like were tantamount to property interests in the state: a perversion of republican principles that would reverse traditional state-society relations as well as corrode the worth and integrity of the group that depended upon such legal language. If the state's arguments did not make this latter consequence explicit, the conservative Pacific Legal Foundation did in its supporting brief.

> The civil rights struggle of the 1950s and 1960s secured the political rights and basic opportunities necessary for black Americans to fully enjoy the fruits of citizenship. Since then, however, the civil rights "movement" has been transformed into an establishment

dedicated to perpetuating itself and expanding its power. The traditional civil rights movement derived its moral legitimacy from
the universality of the rights it sought to establish. The modern
civil rights establishment has abandoned this moral claim by transforming the meaning of civil rights from those fundamental rights
all Americans share equally into special benefits for some and bur-
dens for others. . . . There is no reason to believe that new politically active groups who choose to identify themselves in some
manner will not also seek to parlay nondiscrimination into affirmative duties. (24–25)

Since legal protection granted undue "affirmative duties" that
inflated the power already signaled by the emplacement of local
antidiscrimination statutes, the state argued it was entitled to reassert a
threatened sovereignty. In this manner, the state's brief reconceptual-
ized Amendment 2 as a bulwark against a group's "ability to define the
agendas of all levels of government,"[6] effectively making state authority a minority interest to be protected. Here, the state's vulnerability
models a valid minority position in contrast to a position that gays and
lesbians cannot articulate. Rather than discrimination from this vantage, the state argued that "the intent and effect of Amendment 2 is to
withdraw a deeply divisive social and political issue from elected representatives and place its resolution squarely in the hands of the people," a matter that "goes to the heart of state sovereignty."[7] It is not sexual minorities who are denied political representation by Amendment
2 in this argument, but the people whose rights were trampled by the
court's improper injunction against the amendment: "The right to vote
can be infringed just as effectively by nullifying votes as by preventing
them from being cast in the first place."[8]

The year following the vote on Amendment 2 in Colorado, the
Hawai'i Supreme Court brought down its ruling in *Baehr*. That case
began a series of public interventions including statewide legislative
hearings on same-sex marriage (1993, 1996, and 1997), a commission
appointed to advise the legislature on constitutional involvement in
1995 (which recommended five-to-two against legislative interference),
and legislative debate that culminated in the amendment to moot the
case that was passed in 1998. That legal arguments by the state defending its position in court, and public testimony against same-sex mar-

riage, were impelled by rhetorical reversals like that in Colorado is, perhaps, not surprising considering the nature of the public good being sought. Arguments about the benefits of marriage by conservative activists and state authorities crosscut the claims for its reservation to heterosexuals. If marriage should be encouraged for its ability to discipline human sexuality, to promote social stability, and to augment beneficial socialization, as the traditionalists have claimed, then increasing the number of married couples seems more a virtue than a vice. Yet even if gay and lesbian couples cannot accomplish these social goals—whether on account of an incapacity to embrace "nuptial continence" as the minority report to the Hawai'i legislative commission in 1995 approvingly cited, or because of impediments to conceiving or adopting children, a cart before the horse argued by the state's attorney—why the extension of marriage benefits *harms* society is a matter going to the heart of heterosexual privilege. Much as in the Colorado case, to successfully make the argument of injury depends on demonstrating the vulnerability of state sovereignty upholding this privilege.

One facet of this demonstration can be found in the very idiom of "tradition" that has suffused the campaign against new marriage rights/rites. Tradition, once invoked, as Bauman suggests, charges the discursive field with a defensive tone.

> The paradox of tradition is that once it has been spoken the tradition is no more what its spokesmen claim it to be. Tradition is invoked for the authority of its silence: a silence that neither needs nor brooks argument and which renders all argument superfluous, pretentious and impotent. Yet in order to yield its authority (that is, to be of that use whose prospect had seduced the speaker in the first place), tradition needs to be argumentatively established: its silence must be broken . . . It is said that human conditions do not exist until they are named: but they are not named until they are noticed, and they are hardly ever noticed until their existence becomes a matter of concern, of active search and creative/defensive efforts. (1996, 49)

Rulings directing the supreme court's remand rightly recognized this paradox, discrediting the legal sufficiency of common "creative/defensive efforts" arguing that same-sex marriage threatens tradition (nonetheless carried in several amicus briefs from Catholic and Mormon groups), and that natural law prohibited same-sex unions. Instead, a three-pronged attack was made by and on behalf of the state.

The first prong acknowledged the strong position of the democratic sovereign against the plaintiffs, whose many assertions of privilege had frequently delayed the court case. Gays and courts were forcing an idea of marriage that the majority opposed—a clear case of "judicial tyranny."[9] As the cochair of Hawaii's Future Today, a conservative group that formed after the *Baehr* decision, testified before the legislature,

> given the results of several public opinion polls, it is clear that Hawai'i residents do not want to legalize same sex marriage. . . . It is the responsibility of the legislature to act on behalf of the people to pre-empt a decision by the court. It's times like these that make me grateful I live in a democracy.[10]

The rhetoric of the people is more than an appeal to the legislative branch; it is a demand for sovereign control over public authority and debate, including the newspapers who were steadfast in their support for same-sex marriage in Hawai'i.

> We live in a state rated near the bottom in education and business climate in America. Our cost of living is among the highest in the nation, and our economic base remains perilously tied to one thing—tourism.
>
> We have legislators who openly refuse to represent the voice of the people, and the really sad part is that, by and large, the people have let them get away with it.
>
> Could it be that most of us are too busy just trying to keep our heads above water in this almost impossible economic situation?
>
> But, hey, look on the bright side. At least we'll be the first state in the union to legalize same-sex marriage!
>
> And with the Star-Bulletin omnipotently declaring same sex-marriage legalization is right, it almost makes me want to shout, "This ain't over!"
>
> Come on, people, let's show the elite—including this newspaper—who really is in charge.[11]

At its extreme, such rhetoric permits the sovereign imagination to eliminate the threat of courts and civil rights, *tout court*.[12] If the appeal to tradition discursively depends on the paradox of the authority of its silence, but the necessity of its defense, as Bauman suggests, such tactics of democratic closure on legal debate make sense. The law is easily isolated as the source of sovereign anxiety due to its demands for argument, whereas the legislature can stand up for tradition and silence by constitutionally excluding the impermissible. Gays impudently refuse to acknowledge these legislative and sovereign boundaries according to this position. The minority report of the legislative commission charged to look into same-sex marriage suggested that state jurisdictional boundaries could not contain the consequences of gay activism for the nation as a whole, hyperbolically revealing that "there is even a home page on the Internet where homosexual activists freely discuss this issue across the country."[13] Where silence is sovereign, free discussion is anarchy.

While these fears of the demise of tradition and the broad, unbridled power of gay speech aided by judges beyond democratic reproach reveal much about anxieties over an imperiled sovereignty, they do not tackle directly the issue of why the extension of marriage to gays and lesbians matters for marriage as a whole. A second, more pointed prong can be found in the argument that the state cannot be neutral when it comes to domestic politics, and so must choose between democratic wishes and the antagonistic rights of minorities. As the State of Hawai'i's brief argued, "marriage is too deeply enmeshed in conventional morality to fit neatly into an equal rights analysis."[14] Simply put, this argument relies upon the claim that legalizing same-sex marriages is an endorsement that will promote more same-sex couplings, encourage more same-sex families to have children, and consequentially lead to more social ills. "To legalize same-sex marriage will send a message that will devalue and weaken the very relationship that is critical to draw men to their children"[15] and encourage AIDS, harm women, and confuse children. The State of Vermont followed this same pattern in its justification of state interest in marriage discrimination but added more clearly the utter vulnerability of the heterosexual family and its dependence on the state for survival. The state cited the need to preserve the link between procreation and child rearing (in order to prevent "men perceiving of themselves as sperm donors without responsibilities"), protecting marriage from "destabilizing changes" ("If same-sex 'marriages' are allowed, two elderly women sharing housing and mutual support in a non-sexual friendship might marry each other to obtain certain benefits"), and uniting "male and female qualities" that might otherwise remain distinct.[16] In short, equivocation about the morality of marriage weakens the compulsion that that institution asserts in the benefit of society.

Yet if the endorsement of same-sex marriage was something adults could ultimately choose to ignore, it was the confusion of children and the destruction of stable homes that provided these states' third and most central argument in their defense. Traditional marriage, the Hawai'i attorney argued, is really about procreation and children, and partisan choice would have to be made on behalf of those too weak to defend themselves. Rather than gays and lesbians denied the social good of marriage, it was children who would sustain the greatest impact, suffering separation from "natural" parents, bastardy, bureaucracy in the case of adoption by a nonnatural parent, and instability inherent in gay relationships, among others. It was society's commitments to its next generation and the social institutions affected by children that would be harmed by an extension of civil rights to marriage. Vermont also claimed an interest in children but distinguished its argument from that of Hawai'i:

> Unlike Hawaii, the State is not asserting that children raised by same-sex couples will develop differently in any measurable psychological way. Rather, the State's interest goes to the intangible benefit of teaching children that both men and women share responsibilities in child rearing and participate together in any number of endeavors. The State furthers this interest through its treatment of marriage.[17]

The Political Economy of Civil Rights

These arguments over the social value of civil rights in Colorado, Hawai'i, and Vermont have their genealogy in Foucault's notion of governmentality. Foucault's narrative of modernity emphasizes the historically shifting bases of authority from sovereign sources of "juridical" power exercised on a territory—imagined as emanating from a unitary source in the king, people, state—to the advent of discourses of "population" and "biopower" and the multiple and diverse resultant forces brought to bear on social control. Governmentality, which embraces this vast and more recent tactical realm of the state, accentuates the authoritative importance of political control over space, the public and private realms, political subjectivity, and the like. Whereas sovereignty aimed for the common good, government models itself on the prosperous management of a household or family for its common welfare.

> The things with which in this sense government is to be concerned are in fact men, but men in their relations, their links, their imbrication with those other things which are wealth, resources, means of subsistence, the territory with its specific qualities, climate, irrigation, fertility, etc.; men in their relation to that other kind of things, customs, habits, ways of acting and thinking, etc.; lastly, men in their relation to that other kind of things, accidents and misfortunes such as famine, epidemics, death, etc. (Foucault 1991, 93)

This plurality of aims and identities has implications for the mechanisms of sovereignty (Kuehls 1996, 66ff.). Whereas law and sovereignty were once conceptually inseparable (Luhmann 1990, 11–56), it increasingly became a matter of "employing tactics rather than laws, and even of using laws themselves as tactics—to arrange things in such a way that, through a certain number of means, such and such ends may be achieved" (Foucault, 1991, 95). "It is the tactics of government which make possible the continual definition and redefinition of what is within the competence of the state and what is not, the public versus the private and so on" (Foucault 1991, 103).

The contemporary literature on governmentality has concerned itself with the mapping the emergence of this pluralist space as forms of liberalism and their associated political economies (Rose and Miller 1992; Burchell 1996; O'Malley 1996). Liberalism, from this perspective, emerged in the eighteenth century when government could no longer rely upon the assumption of sovereign control and the self-assured knowledge of rule, but instead upon what Foucault calls "the idea of *society*. That is . . . that government not only has to deal with a territory, with a domain, and with its subjects, but . . . also with a complex and independent reality that has its own laws and mechanisms of disturbance" (1989, 261). From this recognition of the social, a free market could be distinguished: "*Laissez-faire* is here both a limitation of the exercise of political sovereignty *vis-à-vis* the government of commercial exchanges, and a positive justification of market freedom on the grounds that the State will benefit more—will become richer and more powerful—by governing less" (Burchell 1996, 22). In contrast to the naturalized freedom of *homo economicus,* a more contemporary neoliberalism begins from the assumption that regulating government requires the conscious creation of rationalities of freedom: the self-responsible, competitive, and entrepreneurial subject (O'Malley 1996).

In these accounts of governmentality, the idea of sovereignty is frequently eclipsed as law in its classically liberal forms is seen to have continued "a phase of juridical regression" (Foucault 1980a, 144), fading away as a mode of regulation of the self and of society. Governmentality has been variously depicted as an "expulsion" of law (Hunt 1992) and as a "new cluster of power relations, beyond the juridical framework of sovereignty" (Donnelly, quoted in Fitzpatrick 1999, 19). Nonetheless, as Constable (1993), Fitzpatrick (1999), Dillon (1995), and others have made clear, Foucault was strikingly ambivalent about law and sovereignty. Although he is famously noted for suggesting that sovereignty is an inadequate basis for theory ("in political thought and analysis, we still have not cut off the head of the king" [Foucault 1980a, 88–89]), at the same time he saw that with governmentality "the problem of sovereignty is made more acute than ever" (1991, 101).

I take from this more recent understanding of governmentality not the eclipse of law and the juridical for sovereignty practices, but rather its regular return, its competition and collusion with alternative tactics and discourses and its utility for ordering access to those material relations that make up a political economy: "it is the tactics of government which make possible the continual definition and redefinition of what is within the competence of the state and what is not, the public versus the private, and so on; thus the state can only be understood in its survival and its limits on the basis of the general tactics of governmentality" (Foucault 1991, 103).

Colin Gordon has observed that these are concerns about "liberalism as a form of knowledge calculated to limit power by persuading government of its own incapacity; [of] the notion of the rule of law as the architecture of a pluralist social space" (1991, 47). Seen in this light, contemporary conservative stories about both gay behavior and the nature of civil rights are referenda on the model of law as a plastic and nearly unlimited source of liberties facilitating a universal participation in the social contract. In contrast to this liberal pluralism based on the imperatives of self-identity is a view privileging social institutions such as families, local schools, businesses, and churches, and with them their unassailable hierarchies and privileges as the source of what Berlant has called a "hygienic governmentality" (1997, 175ff.) to control the threat of gay bodies and gay rights. This argument for private privilege establishes an alternative allocation of values—of material, cultural, and social things, in Foucault's litany—constitutive of a political economy. Yet there is an undeniably public character to these concerns, as well, seen most clearly in the argument that democratic majorities are the sovereign bodies around which such "traditional" privileges should be maintained.

In order to further understand the tactical mechanisms of this sovereignty politics, I follow the critical lessons of this genealogy of governmentality by delving into the neoliberal economic underpinnings of the antagonism between courts and publics. I examine three basic interests that these states have claimed as their own: protection of limited resources by restricting antidiscrimination enforcement to those "particularly deserving of special protection";[18] protecting "prevailing preferences of the state's population,"[19] particularly property and religious rights; and furthering efficient law enforcement.

Downsizing Rights: The Politics of Scarcity

The supporters of Amendment 2 were acutely aware that laws and policies designed to benefit homosexuals and bisexuals could have an adverse effect on the ability of state and local governments to combat discrimination against suspect classes.
—State of Colorado Plaintiffs Brief, *Romer v. Evans*, 1995

How many new schools would not be built, and how many programs for needy women and children would be sacrificed to pay for the increased public costs associated with luring the same-sex traffic to Hawaii? Who knows what these costs might be?
—State of Hawaii, *Report of the Commission on Sexual Orientation and the Law*, 1995, Minority Report

The equal protection clause is a limitation on the State's power to legislate unreasonable classifications. The Plaintiffs seek to trans-

form the limitation into an affirmative obligation for the State to
endorse same-sex couples as the equivalent to male-female couples.
If this occurs, then traditional marriage becomes merely the "other"
alternative lifestyle.
                    —State of Hawaii post-trial brief, *Baehr v. Miike*, 1996

In the argument that a precarious state sovereignty necessitates a low
priority for the protection of gays and lesbians, the claim that states are
subject to constitutional fiscal constraints in the enforcement of civil
rights plays two supporting roles. The first is to distinguish "deserving" minorities from others, preserving governmental commitments to
traditional "suspect classes" at the expense of "a politically powerful
and relatively privileged special interest group."[20] Such a rhetorical
move supports public testimony that it will be blacks and women who
will be most harmed by the extension of antidiscrimination protection
(Goldberg 1994, 1076–77; Keen and Goldberg 1998, 113ff.). Whether this
is designed to build alliances with other civil rights groups is perhaps
less important than the simulation of a universality of concern (a recognition of "true" civil rights or, in the case of marriage, traditional matrimony) and the reestablishment of boundaries through a reasoned
response to what Rohrer has called the "politics of scarcity" (1996, 56)
that exemplifies this new language.

A second role of this scarcity rhetoric is to transform the images of
sovereignty of the liberal state away from the foundational Lockean
idea of a limited government whose "contracted" authority rests upon
protection of basic and sovereign rights to liberty. These classical liberties are often understood as negative in that they establish formal inhi-
bitions on official power and prerogative. In a strange inversion of this
social contract imagery, it is not rights that are central to liberty, but liberty that is central to rights, a positive conception of rights that works
as a reflexive limit upholding democratic sovereignty. This is clear in
the marriage case, where the State of Hawai'i argued the impossibility
of drawing an equal protection distinction between same-sex marriage,
polygamy, and incest. The state's legitimacy is now seen to stem from a
recognition of its own promiscuity on behalf of personal freedoms, an
Odysseus bound to the mast against the Sirens of social and sexual
need in the quest of its own sovereign destiny.

While the limited state that must draw the line at rights for sexual
minorities is one frame by which support for constitutional limits is

constructed, the other is the deployment of the politics of scarcity to rhetorically invert majority and minority positions. One way that this is done is to demonstrate the zero-sum character of fundamental rights doctrine. The conservative jurist Robert Bork argued in an amicus brief that it was not just the sovereign majority whose rights were infringed by the Colorado courts' nullification of Amendment 2, but those more deserving groups who lobbied for its passage. Protecting groups not sanctioned by suspect class doctrine

> infringe[s] the "fundamental political rights" of those groups, such as Colorado for Family Values, that disagree with "independently identifiable groups" such as respondents. . . . Thus the Colorado Supreme Court truly did "single out" and "disenfranchise" a group of Colorado citizens by denying that group access to a law-making procedure available to all other citizens—the constitutional amendment route.[21]

Similarly, in the case of marriage, it is "the minority infringing on the majority"[22] through the courts, disenfranchising "traditional" families. Not just their vote is nullified, but their policy preferences and political sovereignty are threatened by the governmentalized claim of the fiscal consequences of extended rights. As the State of Hawai'i balanced its future ledgers in its post-trial brief to the circuit court that heard the marriage case on remand: "every dollar spent on a same-sex couple, or a cohabiting couple, of necessity strips a dollar from the State's ability to assist married couples" (34). Vermont likewise saw terrible consequences from the secondary effects of same-sex marriage that would diminish rights for others. Citing the likelihood that increased surrogacy contracts from same-sex couples desiring children would have an "obvious" impact "on the resources of the court system from increased litigation," it concluded that "the Legislature could rationally decide to avoid these issues and costs by denying marriage to same-sex couples."[23]

The politics of scarcity sweeps along within its economic logic a neoliberal fondness for entrepreneurialism (O'Malley 1996). Groups demanding rights should demonstrate not only that their demands little burden the political community, but that they provide concrete benefit to the commonweal. As a leader of the largest "traditional" marriage advocacy group at the time testified before the legislature in 1997,

> In assessing this [amendment to constitutionally block same-sex marriages] we should be discussing the economic and sociological impact same-sex marriage would have on our community. However, debate is continually sidetracked with the issue of civil rights. . . . An equal status for same-sex couples is not supported by evidence of equal contributions to society.[24]

When this entrepreneurial language is used by proponents to argue that same-sex marriage could have direct economic advantage to the state by reaping the pent-up demand for gay and lesbian nuptials,[25] such economic benefits are revealed to cheapen and denigrate sovereignty through the sale of the state's sovereign police powers over health and safety. This, in turn, delegitimates gays and lesbians who would stoop to talking about marriage in such materialist terms. As the state sarcastically argued to the court in its post-trial brief in 1996, "if Hawai'i is willing to legalize same-sex marriage, why not legalize prostitution, gambling, marijuana, or even better, child prostitution? That would probably be even more lucrative—in the short term" (55).

These arguments infuse the claims that rights endanger traditional institutions, values, and their champions at the same time that rights are upheld as integral to the authentic expression of groups whose goal is the conservation of a proper sovereignty. Here governmentality integrates the economic and the legal as separate but reinforcing tactics. Where rights promote inroads into democratic authority, economic rhetoric tames the excess while transmuting antagonism into a defense of the political commons. The difference between patriots and perverts is made all the more palatable, thereby allowing the connection between economic and moral authority to be reinscribed.

Defending Public Preferences

The zero-sum accounting of rights and resources based in the politics of scarcity is the major backdrop for the spectacles impugning "special rights." Both antidiscrimination and anti–"gay marriage" themes in this political genre feature several acts in which putative majority interests are demonstrated to be more fragile and in need of community and state protection than those of more powerful sexual interest groups. Important to this reversal is the manner in which traditional rights to religious and personal liberty and household privacy are shown to protect critical yet vulnerable social institutions (home, church, and property), thus permitting dominant majority political interests to be viewed through a minoritarian lens. As the State of Hawai'i argued along these lines,

> If successful, the redefinition of marriage will be followed by other legal challenges seeking a "functional definition" of parenthood to address perceived inequality in child custody, statutory entitlements and inheritance laws. In short, the orderly structure of laws governing property, domestic relations, and the descent and distribution of property will each be *assaulted*.[26]

This fear of anarchy has resonance with the claim by the State of Vermont that "intractable economic, social and even philosophical problems"[27] would result from same-sex marriage. By implication, it is only through careful husbandry that the state can retain important economic goods whose very genealogy in the *oikos* is once again manifest.

In the Colorado case, these threatened economic interests are argued to be rationally protected by Amendment 2, thus passing a standard level of judicial review.

> Amendment 2 . . . enhances individual freedom by eliminating governmental interference in the choices people make in religious, familial, personal, and associational matters. . . . In truth, these interests are, cumulatively, nothing more than the individual liberty that this nation has cherished for over two centuries. At the heart of that individual liberty is the freedom to make personal choices regarding with whom one wishes to associate, and how one wishes to be governed. . . . Under the ordinances preempted by Amendment 2, individual landlords or employers who have sincere and profound religious objections to homosexuality would nonetheless be compelled to compromise those convictions under threat of government sanctions [and] the implicit endorsement of homosexuality fostered by laws granting special protections could undermine the efforts of some parents to teach traditional moral values.[28]

Examples of such compulsion drive home the point that it is the weakest institutions that are the most threatened by equal protection rights for gays and lesbians. The State of Colorado's brief illustrates this with stories of an "employer sanctioned because his wife gave religious literature to a homosexual employee" (29), and of Aspen churches required by ordinance to open their facilities to homosexual organizations if they allow other community groups access. It also draws upon trial testimony of a Wisconsin woman convicted under that state's antidiscrimination statutes who refused to share her house with a lesbian for fear of "the potential for [unwanted] [*sic*] physical, sexual attraction" (29). Supporting briefs are more colorful in their stories emphasizing not only lurid predation by gay teachers on unwary students and subtle corruption of young minds when "homosexual conduct is . . . accepted as a normal and acceptable lifestyle choice,"[29] but also lawsuits against "conservative Christians for allegedly 'aiding or abetting' discrimination if they should say that homosexuality is wrong or is a sin."[30] In Vermont, one such brief against same-sex marriage worried about the effects on "the religious liberty of persons whose religious beliefs forbid them to rent their property to persons who would engage in acts of fornication or sodomy on the premises."[31]

While the Hawai'i high court refused to give credence to such fears—especially those of churches concerned that they might be forced to conduct same-sex marriages against their will[32]—the Colorado Supreme Court did accept the argument that religious liberty and familial and associational privacy were important if not compelling state interests. Despite this ruling, they held that Amendment 2 was neither necessary nor narrowly tailored to uphold these interests, especially where equal protection violations would result. Significantly, the court also ruled that government does not burden individual rights by endorsing disagreeable views; protecting public morality does not constitute a compelling governmental interest. Nonetheless, as these stories suggest, the political battle is drawn in ways that resist these rather standard legal arguments by illustrating the dangers posed by gays and lesbians to private institutions. This danger is enhanced by reframing the amendment and same-sex marriage as a referendum on public morality. As the attorney general of Colorado argued before the Colorado Supreme Court, challenging the lower court's grant of a permanent injunction,

> The people have not attempted to take away existing federal constitutional rights but have said that otherwise they do not feel that

that issue of homosexuality should be the subject of mandated private conduct, and that is the moral debate that is still going on at this point. It is not resolved. And this court does not need to resolve that moral debate in order to find that it is constitutionally the subject of constitutional debate.[33]

If the "moral debate" is presumed public, it is still the private situations that are definitive. What is claimed publicly is neither the potential criminality of homosexual behavior (although this is the basis of Justice Scalia's dissent in *Romer*), nor privacy rights protecting personal convictions antagonistic to homosexuality. Rather, it is the right to punish sexual minorities privately—to shun, to deprive of a livelihood, to ignore, to erase—reinforced by denying lesbian and gay parents the protection of the private, family realm altogether. As gays and lesbians have shown their ubiquity through acts of coming out, sovereignty is reestablished in the private realm through private action sanctioned by a state attuned to private vulnerability. It is illustrative to note that through this reversal, tolerance for religious liberty is yoked to claims for toleration for religious intolerance and incivility, a far distance from the original claims for First Amendment freedoms.

The Efficiency of Rights

A final legal argument is made on behalf of the rationality of Amendment 2 and the ban on same-sex marriage: its contribution to political uniformity. Elimination of city antidiscrimination ordinances in Colorado protecting gays, lesbians, and bisexuals is argued to promote efficient enforcement, maximize individual liberty, preserve traditional social norms, enhance economic and legal predictability for employers, and ensure, in the words of the Colorado attorney general, "that the deeply divisive issue of homosexuality does not serve to seriously fragment Colorado's body politic."[34] In the case of same-sex marriage these federalism concerns assume a rather bizarre twist. Rather than an interest in state rights to maintain efficient government, the state argues for its duty of moderation toward other states. "The State of Hawai'i must be concerned with how it treats other states. If successful at marrying, same-sex couples will use Hawai'i marriages to foment litigation in the other 49 states and against the federal government."[35] Alaska's legislature argued to the state supreme court that

Marriage and marital status play a role in literally hundreds of government laws and programs in every jurisdiction, both state and federal. Thus, Alaska has a compelling interest in keeping marriage a homogeneous, stable and certain institution. In fact, the smooth functioning of interstate relations regarding marriage and family relations is one of the most compelling state interests shared by Alaska and the other forty-nine states. . . . Alaska's compelling interest in cooperative federalism alone is sufficient justification for refusing to legalize same-sex marriage at this time.[36]

Vermont alluded to the Hawai'i controversy in arguing that it "is not an island unto itself" and that the court must defer to legislative interests in a "rational preference for legal uniformity with other states."[37] Ten states[38] filed an amicus brief in which they saw "severe implications for interstate comity."

This case is not only about how Vermont treats same-sex unions, but it is also about how Vermont treats other States. Any resolution of the same-sex marriage debate in Vermont must take into account the effect that Vermont's action will have on the 49 other states and the federal union. In many ways, possibly including operation of the Full Faith and Credit clause, Vermont's legalization of same-sex marriage would be manipulated in an effort to override other States' and Congress' recently reaffirmed, historically constant, strong marriage policies. Vermont, like its sister States, has a compelling state interest in not drastically redefining marriage in a way that will undeniably create tremendous confusion, imperil the interjurisdictional recognition of Vermont marriages, and produce divisive, coercive pressures on other States that may severely strain Vermont's relations with its sister States.[39]

A similar coalition of states filed a brief with the Hawai'i court that asked for briefs on the consequences of the 1998 amendment in which they argued that uniformity is not just for the sake of comity, but also economy. "Same-sex couples with Hawai'i marriage licenses would have the potential to instigate disruptive and resource consuming constitutional litigation throughout the United States over the interjurisdictional recognition of their 'marriage.'"[40] These arguments seem awkward at first glance because these political fights provide the spectacle for just what they are designated to cure. Yet these arguments also reemphasize the urge toward a seamless sovereign, one whose own body remains unblemished through the exfoliation of those whose bodily practices do not conform to a sanctioned norm.

What is interesting about these claims is their subtle rearrangement of the foundational ideas of political authority and their subversive use of the metaphor of body politic. The locus classicus for this metaphor is Thomas Hobbes's *Leviathan,* where the frightening image of a state of nature in which the solitary, poor, nasty, brutish, and short life devoid of political agreement is contrasted to an artificial image of the self in which sovereignty is to be alienated.

> For by Art is created that great LEVIATHAN called a COMMONWEALTH, or STATE . . . which is but an Artificiall Man; though of greater stature and strength than the Naturall, for whose protection and defence it was intended; and in which, the *Soveraignty* is an Artificiall Soul, as giving life and motion to the whole body . . . by which the parts of this Body Politique were at first made, set together and united, resemble that *Fiat,* or the *Let us make man,* pronounced by God in the Creation. (1968, 81–82)

As God creates man, so man creates the state through a convention constituting the sovereign body politic. This convention privileges the rational. In Bryan Turner's words,

> The Hobbesian problem of order was historically based on a unitary concept of the body. The social contract was between men who, out of an interest in self-preservation, surrendered individual rights to the state, which existed to enforce social peace. However, the regime of political society also requires a regimen of bodies and in particular a government of bodies which are defined by their multiplicity and diversity. The Hobbesian problem is overtly an analysis of the proper relationship between desire and reason, or more precisely between sexuality and instrumental rationality. This problem in turn can be restated as the proper relationship between men as bearers of public reason and women as embodiments of private emotion. (1984, 113–14)

In the democratic—as opposed to Hobbesian absolutist—state, this tension between reason and desire continues, but not precisely in its gendered form identified by Turner. Civil rights shift these boundaries, but by a similar logic rights for new groups will only be protected where reason can dictate an expansion. It was reason that brought men together and legitimated the body politic through a social contract, and it is reason that can breach the divide between men and women, expunging desire from reason in the equivalent of contract renegotiations. Women retain an uncertain status for many groups today promoting traditional families, but race provides a better handle for their argument. As the Colorado deputy solicitor argued before the Colorado Supreme Court,

> There is a major profound choice for society, and voters' felt attitudes about homosexuality should not be mandated by the legislature or by the town council, but that the people should be able to have a vote directly. This is different from all other civil rights issues discussed in all of the precedents before us today because of the lack of national moral consensus. In racial matters, there have been difficulties with implementation of the issue. There have been conflicts, but the moral consensus was decided for all time in the Civil War.[41]

In the Civil War, desire and aggression annihilate themselves, and what remains is consensus or reason around which civil rights protections can be legitimated.[42]

Richards (1998) has argued that the concept of moral slavery won from the Civil War is, indeed, reason to include gays and women under the doctrine of constitutionally protected classes. Politically, this seems to depend upon the unwillingness to see sexual orientation as a sovereign marker of rationality. Yet from these other perspectives that contrast civil rights protections for race, gay rights remain too volatile, too filled with aggression and passion to be included in the body politic. Gays, lesbians, and bisexuals remain within a state of nature, beings defined by their exaggerated and primitive desires, untamed by reason or the countervalences of the opposite sex, and condemned to disease and anarchy (Cooper 1995, 68–69; Herman 1997, 76–82). The additionally implied perversity here is the complex notion that gays do not merely wish to act upon their sexual desires, but they are often wrongly passionate, valuing money above love. As eight Hawai'i legislators argued in an amicus brief to that state's court, "If the State of Hawai'i permits same-sex couples to marry, marriage will be reduced to an entity formed by persons wishing to exploit its tax advantages and other benefits."[43] By protecting the proper value for marriage in Hawai'i, just as Colorado sought to defend private forms of discrimination and aggression, policy revalues the state of nature, asserting a sovereignty denying to the state its right to extend civil rights protections that now must be *reigned* in. As members of the body politic in this logic, we have less to fear from each other than from those marked by a desire that cannot appropriately be, and—as the case against same-sex marriage makes clear—will not be allowed to be, domesticated in common institutions. Instead, aggression and violence play their part in acts of sovereignty that reimagine the violence of the state of nature.

Lord of the Flies—a Note on Children

Legal and political arguments in Colorado, Vermont, Alaska, and Hawai'i have all advanced the state's fiduciary interest in children as a reason to uphold popular or state antipathies toward rights for gays and lesbians. Colorado's solicitor general argued, "The implicit endorsement of homosexuality fostered by laws granting special protections could undermine the efforts of some parents to teach traditional moral values. It is certainly rational for the State to seek to prevent this kind of confusion."[44] A popular television and newspaper ad in Hawai'i during the 1998 amendment campaign implied the same loss of control by depicting a young boy reading from "Daddy's Wedding," a story that takes a matter-of-fact look at a family with two fathers. "If you don't think homosexual marriage will affect you, how do you think it will affect your children?" the narrator of the television version asks.[45] States have argued generally that this harmful confusion is as much a matter of the popularly rejected legitimacy of gay and lesbian families as it is the likelihood that children will be confronted with legal instruments governing surrogacy contracts, subjected to legal uncertainty over their proper guardians, and legally denied access to their "natural" parents, all of which will ultimately make children fail to "adjust." This concern for children provided the main basis for the State of Hawai'i's case at trial in 1996 arguing for the state's compelling rationale for discriminating in the issuance of marriage licenses.

The state's police powers over children's welfare—furthered most
when the state does less to disrupt the heterosexual family sphere—is
ultimately put ahead of civil rights in these arguments. As the State of
Hawai'i continued to argue to the circuit court after it lost its case on
every count,

> It is possible that allowing same-sex marriage may have some ben-
> efits for the same-sex couple. However, it greatly increases the
> exposure of children to family disruption and related develop-
> mental difficulties. At the same time, since the child still must be
> adopted, there is little benefit to the child from the occurrence of
> marriage. . . . Preserving marriages lessens state involvement in
> family matters.[46]

While the alarm rung over child welfare plays upon deep emo-
tions, it also fuels the imagination of popular sovereignty in several
ways. Children serve as a sign of vulnerability, not just for private institutions clumsily trod upon by an unwieldy and overzealous state
whose rights-based intrusions are inimical to security. But also, as
wards presumed to be without judicial voice, children serve as surro-
gates for an embattled majority that has lost its voice in the tactical
maneuverings of the legal process. Children are not just imagined as
the victims of civil rights, but also as models for thinking out the proper
limitations of citizenship. As citizens denied the right to consent to
their own sexuality and to marry, children stand emblematically for the
proper public comportment of gays and lesbians. Children, as are gays,
remain a limited brand of citizen, which some will, but each can, out-
grow with the proper maturity, responsibility, and application of self-
control.

As limited citizens, children also signal the importance of the family as a locus of proper sovereign concern. As a safe, desexualized
space, the family serves as an institutional reminder of the republican
concern for passionate restraint. This takes a particularly gendered
character, as well. The concern for children's welfare is a site for the
particular endangerment that lesbians threaten to the sovereign imagination.

> Lesbians emerge in this scenario as the bad mother. . . . [L]esbians
> induct their children into sin in such a way that their children do

not even recognize it as sin. Appeals to maternal love and examples of happy families will continually confront the fear that their
love will lead their children to accept that which should not be
accepted. Maternal love then becomes not domesticating and
instructive, but seductive. (Phelan 1999, 77)

If protected children serve as a model of sovereignty in a post–civil
rights liberalism, they also reaffirm the state's governmentalized construction of authority. States and publics debate openly not just their
fear of confusion over the fates of children and the loss of tradition, but
the costs and complexities of regulating new experiments in family
structure as well as the future consequences of poor or unknown developmental patterns on procreation, population, and parenthood. Foucault reminds us that families were once the archetype for imagining
sovereignty, but in the governmentalized state families became "considered as an element internal to the population and as a fundamental
instrument in its government . . . no longer, that is to say, a model but a
segment" (Foucault 1991, 99–100). The economic discourse of children
continues this concern with population, but in a manner that discrimi-
nates between families, hierarchizes them, and reprises their model of
patriarchal sovereignty in the name of economic efficiency. Children
link together the themes of sovereignty and of economy that have
played out in these debates.

Conclusion

The insurgent sovereign discourses of modern governmentality have
recently been mediated by the politics of gay, lesbian, and bisexual
identities, and the legal rights around which these identities have
maneuvered. The latest act in this drama is the regulation of access to
the law via stories that recapitulate traditional liberal tensions between
state and civil society, economic and political interests, reason and passionate character. The central theme is a refutation of the model of
social rights that emerged during the New Deal. The Fordist links
forged then between individual and collective liberties and economic
growth that sustained the identity and social justice claims of postwar
social movements have now come under sustained attack as cause and
consequence of a lurching political economy that cannot aspire to universal betterment. Civil rights are no longer seen to be a universal

premise of sovereignty, but are depicted as "special interests," a cultural and economic drag on the promises of the social contract. In short, they are identified with what has always been weak and scarce in the American political landscape: economic rights to the commons. Stories about gays and about rights have been tactically deployed to fuel a growing realm of public opinion that asserts that legal rights and legal identities are best determined by democratic majorities rather than by courts and legal preemption.

It has been the stories of gay and lesbian power, their political agendas, and the minority-like vulnerability of nongays that constitutes the antagonists around which these staggering majorities in Colorado, Hawai'i, and Alaska have been formed. Ostensibly about civil rights and the rational limits to law, these public spectacles have been the pretext for social exclusion and the opportunity for a new governmentality. Public opinion thus serves less as a public sphere in which reason infuses democratic sovereignty (Habermas 1987) than as a realm of unreason. In such a situation, moral languages such as justice and equality are harder to hear, and compromise difficult to establish. This difficulty is revealed most starkly in Hawai'i, where the campaign for the amendment in 1998 was waged with little or no public discussion of the value of marriage for gays and lesbians; rather, debate centered on the consequences for society at large were same-sex relationships granted recognition or denied. Even Protect Our Constitution, the main prorights coalition in the campaign, ran a campaign of analogies, depicting the amendment as a return to the days of Japanese internment and exclusion, designed to reach critical voters of Japanese ancestry.[47] They also added a sovereignty argument of their own: voting on the amendment would put the decision to block same-sex marriage back in the hands of the legislature, where once again the people could be "fooled" (see fig. 2).[48] The League of Women Voters, who urged a no vote on the amendment, argued, "It's not a yes or no vote on same-sex marriage." Rather, their advertisement read,

> When you vote on the constitutional amendment on marriage—be careful. It's NOT a yes or no vote on same-sex marriage. Read the question carefully. It asks, *shall the legislature have the power. . . .* That *power* must remain with our Supreme Court, so that the rights of all Hawaii Citizens are protected from shifting political influ-

Don't Be Fooled!

Mark Davis, Susan Ichinose, Louise Ing, Colbert Matsumoto

A 'Yes' Vote on the Constitutional amendment has nothing to do with traditional marriage.

A yes vote on the constitutional amendment sends the same-sex marriage issue right back to the legislature, where they **will** have to take up the issue all over again. But more frightening to our basic democracy is that a yes vote gives the legislature the power to overrule the Supreme Court and change our Bill of Rights.

Is that what you really want?

THESE ARE THE FACTS:

1. Our State Constitution is clear on the question of who should interpret our Constitution: the Hawaii Supreme Court, not politicians.

2. Those that want you to vote yes are attempting to usurp the authority of our Supreme Court.

3. Special interests want to give the power to politicians whom they believe they can control. They do not trust the Supreme Court.

Who do you want safeguarding and interpreting your constitutional rights - politicians or our Supreme Court?

Vote NO ✓ on the Constitutional Amendment on November 3rd.

PROTECT OUR BILL OF RIGHTS

Paid for by Protect our Constitution/Human Rights Campaign, 870 Kapahulu Avenue, #110, Honolulu, Hawaii

Fig. 2.   Advertisement opposed to amendment to Hawai'i's constitution giving legislature jurisdiction over marriage, placed by Protect Our Constitution and Human Rights Campaign. (*Honolulu Advertiser*, 18 October 1998, A16.)

ences. That's how government works. Changing it puts everybody's rights at risk.[49]

Conservatives argued to the supreme court (which had asked for a
final set of briefs on the consequences of the amendment for *Baehr*) that
the years since 1993 had brought an "earnest debate."

> Advocates on both sides expended hundreds of thousands of dol-
> lars promoting their positions. Politicians, lawyers, editorialists,
> and civic and religious leaders marshaled their arguments. All the
> while, the People of Hawai'i listened and discussed and weighed
> the matter in numerous venues. When a vote was held in Novem-
> ber of 1998, the People of Hawai'i overwhelmingly approved the
> amendment and expressly rejected the possibility of judicially-
> mandated same-sex marriage. . . . *The People have now spoken. The
> debate has ended.*[50]

Yet, no matter how robust the debate was made to sound, same-sex
marriage was rarely ever addressed in ways that advanced an understanding of the men and women demanding such rights. Indeed, same-
sex marriage was often depicted as an absence into which anxieties
should rightfully pour. Where rights advocates were faulted for drawing attention toward civil rights or false analogies, conservatives
depicted same-sex marriage as a self-evident horror whose detrimental
consequences needed no more words, a silence that reinforced the sovereign arguments that had been laid down before. One advertisement
fulfilled its own expectation through the following observation:

> *Spin doctors recommend hiding the same-sex marriage issue from
> Hawai'i families.* People who support the same-sex marriage issue
> rarely ever talk about same-sex marriage. That's 'cause same-sex
> marriages make most Hawai'i voters uncomfortable. It's not an
> idea most of us agree with. So the same-sex marriage people use
> the tried and true political method of deception as they hide the
> real issue, which is preserving traditional marriage between one
> man and woman.[51]

Years of heightened anxiety over same-sex marriage and its effects had
given little room in which to wedge popular arguments validating the
desires and equal worth of gay interests in marriage.[52]

If moral languages are mute, moral positions are nonetheless manufactured through the tactical deployment of economic idioms. A letter to the editor of a Honolulu newspaper in the midst of the highly charged debate over same-sex marriage makes clear the force of these tactics. "What is at issue," the author writes, "is the governmental validation and promotion of homosexuality and the granting of special government privileges and preferences without any evidence of reciprocal contributions to the society that will bear the costs of such privileges."[53] The impossibility of such a balance sheet without a recourse to moral languages only creates the impression that these are excessive demands, thereby crafting their own pseudomoral imperative.

A political environment stripped of an acceptable normative language makes the pursuit of rights less tactically advantageous for sexual minorities (Ball 1997). With morality subsumed under the banal economic language of scarcity, and the victories in *Romer* and *Baehr* sustained without the protective cement of "suspect class" doctrine for sexual orientation, sustained calls for equality or even neutrality are unlikely to be heard in courts, just as they may provoke resistance in the political arena. The entitlement of hostility has its roots broadly planted today.

Chapter 3

The Status of Status

The politics of sovereignty emerging from the same-sex marriage cases and Amendment 2 has affected the terrain for legal mobilization by transforming legal meanings and challenging the contexts for action, fueling the general skepticism about the costs and payoff of rights strategies for gays and lesbians in the post–civil rights era (Bower 1997; Herman 1994; Phelan 1995; Schacter 1997b; Stychin 1995a; Vaid 1995). Until recently, the broad expansion of domestic partnership laws and private agreements providing gays and lesbians some of the benefits of marriage (see Briggs 1994; Christensen 1998; Speilman and Winfeld 1996) promised an alternative strategy, one able to maneuver stealthily below the radar of the opposition. The expectation has changed as domestic partnership has become an increasingly visible element of the debate over rights to public and private space.

This chapter examines the changing forms of modern sovereignty through debates about the meanings of the legal form of domestic partnership agreements, which I characterize as a discursive tension between status and contract. Departing from the modernization thesis that approaches the evolution of individualist contractual rights as an inevitable unfolding of liberty at the expense of status, and from dialectical theories that understand a functional relationship between the meanings of the legal form and economic or social relations, I see discourse about the legal form today as only loosely referential, essentially plastic and unstable, and deeply implicated in the boundaries of political space and the open-ended and uncertain strategies of legal mobilization within it. As tactics of state competence, these discourses about the legal form also have important material effects that further explain their instability. Of significance here are the hollowed meanings of economic contract and client status now that the institutions of wage regulation, collective action, and redistribution preserved by collective bargaining in the Fordist period have begun to wane.

These cultural and economic debates about the legal form raise particular questions that this chapter addresses. Among these are how conservatives have used arguments about the form of law to reconstruct political space and challenge civil rights gains, and why marriage and domestic partnership are now deeply entangled with questions of economic and social reproduction and citizenship. In the discussion below, I draw empirical data from public testimonies and legal argumentation about the political limits to domestic partnership and marriage. In addition, I present interviews I conducted with sophisticated and influential conservative political activists in Hawai'i who are interesting because of their tactical decision to avoid publicly vilifying gays and lesbians and instead cast the issue of marriage and domestic partnership as one of legality and popular sovereignty. I turn first to a discussion of domestic partnership as a vehicle for theorizing about the meaning of debates over the legal form. I then undertake a case study of Hawai'i, where the logic of this politics is most fully developed. Finally, I explore the significance of this research for legal mobilization today.

The Rise and Fall of Domestic Partnership

In April 1997, amid popular protest and legislative maneuvering to derail the marriage case, the Hawai'i legislature passed the nation's first statewide domestic partnership legislation. Hastily cobbled together and passed in an eleventh-hour conference committee facing a constitutional deadline, the law was designed as a counterbalance to a constitutional amendment designed to wrest jurisdiction from the courts over the definition of marriage and lodge it securely in the legislature. This compromise was inscribed in the language creating this new legal status. The Reciprocal Beneficiaries Act (RBA)[1] affirmed that "the people of Hawai'i choose to preserve the tradition of marriage as a unique social institution based upon the committed union of one man and one woman"[2] at the same time that it acknowledged that

> there are many individuals who have significant personal, emotional, and economic relationships with another individual yet are prohibited by such legal restrictions from marrying. . . . Therefore, the legislature believes that certain rights and benefits presently available only to married couples should be made available to cou-

ples comprised of two individuals who are legally prohibited from marrying one another.[3]

The statute goes on to enumerate the contractual benefits and obligations to which reciprocal beneficiaries are entitled,[4] noting that they "shall not have the same rights and obligations under the law that are conferred through marriage."[5] The distinction between marriage status and RB status is reflexively understood in this language as a political difference. Despite the broadening modalities in which individuals find love and meaning with others, the statute talks of a sovereign "people" embracing and unwilling to extend the status of marriage, yet offering tolerance and protection, through their legislators, of diverse alternative forms of commitment forced to remain in the shadow of the law. How might we understand this political difference and the compromise intended here? What is meant by the image of a people defending its status prerogatives against those whose evolving forms of social attachment are seen as needs to be recognized by independent statute?

Domestic partnership managed to avoid the political contrast with marriage for many years. In 1982 the *Village Voice* first established a policy of extended benefits—what they called "spousal equivalents"— as a consequence of bargaining with one of its labor unions. Only a small minority of the affected employees had same-sex partners. By the early 1990s, the number of private companies granting benefits began to rapidly expand, from fewer than a dozen in 1991 to more than three hundred by the year 2001.[6] While private companies and their unions paved the way, they were quickly followed by public unions that negotiated for some benefits in city and county governments across the country and by public and private universities and colleges that granted benefits to their employees. Large cities such as New York, Atlanta, and Chicago now have domestic partnership arrangements for public employees, and San Francisco mandates that private contractors with the city offer domestic partner benefits to their employees and that all companies offering public discounts to married couples extend such benefits to domestic partners as well. Oregon faced a lawsuit by three lesbian nurses in which the court ruled that the state was obligated to provide medical insurance benefits to the partners of all its employees, regardless of sexual orientation.[7] Lambda Legal Defense and Education Fund estimates that nearly one out of every four firms employing five thousand workers or more provides health benefits to nontraditional partners, and over fifty cities and counties and five states provide domestic partner benefits to their employees.

Since the national reaction to the Hawai'i marriage case, controversy has grown, most noticeably in Hawai'i itself, San Francisco, Oregon, and in the case of Capital Cities/Disney, whose extension of benefits in 1996 led to a boycott by conservative Christian groups. Nonetheless, opposition has only infrequently succeeded in overturning such benefits.[8] Arguments against domestic partnership have predominantly taken two forms (Briggs 1994, 758). As in the case of Disney, conservatives have reacted against what they have understood to be a culture war where liberal benefits for gay employees are merely the tip of a dangerous iceberg threatening to sink the fragile *Titanic* of family values. As one journalist for a proboycott organization put it,

> When Disney extended company benefits to the same-sex partners of its homosexual employees, it was following a blueprint developed by Hollywood Supports, a powerful workplace advocacy group that wants to influence cultural attitudes concerning homosexuality. . . . By offering same-sex benefits, companies take the position that homosexual unions are morally equivalent to traditional marriage.[9]

In a second line of attack, it is contractual obligation more than cultural status that has led to some employer opposition because of fears of runaway economic cost.[10] In both cases, whether the concerns be for the social status of legal status or for the obligation of contract, there is an expressed anxiety about the limits of such policies. What connects these two concerns?

Accounting for Status

The advent of domestic partnership in the 1990s suggests to some (both empirically and normatively) a gradual evolutionary approach to equal rights for gays and lesbians beginning with decriminalization of sodomy—and the elimination of the status of the "homosexual"—and ending, someday, in full citizenship symbolized by equal rights to marriage (see, for example, Coleman 1995, 545–47; Sunstein 1994a). This legal odyssey hearkens back to the early modernist ideas of a gradual elimination of status relationships in favor of social regulation by contract. As Sir Henry Maine famously captured it:

> The word Status may be usefully employed to construct a formula expressing the law of progress. . . . All the forms of Status taken notice of in the Law of Persons were derived from, and to some extent are still coloured by, the powers and privileges anciently residing in the Family. If then we employ Status, agreeably with the usage of the best writers, to signify these personal conditions only, and avoid applying the term to such conditions as are the immediate or remote result of agreement, we may say that the movement of the progressive societies has hitherto been a movement *from Status to Contract.* (1917, 100)

Status, in this view, reflects a vision of persons bound into a social order, their obligations and legal duties constricted by their position within familial, occupational, and religious institutions. In contrast to the expected submergence of the rational will to the normative authority of the social unit in status relationships, contract connotes a worldview in which the accretion of social obligation is dissolved in the intentional arrangements of the autonomous individual of the marketplace (Feinman and Gabel 1990, 375). Driven by the interests of *homo economicus,* "every person becomes man in the abstract . . . every subject becomes an abstract legal subject" (Pashukanis and Arthur 1978, 120–21). Society is made to shed its preconscious obligations; "Man [is] the primary and solid fact; relationships [are] purely derivative" (Robert Nisbet, quoted in Bergman 1991, 174).

Viewed from the modernist assumption of a growing contractualism, domestic partnership has an understandable relationship to the enduring status of marriage. Domestic partnership reflects a move toward social recognition of purely intentional arrangements based upon mutual understanding. As Mayor Giuliani recently argued in support of a proposed, dramatic New York City domestic partnership law,

> What [domestic partnership] really is doing is preventing discrimination against people who have different sexual orientations, or make different preferences in which they want to lead their lives. Domestic partnerships not only affects [*sic*] gays and lesbians, but

they also affect heterosexuals who choose to lead their lives in different ways.[11]

Those corporate and governmental plans (such as Hawai'i's RBA) that are gender-neutral—that is, that do not discriminate based on the sex of the partner—acknowledge the inventiveness of social choice (and the movement toward contract) through their disregard of marital status perhaps more than plans that deny benefits to heterosexual partners. This evolutionary/contractualist perspective might also be bolstered by recognition of the innovations in marriage law itself that have retained marriage as a dubious status with fewer social interests— hence, less obligation—than in its earlier incarnations. For example, unmarried cohabitation is no longer illegal, marriage is more easily dissolved, the legal significance of bastardy has declined along with its social condemnation, fornication and adultery are rarely prosecuted outside the military, penalties against homosexuality have been expunged or remain unenforced, and racial barriers to marriage have been eliminated. As marriage has assumed a more intentionalist character in this view, "heterosexual marriage superficially appears to retain its central position in the social order [but] in reality, it has been largely undermined by the rise of the pure relationship and plastic sexuality" (Giddens 1992, 154; see also Luhmann 1986). The legal consequences of this perspective are seen as a search for "a new model of status[;] how we might use status in a way that is sensitive to both the egalitarian ideal and the pluralistic character of contemporary family life" (Regan 1993, 118). In the words of one same-sex marriage advocate in Hawai'i,

> Gone is the barbaric idea of a wife who is by law the property and completely under the control of her husband. Now a wife is an equal partner with her husband, both in fact and under the law. We call for further enlightenment.[12]

For many advocating this "silent revolution" (Jacob 1988), it is understandable why domestic partnership laws in combination with loosening legal bonds on marriage itself might be seen by some gay rights activists as "a logical next step as the process of law reform continues" (Coleman 1995, 545)[13] especially because these social policy reforms are anchored in the popular legitimacy of legislative action and not adjudication.[14] For Richard Posner, the mature development of domestic part-nership laws such as exist in Scandinavia constitute "in effect a form [of] contract that homosexuals can use to create a simulacrum of mar-riage" (1992, 313–14). In this view, contract has now become the sole basis of status.

This modernist and, indeed, realist perspective has significant explanatory limits, however. While the availability of domestic part-nership surges, and as marriage is gradually hollowed out of its unitary legal character, marriage as a status concern has become culturally magnified, dominating state and national politics. Since the prospect of legalized same-sex marriage in Hawai'i, forty-eight states have consid-ered bills to restrict marriage to heterosexual couples; twenty-seven of these have been enacted as of this writing. Congressional Republicans have tried to make political capital over the "marriage penalty" in the income tax. Oklahoma, Ohio, and other states are considering the lead of Louisiana, which has instituted a "covenant marriage" status designed to restrict rights to divorce for any

> one male and one female who understand and agree that the mar-riage between them is a lifelong relationship. . . . Only when there has been a complete and total breach of the marital covenant com-mitment may the non-breaching party seek a declaration that the marriage is no longer legally recognized.[15]

Indeed, the politics of status today demonstrates an "evanescent anxi-ety" over the disappearing vestiges of status obscured by the expansive presence of contract.

For some observers, this growing anxiety over status is less a har-binger of something new as much as it represents an inevitable dialec-tical reassertion of the need for authority and legitimacy amid social change.

> Status and contract are both representative of a social need: status represents the need for legitimacy in legal adjudication; contract the need for formal legal categories which transcend the substan-tive issues of the particular case. In times of social change, the need for formal categories is preeminent because a stable and unbend-ing legal referent is necessary to regulate dynamic social relations. . . . Status considerations return to ameliorate the effect of social

change and bolster the formal legal categories with substantive considerations of justice. (Bergman 1991, 216; see also Pound 1909; Unger 1987, 70)

This dialectical account of the movement between status and contract has explanatory affinities for broader economic forces impinging on social change. It helps explain why a limit to contract was reasserted earlier this century when individualism was recognized to dangerously increase state and corporate power (e.g., the rise of the legal labor union and the traditional family regimes that higher wages produced; see Gabin 1990) and why global economic needs for flexible specialization involve an attack on the ideology of unions as well as tolerance and support for newer forms of social and marital relationships (Stacey 1996).

While the dialectical approach accounts for the ontological security that status relationships can provide in a changing world, its functionalism tends to overlook the significance of the discursive character of the legal form that today obscures the mapping of social need to legal instrument. Status and contract today are entangled one with the other, simultaneously valorized by all parties in debates over domestic partnership, making the very categories of the legal form discursively unstable and increasingly mutually interdependent. For instance, domestic partnership agreements are identified by some opponents as signs of illegitimate social status in one breath and castigated for extending obligations of contract in the next, while for proponents it is the possibility of contractual duty that signifies the status of citizenship. Haunting this uncertain referentiality is both the fantasy of marriage between same-sex couples that does not yet exist, and the uncertain significance of contract to economic relations. Nonetheless, this ambiguity of the legal form of domestic partnership agreements creates a policed division, a boundary around which is created the real by conflating it with the imaginary (Hughes 1998).[16] What limits the dissonance in these debates are new and exclusionary languages of sovereignty and new practices of statecraft, a new spatiality within which support for equal rights and limitations to marriage are made to echo melodiously. Donzelot has explored the historical roots of this tactical collusion, a "harmony between the order of families and the order of the state" (1979, 25) that is once again a dream of new sources of power. When Ross Perot restricted benefits for the gay and lesbian partners of all his new employees, he maintained that "[i]t has nothing to do with gay rights[;] it has everything to do with fairness and equity" (Myerson 1998). This equation between denial of rights and strengthened ideals of a democratic sovereign only balances because of this new power produced in the imagination of marriage as the privileged and official form of family-state relations.

If, as I argue here, contract and status have now become discursive categories with mutual investments in each other and in the production of state sovereignty, what characteristics differentiate the two in these debates? In this chapter I use the terms to indicate different conceptions of identity and the political theories and economic realities in which they are embedded. Contract explicitly interpellates and binds an abstract identity such as the juridical self or the worker self. These identities are imagined to lie in parity within the contexts of democratic equality (e.g., blind justice or the market) and encourage negotiated and egalitarian family relations. Status, in contrast, is a gesture toward the whole, socially integrated self (paradoxically, understood as a necessary legal fiction). Since the whole is always limited by the social horizon, status presumes an implicit social boundary.[17] For this reason, where contract assumes a democratic veneer, status relationships are often defended in republican or communitarian ideology based on a notion of respectable citizenship imbued with social values over and above legal rights.[18] Through this republican mantle, legal status gains *social* status in its articulation of boundaries by contrasting itself to the limitless democratic character of contract. This contrast may be less significant for labor unions whose declining influence militates against a demonstration of the contribution their legal status makes to the social and economic good, than it is for such elite statuses as corporations on whose increasingly unchallenged economic hegemony marriage as status is modeled. Nonetheless, just as identity imagined through the lens of contract is partial, so too is status since the social horizon is an open boundary, never fully articulated. As Weitzman observers in the context of marriage,

> The marriage contract is unlike most contracts: its provisions are unwritten, its penalties are unspecified, and the terms of the contract are typically unknown to the "contracting" parties. Prospective spouses are neither informed of the terms of the contract, nor are they allowed any options about these terms. In fact, one won-

ders how many men and women would agree to the marriage contract if they were given the opportunity to read it and to consider
the rights and obligations to which they were committing themselves. (Quoted in Robson and Valentine 1990, 528)

As Pateman has argued, these "repressed dimensions" (1988, ix) of
marital status run in two directions. The explicit abstractions of the
marital relationship have their counterparts in the unarticulated
dimensions of status in the democratic, contractarian tradition.

The unspoken aspects of marriage law permit competing discourses about the necessarily ambiguous legal form to have unpredictable, but significant consequences. Marriage can be articulated in
the terms of social status (what I call the status of status) when it is
defended in republican or communitarian language designed to firm
social boundaries by narrowing legitimate conceptions of the common
good. But marriage can also be articulated as contract: as a series of discrete obligations democratically available to citizens capable of demonstrating their abstract capacities to rationally assume such responsibility. Compounding this categorical slipperiness are transformations in
the economic foundations of capitalism that alter traditional meanings.
The replacement of contract with ersatz post-Fordist discourses of flexibility (Esser 1996), adversarial bargaining relations with corporate
"team" and "family," and worker-as-producer with worker-as-con-
sumer (Amin 1994; Casey 1995)—all within the context of growing
social inequality and economic scarcity (Oliver and Shapiro 1995)—
have further obscured the distinctions between status and contract, and
made the meaning of the social contract available for revision. Contract
today can become a sign of economic profligacy endangering the common good as much as it can remain a marker for the limits of the sovereign body. Drawing from political theory and from political economy,
the debates over the status of status and the place of contract thus form
a site for the articulation of governmentality. Domestic partnership,
particularly the legal form that it has assumed, has become enmeshed
in these debates, as I show in the next section of this chapter.

A Sovereign Partnership

In this section I examine debates over the legal form of domestic partnership. I look particularly at the case of the RBA in Hawai'i since that

law was historically developed as a bulwark against the marriage case, thus intensifying the increasingly common types of discourse I am interested in here. But Hawai'i is uniquely situated for this type of study for other cultural reasons. A Hawaiian wedding has long been a romantic dream in American culture, celebrated in film and song. Today, however, a Hawaiian wedding is as likely to conjure images of gay or lesbian couples as it is the heterosexual celluloid fantasies of Hollywood. In part, this is influenced by its own apparent cultural logic. Hawai'i has long been celebrated—and celebrates itself—for its tolerance and openness, and this certainly is part of its appeal as the place of romantic dreams. It has long been depicted as a mythical paradise where beautiful and exotic Polynesians have been available to Westerners for sexual and marital purposes. This myth of openness immediately confronts the visitor to the islands. Since the end of the plantation era, Hawai'i has been a true ethnic melting pot where interracial relationships have become the norm rather than the exception. This social tolerance is reflected in the law that has valorized a declining emphasis on status exceptions. Hawai'i has no law against sodomy. It has its own constitutional protection for equal rights on account of sex. It prohibits discrimination based on sexual orientation in public and private employment. And it had the pending *Baehr* case that would extend marriage to gay and lesbian couples. How the RBA reinforces or works against the grain of this cultural and legal logic expansive of contract is therefore of significant political importance.

I develop this political significance by following three tactical dimensions of the debate about domestic partnership. First, I discuss the discursive construction of social boundaries in debates about the legal form that buttress a status of status for "traditional" marriage and a demand for sovereign intervention in opposition to equal rights to marriage. Next I examine the valuation of space over time in litigation about the RBA that also aids the construction of exclusive social boundaries. Finally, I turn toward some issues of identity construction articulated in the debate. All three issues go to the heart of sovereignty concerns, hearkening to a new Hawaiian—and national—political landscape.[19]

Phenomenology and Ontology

Contract and status have a peculiar and ambivalent relationship in liberal thought. On the one hand, the discourse of contract is central to the

liberal imagination of sovereignty, for contract presumes the subjectivity essential to liberal authority. For John Locke, contract is the basis of
authority when it provides for a stable currency, a growing economy,
and ultimately a means of protecting individual wealth and security
through mutual agreement.

> And this puts men out of a state of nature into that of a common-
> wealth, by setting up a judge on earth, with authority to determine
> all the controversies, and redress the injuries that may happen to
> any member of the common-wealth; which judge is the legislative,
> or magistrates appointed by it. And where-ever there are any num-
> ber of men, however associated, that have no such decisive power
> to appeal to, there they are still in the state of nature. (1980, 48)

In Locke's theory, then, contract eliminates the vestiges of many earlier
social obligations, building new forms of social intercourse and authority based on self-interested acts of will. On the other hand, contract in
Locke's account also signifies an important status relationship, here
envisioned as the distinction between membership in the common-
wealth and the civic virtues of restraint on which it rested, and the non-
identities of the state of nature. For Kann (1991) this Lockean ambivalence is the origin of enduring American liberal and republican
traditions.

Feminist theorists have shown that marriage, for Locke, retains a
similarly ambivalent relationship to contract (see also Grossberg 1985).
Marriage retains this prepolitical flavor, an island of "paternal right" in
a sea of "political right" (Pateman 1988). It also marks the limits of community by institutionalizing the flow of property to successive genera-
tions. Nancy Fraser has recently questioned whether social and economic organization should continue to be seen as more than an
enduring double dynamic of contract and patriarchal status. In the
present, "post-socialist condition" gender dynamics are ambivalent,
subjectivity constructed both by the legal meaning of contract and the
materialism of the market.

> Even as the wage contract establishes the worker as subject to the
> boss's command in the employment sphere, it simultaneously con-
> stitutes that sphere as a limited sphere. The boss has no right of
> direct command outside it. . . . [I]n those arenas which are them-

selves permeated by power and inequality, the wage functions as a resource and source of leverage. For some women, it buys a reduction in vulnerability through marriage. . . . Gender inequality is today being transformed by a shift from dyadic relations of mastery and subjection to more impersonal structural mechanisms that are lived through more fluid cultural forms. One consequence is the (re)production of subordination even as women act increasingly as individuals who are not under the direct command of individual men. Another is the creation of new forms of political resistance and cultural contestation. (Fraser 1997, 230, 234–35)

My goal below is to further examine this political resistance and cultural contestation. Rather than limiting the impact of status, as Fraser seems to suggest, status returns in a manner that Locke might understand, even if in a form he might not recognize. While these new dynamics are unique, they remain connected to the discursive dynamics of the modern political economy. Judith Butler has recently made this point in her argument that the cultural dynamics of sexuality should not be seen as "merely cultural."

Is it possible to distinguish, even analytically, between a lack of cultural recognition and a material oppression, when the very definition of legal "personhood" is rigorously circumscribed by cultural norms that are indissociable from their material effects? For example, in those instances in which lesbians and gays are excluded from state-sanctioned notions of the family (which is, according to both tax and property law, an economic unit); stopped at the border, deemed inadmissible to citizenship; selectively denied the status of freedom of speech and freedom of assembly; are denied the right (as members of the military) to speak his or her desire . . . do not these examples mark the "holy family" once again constraining the routes by which property interests are regulated and distributed? Is this simply the circulation of vilifying cultural attitudes or do such disenfranchisements mark a specific operation of the sexual and gendered distribution of legal and economic entitlements? (1998, 41)[20]

I intend to offer some answers to these largely rhetorical questions in my examination of the interrelationship between status and contract in Hawaiʻi. My technique is to start at the phenomenological level, where issues of identity and security motivate the tactical deployment of economic and political discourses to limit the impact of rights groups. Such groups use rights to challenge privilege. As explored in the last chapter, it is because languages of privilege are inherently suspect in democratic societies, and because the invention of such languages where words were never before needed ironically assumes a defensive position, that the reestablishment of privilege is best obtained by restoring the ontological comforts of silence. As a form of governmentality, this technique seeks not to build security through the costly normalization of a deviant population, but to manage through political exclusion and the deterrence of debate.

In Hawaiʻi, it has been the political demands of gays and lesbians that has focused the phenomenology of insecurity.

> There's just something really special between me and my husband. ... How do we preserve society the way it is? I guess, when people see our culture going through a lot of changes, they're saying we need to draw the line somewhere. They're trying to draw it in other social issues. Gun control and things like that. Well, we need to draw the line here, too. I guess it's one way of society saying: this is where we're going to stand for now.[21]

> I can think back of being at the legislature in '94, '95, whatever it was, with a lady I know who is a pure Hawaiian. She was up there in tears. She doesn't know anything about law. She was just saying, "I go back to the beginnings of time here with my family. I might have to leave." That to me is kind of a radical approach, but she said, "You know, I never thought I'd want to leave my ʻāina, my home." It's just—the whole idea of same-sex marriage, to a lot of people, I'm not saying me now, to a lot of people is very hard to fathom. Hard to accept. I talked to a Hawaiian leader, actually I won't mention his name, but a Bishop Estate trustee. And he said, "You know Jack, we are a very open people. The Hawaiians have opened their shores, opened their homes. My wife is Hawaiian. You know we accepted all cultures, we have freedoms that a lot of states don't have, as you know, even with sexual orientation." But he said, "This is crossing the line," to quote him. Crossing the line.[22]

Hawai'i has been changing a lot. Quite frankly, people are saying
not for the better. We have more crime. People aren't as nice. . . . I
grew up here. . . . We used to keep things unlocked. You never worried about churches being broken into. Now we have rectories that
have bars on the windows. The poor rectories. It's not like there's
anything in them. This is not Philadelphia. . . . On top of that, the
economy stinks. I think people are saying, wait a second, someone's
determining social policy. Someone's determining what Hawai'i's
going to look like. It ain't us. We are not benefiting. . . . At a certain
moment I think people started to think, wait a second. The gays
aren't just asking for protection of housing and employment. . . .
We're OK with that. But now you want us to redefine marriage for
you? Wait a second. You said you weren't going to do that. . . . I
think people really started to feel that they were out of control.
They're not asking for a few things and we'll give a little, and get a
little. They want everything. This is really it.[23]

The fear that gay and lesbian demands for rights are responsible
for individual perceptions of being "out of control," demanding
"everything," is met by efforts to "draw the line." In many ways, this
boundary politics is a mutual construction between social movements
with important phenomenological and legal components, as Blasius
has made clear in his experiential account of "coming out."

The concept of coming out can be crystallized into three axes of
experience. . . . First is the axis of subjectivity—one's relationship
to one's self in coming out to oneself through one's erotic relationships. . . . Second, there is coming out to others socially (in family,
occupation, and other social interactions), corresponding to the
axis of experience that consists in exercising and submitting to
power in relations that engage the legal system and other institutions, which corresponds to . . . the assertion of lesbian and gay
rights. Finally, there is coming out in one's imagination or understanding of the world the way it is lived by a lesbian or gay person.
(1994, 210–11)

To the extent that legal rights for gays and lesbians have been secured
without a "protected class" status, power (and with it, as Foucault has
shown us, resistance) has taken novel legal forms. Rights provide the

requisite subjectivity for contract, and the basis for social recognition within the status of nation. As Marx once characterized this notion,

> The state abolishes, after its fashion, the distinctions established by *birth, social rank, education, occupation,* when it decrees that birth, social rank, education, occupation are *non-political* distinctions; when it proclaims, without regard to these distinctions, that every member is an *equal* partner in popular sovereignty and treats all the elements which compose the real life of the nation from the standpoint of the state. (1978, 33, emphasis in original)

For this reason, it is common to hear in response to supporters of *Baehr*[24] that protection for gays' citizenship rights is not in question by those seeking to overturn it. As one conservative activist told me, "We're not antihomosexual at all. They have every right under the constitution that you and I . . . anybody has,"[25] rights legitimately acknowledged by Hawai'i's antidiscrimination statutes. Instead, it is the articulation of status differences based on the extension of these rights that re-creates security and resists the realization of the imaginary world that Blasius understands these rights gains to help produce.

One way that this status is constructed is through self-positioning. Attempts to prevent same-sex marriage are best fought out in the rational middle of the road, eschewing obstacles of passion. "On this issue in particular, and a lot of these hot-button issues, it's the extremes that are a problem. They tend to define the issues. Extreme Right and extreme Left. Neither one I find very desirable."[26] For this reason, the main conservative opponents distanced themselves from religious labels despite the enormous economic and organizational support of churches.[27] "It became very difficult for us to publicly say, 'Yes, we have religions that are supporting us'; . . . it's not something we've gone and said to the community."[28] Early rallies in opposition to marriage were carefully contained. As one activist recounted,

> We had to ask a few people to leave who had signs that we thought were offensive to people. Because our point was never to be offensive. In fact what we always tried to do at Hawai'i's Future Today as well as Save Traditional Marriage '98 was keep it on a civil, rational kind of argument, not being attacking of other people.[29]

In fact, to preserve this positioning when campaign maneuvers were at their most unpredictable, Save Traditional Marriage '98 would call upon Mike Gabbard, known as a loose cannon in the campaign, to shoot several extremist shells across the public bow, thus permitting the proamendment forces to publicly declare their reasonableness.[30]

This centralist positioning works well in an island community feeling the threat of social change. Even in a tourist economy that ironically tends to subvert the imagination of sovereignty in its economic dependence on strangers, it is the threat of the extension of the political community to outsiders and the mixing of cultural with political citizenship that helps reproduce status boundaries.

> We wanted [a group] that was nonreligious, that was kind of ordinary, middle-of-the-road people. People that live here. Because the polls . . . showed that those who supported same-sex marriage were those who were from outside. The most recent moved here tend to be Caucasian. The Orientals and those who had lived here were those most opposed to same-sex marriage. Even the Hawaiians were overwhelmingly against same-sex marriage. So we wanted something that would represent us. . . . We wanted it focused on what was really an issue for Hawai'i. We wanted us to have a word. Not the courts. And to a certain extent, not even the legislature. We wanted them to represent us the people, the middle, the silent majority.[31]

The imagination of a bounded community pursuing a reasonable, centrist course, responsive to threats to individual and collective security is furthered by legal arguments contrasting contract to status. The RBA serves as a unique and ambivalent handle in this regard. In as much as the RBA establishes an ersatz "marriage" equivalency, the two statuses appear as competing estates threatening to erase the significance of their differences. As one attorney voiced the problem with this equation, "domestic partnerships are the means of conferring preferred status upon homosexual couples, but without calling it marriage. It will thereby dilute the significance of marriage."[32] For some, this dilution is a consequence of special rights conferred on gays that smuggle in the denied suspect class status that they seek.

It's the equal rights thing. We have no equal rights. If you say that, then you give them a special status, and they don't have this. They call it a . . . suspect class, which would be the equivalent of your skin color, your religion, and your sex, male or female. They don't have that, so they don't have the rights for that. In essence, what a domestic partnership is, it's giving a particular class to people, homosexuals, all of the rights of marriage except the license. I don't think that will fly.[33]

One reason that RB status is seen as unfair is due to the ways in which it is unavailable to heterosexuals able to marry.

If a reciprocal beneficiary does not include qualified unmarried people, then opposite-sex unmarried couples would again be disadvantaged, and reciprocal beneficiaries would be elevated above parents and placed closer to married status in the [social] hierarchy.[34]

However, because the RBA is not limited to gay or lesbian couples but valorizes any two life-partners—even partners residing out of state—it can also serve as a metaphor for a loss of rational boundaries threatening republican restraint and its benefit to economic health.

The reciprocal beneficiaries, that pretty much gives [recognition to] couples . . . not necessary gay couples but people that are not permitted to marry. . . . Apparently this has opened a unique can of worms. Because [now] we're only limited by our imaginations. That's probably not what the legislators intended when they did it. . . . But it just goes to show you what happens. [We're] in enough trouble with the economy that it would just put another nail in the coffin.[35]

What's at stake [in the RBA] is the cost. I mean, the government, the city, the state, the county government would all have to offer that. There go your costs of government. It's a cost. It's a cost to business. To me the economic aspect of it is at stake, especially with this economy.[36]

Where do you draw the line in this whole area? . . . What if two brothers live together or a mother and a son live together or a daughter and three sisters—all these combinations? It could be devastating to our economy because many times with things like that when there are those kinds of rights, and they're not orderly looked at, the abuse is unbelievable.[37]

I think people see a limit is being crossed when the absurd starts to become possible.[38]

Formless, this new status threatens to escape democratic control.[39] On the social front it may consume the newly established middle ground: "the [RBA] is a foot in the door for homosexual activists to achieve their ultimate goal—societal acceptance of homosexuality on an equal basis as heterosexuality."[40] The result is a loss of self-recognition in the very forms of the political debate. In reference to the November ballot amendment to wrest control of the *Baehr* decision, one activist remarked,

> In the old days, when you said marriage, the popular assumption was a man and a woman are getting married . . . When I read the amendment statement [I'm lost. It says,] "Opposite sex couples." Believe it or not, "opposite-sex couples" is a real stumbling block for people. That's normal folks. It seems strange for something to be worded as "opposite-sex couples." We're used to hearing "same-sex couples." We've heard "same sex-couples" for three years. And now "opposite-sex couples" seems odd.[41]

Since RB status is really like contract, lacking any natural social boundaries, it may engender its own necessity and the involvement of the legislature with further severe consequences for individual security.

> The language and effect of this bill is to establish a category which is parallel to marital status in all but name. It gives certain rights and benefits to this status which can be added to, each year, on an incremental basis, so that eventually what we know as "marriage" may become a subset of this status. We realize that this is not the intention . . . but unfortunately, due to the structure of this bill, we think that this end is virtually unavoidable.[42]

> For the state government to go ahead and give them the status of the suspect class [via entitlements to domestic partnership]—what will happen then is they will say, "Oh, now that you've given us all

of the benefits, the only thing we're lacking is this marriage license, so give us the marriage license."[43]

Courts are not immune to this expansionary logic. As one social worker testified about the RBA, "A court which can find a right to homosexual marriage in our constitution can also be expected to stretch reciprocal relationship statutes beyond any intentions we can presently imagine."[44]

This vulnerability to political institutions is also obtusely mirrored on the part of gay rights' proponents. For some, the RBA is "a right step in several directions" in part because it might "escape the politically laden phrases such as marriage and domestic partnerships,"[45] thereby ensuring a more rational debate over civil rights. Yet, for many proponents, the productiveness of this debate is in question for the very reasons that conservative opponents mistrust the judicial and legislative processes. "Domestic partnership as suggested leaves open a Pandoras [sic] box of judicial decisions about who qualifies."[46] Where opponents to domestic partnership see status, many gay rights supporters see the legislature as only able to provide contract, and insufficiently at that. For these activists, the RBA is a "feeble attempt at providing far too few rights to the gay and lesbian community in lieu of granting them full and equal rights provided in state sanctioned marriage," and in this regard the meaning for citizenship is second-order, no better than "allowing Rosa Parks to 'have a seat in the back of the bus.'"[47] As one activist phrased it, "Out of the entire supermarket of rights and benefits, you've served up four cans of soup. That's four more than we had before, but it's not a balanced diet. It's a measly meal on a place mat of fear."[48] It is the contrast between full marriage rights, precluded by the proposed amendment, and the limited scope of the RBA that demonstrates for these activists that domestic partnership is discriminatory.

With different valances, the mistrust of how political institutions handle issues of status and contract tends to foreclose domestic partnership options for opponents and proponents of equal status alike. For gay rights advocates, the avoidance of institutional uncertainty ultimately demands the affirmation of equality by unconditionally upholding the ruling of *Baehr*. Conservatives ignore the mutual unhappiness with the RBA, resurrecting it as a Frankenstein demanding increasingly more legislative appeasement. This helps make the case for the direct involvement of the people to reclaim their threatened sovereignty by means of a constitutional amendment restricting marriage to heterosexual couples. Yet, for conservatives, the multiplicity of legal statuses valorized in these images of the RBA and domestic partnership movement still demands that "traditional" marriage be differently valued, that the state be held accountable for its preferences.

In order to make the claim that the RBA is a status of a different sort—and not, qua status, equal to the status of marriage—the idea of domestic partnership is rhetorically contrasted to (fictive) claims for marriage status. The model for this argument was advanced by Governor Pete Wilson of California when he refused in 1994 to sign Bill 2810, which would have established domestic partnership. He wrote then,

> We need to strengthen, not weaken the institution of marriage. In virtually every culture, marriage has been deservedly celebrated as a relationship demanding commitment and unselfish giving to one's family—especially to one's children. Government policy ought not to discount marriage by offering a substitute relationship that demands much less—and provides much less than is needed both by the children of such relationships, and ultimately much less than is needed by society.[49]

Despite the Hawai'i trial decision finding no merit in these reasons to prefer marriage over other partnerships in 1996, the RBA has become the rhetorical substitute to demonstrate the continuing necessity of such a preference. Much as Governor Wilson has suggested, marriage is distinguished for its social connotations, especially the expectation of responsibility and "restrained citizenship" (Kann 1991, 15) that it is supposed to signify.

> I think it's problematic . . . creating this whole new category of law that leaves undertones of sexual categorization without a clear distinction between why we benefit certain relationships and why we don't. I think it's problematic. The better way to do it, which I agree is more complicated, which is why the legislatures want this quick, is to look at the different benefits and decide which ones could be extended and which one should be extended and which ones ought not to be . . . to do the hard work.[50]

There may be a case for domestic partnership laws, but I don't think in the homosexual context. Basically, [their] agenda is to be on par and equal with a heterosexual couple. I don't think they should permit domestic partnership for a guy and a girl that are living together, two men living together, who are sleeping together, or a guy and a woman living and sleeping together. The Bible calls it sin. I'm not going to say, "Oh, these guys." Or say, "Give domestic partnership for the heterosexuals." No. Wait a second. Let them get married. Let them go through all of the stuff that marriage entails.[51]

[Traditional families] tend to build a stronger society. And produce a citizen that we would like to see. . . . Fragmented families or new families have shown that [they don't] produce the strong individuals that you need to hold society together. In a society like the United States, we have a lot of personal freedom, but with it comes a lot of personal responsibility. [You must] be willing to give up personal gratification for the betterment of the society.[52]

Public arguments make it clear that the legal form of RB status signifies this lack of responsibility and lowered social value of these newer relationships.

I note that this bill [RBA] does not appear to confer any fees or costs on the reciprocal beneficiaries it seeks to embrace. Clearly, parties to marriage receive no such freebies. Therefore, as written this bill appears to discriminate against those who are permitted to marry.[53]

One opponent of San Francisco's Proposition S, which would have created limited domestic partnerships, echoed the same concern.

The draft ordinance states that "domestic partnerships" are relationships which can be minimally defined by six-month periods. The ordinance does not see "domestic partnership" as entailing any of the manifold legal rights or duties created by marriage; rather domestic partnerships "create no legal rights or duties from one of the parties to the other." Thus domestic partnership in the proposed ordinance seeks to provide domestic partners all of the public benefits of marriage while imposing none of the legal obligations of marriage.[54]

The anxious equation of legal status with social status, the expressed fear that "equal economic benefits [for gays and lesbians are] merely a first step," that they "will not be satisfied until they have equal social, religious and economic status with heterosexual couples,"[55] is modified by arguments about the legal form these status relationships take. This rhetorical positioning uses the relative openness of domestic partnership status laws—both the undefined nature of the relationships they cover and their incompleteness that is yet to be perfected by future legislatures—to make a contrast with marriage and draw a limit. In the logic of status, it is those legitimately burdened with the responsibility for community who must take in hand their political responsibilities and reconstruct their own security at the ballot box. Majorities are crucial in this realpolitik, but so are sovereign discourses about law and its relationship to cultural values.

One important aspect of the debates about the cultural status of status is that the social advantages that accrue to heterosexual married couples do so because they represent an authentic sovereignty. Rather than the social contractarian imagery of individual equal rights predating the social body, it is society and its status relationships that provide the basis for the reconstituted political body delimited by adherence to the norms of heterosexual status. This rhetorical inversion is deeply layered in that law is invoked to substantiate the original claim for status, but status is then fetishized as the solitary claim for law, able to redeem law.

> Part of the problem [since the *Baehr* case] relates to Hawai'i's constitution, which was changed at the last constitutional convention [to include equal protection on account of sex]. By doing that, I guess it was really us, we the people did that . . . whether unwillingly or intentionally, we did that. We essentially opened the door for the court interpretation that we got. Now in retrospect we're going, "Wait a minute, that wasn't what we meant." . . . You have law and justice . . . and justice should be interpreted culturally.[56]

> I think . . . implicit in some of the desires to redefine family is that for anything to be legitimate it has got to be recognized by law. And I would say, well, *no*. I mean, law has to recognize those things which are necessary for the common good and for the basic protection of individual rights—which, of course, is always in con-

nection with the common good . . . I am not defined just by my
rights as a human being. I am defined also by my responsibilities.
To other individuals, to myself, the environment, to the community, to institutions within the community as well.[57]

The idea that rights are dependent upon proof of the common good
inverts the usual argument that gays and lesbians are seeking "special
rights." To the contrary, it is heterosexuals who deserve special rights,
especially the special status of marriage.

Time, Space, and the Legal Form

The open-ended nature of the RBA, especially its broad eligibility
requirements, has an equivocal meaning. On the one hand, broad eligibility is a surrogate for citizenship, its status providing benefits useful
for asserting individual and social rights around which community can
be imagined. On the other hand, the lack of limits when combined with
arguments about the economic costs of contract can invoke a tightly
bounded community (Merelman 1984) deserving status because of its
temperance and prudence. This latter rhetorical move best describes
the politics surrounding a legal challenge to the RBA that left its material benefits nearly gutted. In this section I want to trace the legal
rhetoric around this case and examine its meaning.

In July 1997, just as the RBA was to take effect, the Bank of Hawai'i
and twelve other businesses brought suit to enjoin the act. The plaintiffs
made their case in the newspapers as well as in the court. In a newspaper advertisement, the bank president recognized that the suit could be
seen to disparage the rights of gays and lesbians. "Let me stress that this
is not a moral issue of gay and lesbian rights. This legislation goes far
beyond domestic partners. It is, instead, an issue of how this legislation
will affect all the people of this state."[58] If the sanctity of equal protection
for health care benefits was not to be a sufficient basis for civic duty,
opposition to the unrestrained character of the RBA was, and would
provide a ready handle for legitimating the plaintiffs' interests.

We believe it is important for everyone in our community—individuals, unions and businesses—to aggressively address issues
which impact the people of this state. Our ability to provide eco-

nomic opportunities in Hawai'i for our children and ourselves is at stake.

The law mandates that we provide health care benefits to designated "reciprocal beneficiaries" of our employees. Under this legislation, contrary to what was said during the legislative session, anyone who is single and prohibited from marrying by law can be designated a "reciprocal beneficiary"—regardless of their relation or whether they live in the same household. This law opens the floodgates in terms of who qualifies for health care benefits. As an example, someone could designate a resident of another state already diagnosed with a major medical problem. This is not the intent of dependent or domestic partner health benefits.[59]

The image of RBs straddling state lines—an ocean in the case of Hawai'i—is used to evoke a political community in dire need of reasonable boundaries. Combined with an invocation of economic scarcity, the imperative of immediate action is invoked.

Companies will no longer be able to control or even predict the cost of health care benefits. It will raise the costs of providing important benefits to those that are truly deserving and make it more difficult to provide quality dependent benefits. Indeed, this legislation may have the effect of reducing dependent coverage—not increasing it. This law could force us and other companies to cut back on our family benefits or even curtail our staffing. We do not want to face these alternatives but we must maintain a cost structure which allows us to provide cost-effective products and services to our customers and to compete in today's global economy. This law erodes our ability to do that.[60]

This public reasoning was privately confirmed as the motivation to mobilize the law.

We felt that reciprocal beneficiary's law that was passed by the legislature really was not a good law. Maybe the intention was noble, but the way it came out was terrible. Because taken literally, anybody in the country [could use it]—there was no residency requirement. I told people that if I were single I'd go onto the Internet,

advertise for somebody—literally I could do it. As stupid as it
sounds—I would then pick up somebody who was dying of cancer
or of AIDS or of some terminal disease and put them on my policy,
and they'd pay me. I could maybe negotiate a thousand bucks or
five thousand or something.[61]

The lawsuit took aim at these open-ended obligations of the RBA
affecting "every pair of unmarried, adult individuals, wherever residing," without demonstrated requirement of shared residence, "income
or expense," dependency, state residency, "relationship of a close,
social or emotional nature," or "any connection to or with each other
except for their declaration of reciprocal beneficiary relationship."[62]
Interestingly, few of these requirements are necessary for legal marriage, either. Nonetheless, it was the demand for equal treatment
between RB status and married status—the conflation of status with
contract—that was argued to be the major legal problem. Specifically,
the suit complained about an informal advisory opinion proffered by
the attorney general to the effect that the state's requirement of prepaid
health insurance for all employees was now extended by the RBA:
"There is no requirement . . . that employers either offer or pay for
health care coverage for individuals other than their employees. But,
under Section 4 of [the RBA] if employers choose to offer family coverage, they must also offer reciprocal beneficiary family coverage."[63]
    In order to defeat this obligation, the plaintiffs argued that they
would incur administrative and economic hardships and that the RBA
was preempted by issues of federal constitutional supremacy.[64] Specifically, they claimed that companies were required to abide by federal
laws related to continuing retirement benefits (COBRA and ERISA)[65]
and family and medical leave rights,[66] which limited the state's ability
to modify employment contracts. Federal tax requirements, in particular, made some benefits to RBs accountable as income unless dependency was demonstrable; employers would thus be liable for the differences to comply with state nondiscrimination law and might incur
liability where trust funds were used to pay benefits to individuals
qualified under RBA but not federal law. Importantly, it was also the
Defense of Marriage Act that clarified the federal supremacy issues that
limited the employers obligations. All of the sworn affidavits of the various plaintiffs contained a passage such as this: "Following the Defense
of Marriage Act (1996), it is clear that reciprocal beneficiaries would not

be eligible for federally mandated rights, such as COBRA coverage and FMLA Leave."[67]

The state's response to save the RBA could have rested upon an assertion that some of the challenged relationships established by the act *did* meet federal guidelines for dependency and that state sovereignty over marriage could be extended to newer status forms as well. Despite the fact that one of the federal statutes is known to be "the most sweeping federal preemption statute ever enacted by Congress,"[68] there are state sovereignty issues upon which ERISA is now open to challenge.[69] The lack of a challenge to federal supremacy (and to DOMA) has its genealogy in the marriage case. There, the attorney general argued against equal rights to marriage in an inversion of federalist logic: "The State of Hawai'i must be concerned with how it treats other states. If successful at marrying, same-sex couples will use Hawai'i marriages to foment litigation in the other 49 states and against the federal government."[70] The belief that state sovereignty required no assertion of prerogative led to the state's response in this suit that the RBA was defensible, but only in a truncated form. Therefore, despite the rhetoric that the RBA was originated due to the legislature's commitment to "fairness [that] requires that close relationships which provide a special bond be allowed rights similar to those of a marriage"[71]— an argument that was essential to justify the claim that the RBA was a substantially equal-status alternative to marriage—the attorney general argued that the specific language of the act was intentional. According to this theory, the legislature had been careful to specify only equality of health *insurance* benefits for RBs, and not health benefits stemming from HMOs (Health Maintenance Organizations) or other mutual benefit societies since states are allowed to regulate insurance without intruding on federal jurisdiction under ERISA. Arguing this limitation, the attorney general issued an advisory opinion one month after the lawsuit filing that concluded that the RBA applies only to insurance companies.[72] This opinion made it clear that of the approximately 320,000 employees who obtain coverage through their employers—including public employees who were not part of this suit and were later told to repay benefits they received from the state[73]—only about 1,800 had coverage through an insurance company and so could take advantage of the RBA's health coverage provision.

The state's defense turned upon this opinion, arguing that the plaintiffs had no standing to sue since it was only the insurance companies, and not employers, that incurred any obligation under the RBA. The case was resolved in a consent order that acknowledged this lack of standing and stipulated that "private employers that have not contracted with insurers have no legal duty or obligation under [the RBA] to make reciprocal beneficiary family coverage available to their employees."[74] If the suit forced the state to admit that the RBA created a trivial health insurance benefit compared to marriage, it failed to recognize that the underlying issue of equal protection that had generated the RBA was itself responsible for the supremacy issues that had come back to limit it. Hidden in this case was the history behind DOMA, particularly the reaction to the Hawai'i marriage case that had asserted a traditional right of states to determine the parameters of marriage. DOMA has disallowed these state prerogatives, in part by turning an issue of equal protection into a consideration of process and the limitations of status. The repression of the original history seems evident in the excessive protests of the district court judge.

> This has nothing to do, and I mean absolutely nothing to do with questions of rights for people of any particular sexual orientation. None. Nothing. This court will protect the rights of every American, regardless of their sexual orientation; and I have. And if this law was drafted in such a way that it didn't violate ERISA, I would uphold it without question. That's not the issue.[75]

Indeed, in almost every way, this case has everything to do with rights. Why, then, is this so obscured? Why does this judge protest too much that he is a champion of rights just as others have loudly declared that their opposition to gay and lesbian benefits has nothing to do with their commitment to rights?

Marx argued that the legal form of contract obscured the true underlying social relations of production by couching the vertical nature of exploitation in the horizontal ideology of shared and equal liberty perceptible in the calculus of economic exchange. Lost in this abstraction are historical relations and material advantages: the property interests around which, in this case, entitlements to retirement and family leave are embedded. As Balbus remarks, "The 'blindness' of the legal form to substantive human interests and characteristics thus parallels the blindness of the commodity form to use-value and concrete labor[;] the legal form functions to extinguish the memory of different interests and social origins" (1977, 576; see also Feinman and Gabel 1990; Fine 1984; Gavigan 1999; Picciotto 1982; Robson and Valentine 1990, 523). By removing the interests and origins from political existence, what remains is a renewed view of social equality on which sovereignty claims can rest.

Equally concealed in the professed commitment to equal rights are the various layers of popular sovereignty whose compression in this case traded off temporal complexities for spatial ideas of jurisdiction. In essence, the court refused to give credence to state sovereignty to create status relationships that are constitutionally recognizable in all other states. Rather, relying in part on DOMA's assertion of federal sovereignty in face of an imaginary right to marriage, the spatial imaginary alluded to by the court—the claim for a federal supremacy—suppresses the underlying impulse on which that supremacy is in part constructed. Indeed, despite the denials, this case is all about rights. So thoroughly, in fact, did it eviscerate those rights most attractive about RB status, that few signed up for the status. Publicly, the state department of health anticipated twenty to thirty thousand RB registrants within the first few months of the RBA (Essoyan 1997); two years later only 435 applications had been filed and approved.[76] Interestingly, now that the issue of status rights is resolved, three of the original plaintiffs decided to offer identical benefits to opposite-sex and same-sex partners of their employees on the same basis as married spouses. For Hawaiian Electric Company the decision was in defense of business prerogatives.

> Companies object to the mandatory, mandating you do this, mandating you do that. And so I thought it was important to send a message back to whoever's listening that, left to our own devices, you might be surprised at some of the things we do because we think they're the right thing to do. I mean we implemented a domestic partnership policy which addresses the people you should address, that is, local residents, [and] requires that you live together here in the state of Hawai'i for a twelve-month period. And we did not limit it to same sex. We opened it up to anybody, because even though it increases your costs, I couldn't say to a heterosexual couple that chose to live together and not get married— why should they be discriminated against?[77]

As an executive of the Bank of Hawai'i explained their decision to offer benefits, "It's not a political issue; it's a business decision."[78]

The denial of local politics bolstered by the discursive appeal to a larger sovereign has affinities to the tactics of those activists opposed to same-sex marriage. In an effort to derail the *Baehr* case through the passage of the constitutional amendment, an argument about popular sovereignty is made to substantiate the prerogatives of publics over courts in the setting of status boundaries. As one brochure expresses this idea, "The question of whether or not the state should legalize same-sex 'marriage' is one that should be decided through the people via their elected representatives—not the courts."[79] Nonetheless, this entreaty to the voters of Hawai'i to empower their legislators in this matter is often couched in the rhetorical appeal to imaginary communities wider than the local electorate. As this same brochure remarks in large black letters, "Your Vote is Important to Traditional Marriage Supporters Around the WORLD," also exhorting readers, "The eyes of The Nation are on Hawai'i—Don't let them down." When sovereignty is seen to be lodged in these larger communities, whether they be federal jurisdictions or moral communities, it is apparent that individual rights are valorized at the same time that they are effectively nullified. From the vantage point of these wider imaginaries, having individual rights no longer poses a threat. Particularities—especially sexual differences—are erased, as rights are reducible merely to those applicable to the abstract juridical subject.

Of course, a deep ambivalence marks this case, one that is not resolved by its outcome. On the one hand, the failure of the RBA to provide meaningful health benefits is a major loss to many who awaited this contractual right as a source of protection for themselves or their partners. This denial reaffirmed an economic caste system in which some citizens would be differentiated by their strategies of survival. On the other hand, this affirmation also proved many activists' point that there was no substitute for full access to marriage rights.

Sovereign Identities

The common tirade against "special rights" for gays and lesbians works against a background of neoliberal economic discourse to produce a rhetorical reversal critical to the construction of political identities. As we saw in the last chapter, by claiming a surfeit of rights and a limit to means, the costs of rights enforcement, the need for efficiency, and interference with private property can all be identified to position a broad majority as an embattled minority, itself in need of the protection of a limited state. This argument is modified in the politics surrounding domestic partnership. The open-ended and inclusive form of domestic partnership agreements—as contract—does raise significant and similar issues of cost (even though, as the RBA plaintiffs realized in the end, it may still be good for business). However, understood as a competing status, one recourse as we have seen is to articulate the status of status. This tactic relies upon the creation of a republican identity—also fully functional in the electoral politics that surrounds these events—in which marriage is acknowledged to be itself the ultimate "special right" of remarkable citizens. This tactic may have efficacy in political mobilization, but as the trial portion of the marriage case has revealed, it makes little headway in the courts. If the doors to the court are closed, how are identity claims for remarkable citizens protected?

Identity politics in the liberal state often justifies a reliance on courts to uphold what cannot be determined by a majority. Paisley Currah has noted that "identity claims, although emerging in a now enlarged public sphere, remain non-negotiable; that is, they are phrased as fundamental rights that cannot, in accordance with the liberal rule, be subject to political deliberation and be adjudicated in accordance with the larger common good" (1997, 235). In this section, I want to examine an emerging identity discourse that has sustained the claims for a status of status by borrowing from this traditional political frame for minority equal protection, a comparison raised by the specter of domestic partnership as a competing status to marriage. One activist working against same-sex marriage explained to me that she was not opposed to some status for gays and lesbians who wished to have their relationships recognized by the state. But this could not be called marriage, nor could it assume the common or statutory law of marriage, for that would challenge what lies at the heart of heterosexual identity, an identity as nonnegotiable as any other.

> It's interesting how identity is a very mobilizing factor. And it tends to be looked at as a minority's mobilizing factor. The [heterosexual] majority hasn't had to look at what it is that unifies

them. So I'm trying to step out of the minority and look back over here now and say, what are some of the issues that are as vital to you that seem to be as vital to me? And are they equal in argument? Or are they not?

The idea of an identity seems to be terrifying to a lot of people. To have their identity co-opted into a new meaning [as would happen if we declare] homosexuals to be exactly the same as heterosexuals, in their relationships and their lives and therefore they can use the same terms for the same meaning. It loses the meaning. Where marriage may have a strong meaning now to the heterosexual community, it could lose all meaning, when it is completely devalued. . . . To me, that would throw out a powerful identity. I don't mean to misconstrue what I'm about to say so I want to be careful. . . . I disagree a family has to be male, female, children. I have come to understand family as people who work together . . . and hold themselves together. I understand that principle. Yet today we don't know what we mean by *family*. People call a family, and the first thing you start doing, you say, Could you explain your family? Single family? Mom is home? Dad is home? . . . I can't just say "family" and you automatically know what I'm talking about. I've done this at times to define the family I speak of. Marriage is such an identity in my perception to heterosexual relationships that that loss of identity will keep them united in a very strong sense.[80]

The function of heterosexual identity maintenance is to build individual and group security by limiting the need to constantly clarify one's sexual orientation through language discriminating one relationship from another, a task fraught with the danger of illegitimate insult in the context of liberal legalism and its hegemonic commitment to equal rights. Legal categories such as marriage thus become a linguistic shorthand for sexual identity where they might otherwise conflate status relationships. Nonetheless, such a move is not without its call to discourse, for the meaning of marriage is unstable when courts are willing to intrude. Legal difference can only be legitimated from a renewed democratic sovereignty that can rely upon the trump of identity rights to preserve heterosexual identities through these markers, but then must negotiate status differences among ostensibly equal, but different, identities.

Activist. [I want to] find a discourse to start from . . . a courtesy
discourse. The whole idea of a conflict resolution or a win-win
negotiation, is to have people come away from the table with
agreement of the most important kind resolved. . . . I still
believe that could happen without [abandoning] marriage as an
identity for heterosexuals. And finding the identity of homosexuals. And having that identity be accepted. . . . This goes
beyond acceptance, beyond tolerance. This is a norm. . . .
Because the community has to come together and . . . go
through this process, one [priority] for [Hawai'i's Future
Today] has been the court [that is now] eliminating that dialogue, eliminating the people coming to the table. That is such
an important element to change. Some of the dialogue, some of
the discussions I think get to take place. So rational speaking
isn't allowed to occur. It's still emotion based, fear based.

J.G-H. Let me pose a problem. The idea of a courtesy discourse
seems to be predicated on the notion that identities of heterosexuals should be preserved because they are entitled to their
identity as much as anybody else might be entitled to theirs. It
also suggests then, that what marriage means is almost always
thought of in contrast to homosexuality, that which cannot be
heterosexual. In that sense, it tends to preserve some of the tensions that the idea of a courtesy discourse is intended to eliminate. . . . It suggests that what is heterosexual and what is
homosexual will be rather enduring positions. . . . Is that problematic? Does that tend to work against a courtesy discourse?

Activist. I don't see it as problematic as much as I see it as reality.
For example, I cannot participate in reciprocal benefits [the
RBA]. I can't. I will never be able to. Not as long as my husband
is alive. I won't be able to. Does that make reciprocal benefits
wrong? And marriage right? Or does that make marriage
wrong and reciprocal benefits right? No. It [only] makes . . .
reality of the hoops we have to go through in order to have
these benefits. That's where I hope to develop the language that
is common, and comfortable, and right. I may not be the one
who can develop it as much as I can put it forth, of what it
means to have a homosexual union . . . for lack of a better word
at this point. There is a need for a [terminology for the] relationship between women in love, for the relationship between

> two men in love, without giving it a right or a wrong, or . . . a
> second-class position. [We should be] trying to eliminate that
> barrier and give it it's own identity for what it is and a sense of
> respectability.[81]

The imagination that a "courtesy discourse" could preserve heterosexual identity and yet eliminate a second-class status ultimately depends upon the preservation of legal concepts such as marriage to serve as identity markers and the simultaneous elimination of legal access to challenge their restriction. This is a through-the-looking-glass worldview in which courts are the threat to identity groups, legislatures and democratic majorities the benevolent, sovereign protector. Cleansed of the influence of judges and legal norms, the discourse in which identities are to be courteously negotiated (while freeing heterosexual identities from actual transformation) is imagined to float freely in a normative and political space forever fractured by sexual orientation.

The RBA is an example of the kind of status likely to emerge in such a negotiation, as this activist makes clear. Again, its legal form is significant. The openness of the RBA to nonsexual and familial relationships allows it to preserve heterosexual identity (the one relationship that it explicitly excludes from eligibility) without necessarily embracing homosexuality. The diversity of relationships comprehended by the RBA also tends to hide the diversity of heterosexual relationships behind a facade of homogeneity with utility for building political majorities and for warping what a true courtesy discourse might look like.

The positioning of heterosexuals as an identity group threatened by legal standards of equal protection for the right to marry impels the political strategy now pursued: the elimination of the voice of courts. Shorn of one vestige of a vertical dimension to citizenship involving the connection between citizen and constitution, the argument instead substitutes another more powerful horizontal dimension—that cultural nationalism that exists between citizens. On this horizontal terrain, the discourse of courtesy is an imagination of duty to, and establishment of justifications for, legal sanction of relationships. Couched in a language of good manners, courtesy discourse recreates a sense of vertical hierarchy, what Nietzsche understood as "the happiness of 'slight superiority,' involved in all doing good" (Nietzsche 1967, sec. 3, p. 18). This is a discussion about what is due others; heterosexual privileges are not on the table. Instead they are locked silently in the vows of marriage, an oath metaphorized as the sacred oath of citizenship.

Herman has made it clear that strategies for achieving different identities highlight the normative, hegemonic power of liberal legalism. This is as true for gay and lesbian rights activists as it is for opponents of liberalized rights whose legitimacy depends on conceding liberal legal categories (such as formal equality of the sexes) that obstruct the voicing of their full fury at sexual deviance (Herman 1994, 112, 118). The argument for a "courtesy discourse" is an attempt to weave within this liberal discourse what we might call the "contract of status." Status here is a marker for collective boundary making in two ways: as marker of identity, it defines the procedural mechanisms for reasserting the social contract in the absence of rights politics. As a signifier for particular identities it preserves the functionalist distinctions and, necessarily, all the social advantages that have accrued to "traditional" identities, while relegating newer identities to search a thin veneer of new and awkward terminology lacking legal significance.

Making a Mockery of Marriage

Gearing up for the 1998 amendment campaign in Hawai'i, the coalition of opponents operating under the banner Protect Our Constitution hired a consultant to conduct focus groups and detailed polling. One notable finding was that voters were "adamant in their belief that everyone should be treated equally" at the same time that marriage for lesbians and gays was, for some, an undesirable "crossing [of] the line."[82] The simultaneous commitments of electorates to equal rights for all and to a limit for gay and lesbian rights in Hawai'i is not perceived as a contradiction because the dissonance is eliminated through a reimagination of sovereign political space. Domestic partnership has played a mediating role in this new cartography by modulating the debate over equal rights to marriage, permitting new arguments about the limits to equality and the power of status to reconstitute the political body.

Central to this reactionary response to domestic partnership is the articulation of a slippery interface between status and contract. When domestic partnership is argued to be a fair source of protection for lesbians, gays, and others who have no benefit of marriage, languages of contract are tactically deployed, depicting now the material danger of an unfettered extension of obligation amid economic needs for restraint, later the open horizon of legal status demanding social limits to reclaim political space and reconstitute a more authentic social contract. When domestic partnership is argued to be a status equivalent to marriage or when it is argued to be a stepping-stone to full participation in citizenship for gays and lesbians, heterosexual status is conflated with citizenship by again playing off the legal form: the apparent cost-free nature of new legal statuses or their ersatz quality due to their open membership. Reinforced by the convergence of liberal contract theory and by republican and communitarian ideologies, equality and status differences are reimagined to reinforce new majorities and a new governmentality.

The elections in November 1998 demonstrated the force of this new mapping of political space when, after a hard-fought, multi-million-dollar campaign that dominated all other statewide contests,[83] nearly 70 percent of the electorate voted for a constitutional amendment intended to derail the *Baehr* case. The day following the election the Democratic governor, reelected with the slimmest of majorities in a race in which both he and his opponent supported the amendment, declared his intent to revivify the domestic partnership law as a sign of his party's (belated) commitment to equal rights. The reaction by anti-marriage activists was swift and fierce. The chair of the Alliance for Traditional Marriage condemned those trying "to make a mockery of marriage."[84]

> It's a sad day for democracy in Hawai'i. Just one day after the people made it absolutely clear that we don't want same-sex marriage, the Governor declares that he will push for legalization of same-sex marriage in the legislature, but in the disguise of a different name; same-sex union or domestic partnership. This is an outrageous attempt to undermine the will of the people.[85]

One outraged citizen echoed the reaction:

> I voted for [the governor] and the marriage amendment, so I'm bummed. Throughout the campaign [he] said he was against same-sex marriage. Then one day after the election, he says he wants a domestic partnership law. Any idiot knows this is just

another name for homosexual marriage. . . . Governor, you
betrayed 70 percent of the people. . . . Shame on you.[86]

Support for domestic partnership by some of the leadership of Save
Traditional Marriage could not stem the tide of opinion. As one letter
writer accused,

> This is abdication. By negotiating the particulars [e.g., parental
> rights] you concede the principle. The objections to legalizing
> same-sex marriage were not over the particulars of what marital
> benefits to bestow or withhold, but upon the principle of non-
> recognition of homosexual couples as a special protected class.[87]

The governor's response was equivocal. As his communications director explained,

> [The] Governor . . . supports domestic partnerships, which are by
> no means the same as same-sex marriages. Domestic partnerships
> extend such rights as hospital visitations and shared insurance
> benefits to people who have formed long-standing domestic rela-
> tionships. A domestic partnership law will not place such relation-
> ships on a par with traditional marriages. By asking next year's
> Legislature to create a workable domestic partnership law, [he] is
> working to provide equal rights for everyone without altering the
> institution of traditional marriage.[88]

That domestic partnership can be portrayed as a compromise, one able
to preserve the status of traditional marriage while providing "equal
rights for everyone" suggests the cultural interplay of contract and status will continue to define a political space in which the denial of citizenship for a few can be made in the name of citizenship for all.

For the Hawai'i legislature, these cultural dynamics were para-
lytic. The 1998–99 session saw neither legislation declaring marriage
between a man and a woman as the recently passed amendment had
authorized, nor any attempt to repair or replace the RBA. One key leg-
islator noted that the senate Judiciary Committee stalled because the
two issues were inextricably linked together.[89] As parts of the RBA
expired, employees with reciprocal beneficiaries were notified that

benefits were being withdrawn. The next year's session saw some attempt to restore the insurance benefits to the RBA, but the bill died before reaching a floor vote in the house along with a bill designed to strengthen antidiscrimination protection for gays and lesbians. The threat to marriage swept away by the 1998 amendment was nonetheless resurrected by religious opposition to the legislation as well as the sense that "the members [of the house] were very much concerned about the financial impact" (Kua 2000).

How to tactically exploit such paradoxical terrain is unclear. Perhaps what has been experienced in Hawai'i may encourage a deconstruction of the very terms of citizenship, revealing its exclusiveness, privilege, and ultimate indeterminacy in both its democratic and republican guises. As Shane Phelan has pointedly noted, "The political goal of equality . . . cannot be achieved without thorough examination of the structures of thought and society that have made political equality seem scandalous" (1999, 56). That interrogation, she demonstrates, is likely to make alternative conceptions of citizenship based on republican ideas of work, on tropes of reasoning and passionate bodies, and on democratic notions of abstract rights face the same problems of exclusion encountered by a politics of access to marriage and domestic partnership. Progressive struggle now is likely to have to work on the interstices of these various legal and political discourses. As an example, individual security and collective recognition may advance less through a direct engagement of marriage rights in courts and legislatures, than through ancillary struggles that make access to health care, shelter, and the like, independent of domestic status. This interstitial politics—although difficult—might best revalue the sovereign discourses of contract and status that have themselves made a mockery of marriage.

Chapter 4

Laboring for Rights

We in the labor movement don't believe that civil rights is a special interest. It's all our interest. It's the interest of all of us to ensure that equality and freedom is extended to all the citizens of our country.
John Sweeney, AFL-CIO convention, 1983

[The AFL-CIO] supports enactment of legislation at all levels of government to guarantee the civil rights of all persons without regard to sexual orientation in public and private employment, housing, credit, public accommodations and public services. Affiliated unions and state and local bodies should take an active role in opposing measures which reduce the rights of people based on their sexual orientation and should participate in appropriate coalitions in order to defeat such measures.
AFL-CIO convention resolution, 1993

The strategies that have brought the labor movement in the United States to the same table as lesbian and gay organizations to dine on the fruits of common interest have had mixed success. Political initiatives to deprive gays and lesbians of their civil rights in Maine, Oregon, and Idaho in recent years have been met by coalitions between labor and other progressive forces that helped defeat each, although by very slim majorities. In some public and private contract negotiations, labor has supported the extensions of benefits to gay and lesbian partners, encouraging a "silent revolution" of progressive social policy even where public policy has officially remained mute. And at the national level, in 1997—fourteen years after first going on record in support of gay and lesbian civil rights—the AFL-CIO under the leadership of John Sweeney made Pride at Work an official "constituency group" within the organization in order to foster mutual understanding of gay and labor issues and to urge coalitions designed to promote civil rights.

Despite these political successes and organizational achievements, the limits to cooperation and understanding have become increasingly evident. Spontaneous coalitions such as the one that defeated Oregon's discriminatory Measure 9 in 1992 have been short-lived, and gay political action groups that emerged from the fight such as Oregon Right to Privacy have not always reciprocated later in support of labor's declared issues (Osborne 1997, 226). In Hawai'i, where the *Baehr* case has offered a tremendous opportunity to renew civil rights commitments and where the opposition has threatened to submerge far more than just the legal progression of the marriage case, labor has remained a nearly silent voice. In Hawai'i, the table of common interest is not yet set. This chapter asks the question, What accounts for the present limits to cooperation between labor and lesbian and gay groups?

From the Universal to the Particular

Organized labor's national decline in power, prestige, and representation can be measured in more than its sinking density, which now hovers around 15 percent of the working population, down from a high of 34.7 percent in 1954. Buoyed by these higher numbers in the past, organized labor rose to take a prominent economic and social role in the United States, pushing wages higher and maintaining the means and norms of private, family-based consumption that undergirded the expansion of industrial capitalism. High demand led to increasing opportunities for profitable industrial manufacturing on ever-increasing scales of production, cheaper goods, and even broader consumption. This seemingly virtuous capitalist cycle—called Fordism after Henry Ford's pioneering high-wage policies in the 1920s—provided the terrain for consent to the neoliberal capitalist order (Aglietta 1979; Gramsci 1971; Rupert 1995), one in which private pursuit of worker interests was rewarded with broad-based economic gain in many social sectors on a national scale. From the Second World War until about the mid-1970s, what was good for the United Auto Workers (more than for General Motors) was good for the country.

However, once capital was able to organize on a global scale, it was able to rely on inexpensive third-world labor to maintain profits, weakening the dynamic national relationship of labor to capital (Brenner 1998). The resulting deindustrialization at home made unions weak in relation to capital and their rights to organize and strike the targets of increasingly hostile state and corporate authorities (Levy 1985; Sexton 1991). Labor's representation of the working class, its abilities to command wage premiums, its attention-getting political voice, and its internal cohesion began a long decline from which labor has not recovered (Davis 1986; Moody 1988; Rogers 1992). As labor's power wanes, and as the tie between productivity and income has been severed, unions are no longer the measure of collective action (Eder 1992). Since the period of stable Fordism, other social movements on behalf of civil and human rights for people of color, native peoples, women, gays and lesbians, and the disabled, along with dramatic movements for peace and disarmament and the environment, have organized themselves around (and sometimes with) the labor movement (Boggs 1990; Brecher 1990; Melucci 1989; Scott 1990; Waterman 1993). Lost amid this plurality of action has been a sense of universalism.

Unions always were, in many ways, "particular." As many critics of the American labor movement have observed, labor was primarily an "aristocracy" of white, male workers, although struggles for inclusion of other identities and movements were still vital aspects of labor's history (Cook, Lorwin, and Daniels 1992; Davis 1986, 81ff.; Draper 1994; Gabin 1990; Goldfield 1997, 1993; Kingsolver 1989; Levy 1994; Osborne 1997; Roediger 1991, 1993). Indeed, labor unions today are much more diverse than they were in the 1950s and 1960s when Fordism was at its heyday (Milkman 1997; Moody 1997b). Nonetheless, Fordism permitted unions to articulate a more universal stance for two reasons. First, the preservation of a beneficial cycle of capitalist accumulation encouraged primary and secondary institutions that benefited a wide segment of the working class and society at large. Strong unions and collective bargaining principles gave protection to marginal groups fortunate enough to be employed in unionized sectors, protection revealed by their differential success once union power was diminished in the 1980s (Milkman 1997). Welfare state institutions were a secondary benefit to marginal social groups and were widely supported by labor and the Democratic party. Second, the integration of labor and the working class was reinforced by involvement in markets and struggle over surplus. Today, by contrast, many identity groups gain cohesion through consumption aided by a capitalism thriving on "customization" resulting from flexible production methods (e.g., Evans 1993). There is, thus, rarely an attempt to engage market failure, and so an unwillingness to address the material basis for universal claims.

Despite these changing economic and social dynamics and the

long slide in power and representation, the labor movement has been criticized—from within and without—as unresponsive. During the Fordist period, the AFL-CIO was adamantly opposed to increased expenditures on organizing since it did not make much difference to the political and social position of the labor movement even during a decrease in membership (Voos 1982). As George Meany, the president of the AFL-CIO from its inception in 1955 through the beginning of its decline in 1979 once said, "Frankly I used to worry about the membership, about the size of the membership. But quite a few years ago, I just stopped worrying about it, because to me it doesn't make any difference" (quoted in Rogers 1990, 1). Today, as unions have recognized that rebuilding their threatened organizations does make a difference, they have had to confront their own history of neglecting women and minorities as they discover that these groups are now most disposed toward joining unions (Crain 1994; Goldfield 1997; Meiksins 1997). The recognition of the need for organizing and participation in coalitions with other social movements has been one of the lessons urged by the present head of the AFL-CIO, John Sweeney. As president of the Service Employees International Union before his election to the AFL-CIO, Sweeney's union grew dramatically with a commitment to organizing those who had been long neglected. Included in his formula for restrengthening the labor movement has been an admonishment to create viable linkages with other movements by supporting civil rights struggles, including those of lesbians and gays. That strategy has shown some signs of success as membership has held steady or grown in the past few years.

The Hawai'i labor movement has faced this national directive to organize workers from a relatively privileged position. Hawai'i presently leads the nation in union density; 26.5 percent of workers were organized in 1999, almost twice the national average. Those numbers are the legacy of a dramatic labor history dating from before the state's inception. The many years of ethnic-based divide-and-conquer strategies to control labor in the sugar and pineapple fields in the early twentieth century made union organizers keenly aware of the centrality of antidiscrimination principles in the construction of solidarity (Beechert 1985; Lal et al. 1993). The postwar political economy that emerged from labor's victories in agriculture and the tourist industry was based on relatively high wages and generous workers' rights, social rights to a bountiful welfare state, and strong support for immigrants. This rights-based social tolerance built the foundations for nearly four decades of uninterrupted Democratic party rule and labor influence in the islands. As a reflection of labor's ability to speak for universal interests, Hawai'i became the first state to offer universal health care, and the first to vote to ratify the Equal Rights Amendment. Hawai'i also instituted one of the nation's strongest antidiscrimination policies for gays and lesbians in employment and state services. In addition, the special character of the tourist industry predicated on the allure of a preserved Polynesian culture for a global clientele has made an appreciation for the civil rights of all an integral part of what makes Hawai'i work. Why, then, this progressive legacy have been squandered when it comes to gay and lesbian demands for marriage requires both analysis and strategic consideration.

The need for inclusive strategies is particularly apparent under the present economic climate. With economic recession in Japan, tourist arrivals from Asia began to plummet, and Japanese investment in real estate declined precipitously, tossing Hawai'i into a downward economic slide at the same time that economic indicators were beginning to soar on the mainland. The state government, overflowing with surplus in the 1970s and 1980s when growth was as high as 13 percent a year, was forced to adjust to declining revenues as growth went negative, or hovered above the line at just 1 or 2 percent. As recession gripped Hawai'i during the 1990s, Hawai'i's labor unions realized that their visible strength could quickly become a lightning rod for discontent. With neoliberal economic solutions preoccupying the Hawai'i Democratic party, union prerogatives—especially those protected by the state's strong public unions—have come increasingly under fire, straining relationships between the party and the unions. One Honolulu newspaper ran a weeklong series of front-page exposés in 1998 excoriating unions as "the untouchables," and remarking on "an inefficient system" that protected the fiddler of union work rules while Hawai'i's economy burned.[1]

Although American unions have long weathered poor public opinion and bad press (Lipset 1986; Puette 1992), Hawai'i's unions had particular concern over the political process. Under the Hawai'i constitution, the call for a constitutional convention must be placed before the voters at least every ten years. That question was on the ballot in 1996, a year in which the discourses of sovereignty and economic efficiency were making supporters of unions, same-sex marriage, and Hawaiian rights decidedly nervous. Opposition to same-sex marriage was used in the campaign to support a convention, but unions and Hawaiians knew there was only a small gap between resistance to "special rights" and to "special interests" that could be exploited in a convention. Union supporters feared a general attack on workers' rights and, in particular, support for "privatization" of some public services that would threaten public union jobs. Native Hawaiians were concerned over the growing opposition among some developers to the supreme court's 1995 decision[2] upholding the rights of Native Hawaiians to gather traditional resources on private land, rights that had been asserted to delay and obstruct new hotel developments. The fears of boiling alive in a common pot did not induce cooperative strategies in 1996, even after the convention was narrowly passed by the voters.

In a strategy that risked exacerbating the concerns over political sovereignty, the state AFL-CIO on behalf of fifty unions challenged the 1996 convention vote in court after the attorney general certified the election results. The state supreme court ruled on that challenge in early 1997, deciding, contrarily, that the large number of spoiled ballots denied the clear majority mandated by the constitution to call a convention.[3] In reaction, several businessmen filed suit in federal court in an effort to uphold the original vote. Although their probable target was union power and Native Hawaiian rights, same-sex marriage was again used to gain popular support for this latest intervention. The federal court ordered a new vote on the basis that, without advanced publicity about the status of the spoiled ballots, the original vote was fundamentally unfair, a decision later overturned in the Ninth Circuit Court of Appeals.[4] Concerned over the seesawing in the courts, and the growing anger of the public represented by the groups Let the People Decide, and Citizens for a Constitutional Convention, the Hawai'i legislature put another vote on the ballot in 1998. One senator explained his decision in the language of sovereignty: "This is an opportunity for the public to have a say on their document, which is the Constitution."[5] In November of that year, the people spoke against a convention but in strong support of the same-sex marriage amendment.

In the discourses comprising the convention campaign, unions in Hawai'i were faced with a clear realization that they no longer represented the universal interest of either the Democratic party, or the working class fearful of a stagnant economy. Yet, neither were unions, Native Hawaiians, or civil rights supporters easily able to forge a broad response to the universalist language of sovereignty through the combination of particular concerns. In the following chapter, I examine the problems of coalition from the perspective of Native Hawaiians. Here, I want to look in depth at the difficulties labor unions faced. Even amid the convention politics when public opposition to same-sex marriage threatened to weaken union rights, and when millions of dollars were flowing into the high-profile marriage campaign, few unions openly or even covertly supported same-sex marriage.

Writing about the negative case—why union action to support the rights of gays and lesbians has *not* materialized—is an onerous task. The absence of evidence is paradoxically the best evidence, yet it necessarily speaks little. What it presents, I think, is an opportunity to see how political language constructs the issue as a nonproblem, that is, a problem not fit for labor's intervention. In order to develop this framework for understanding, I first evaluate the nature of political argument in order to make sense of interviews I conducted with several of Hawai'i's union leaders to learn why they have failed to support the marriage case. Comparing these unions with the few that *have* committed themselves to support, I speculate that unions with a strong democratic culture that encourages coalition building and tolerance for open gay and lesbian identities may have more success in envisioning gay rights, identities, and citizenship in harmony with workers' interests.

A Beneficial Union

The Commission identified the following major legal and economic benefits [of marriage]: Spousal and Dependent Support. . . . Health Insurance. . . . Retirement. . . . Workers compensation. . . . The Commission can not claim that the list of major legal and economic benefits that are extended to different-gender couples but are not extended to same-gender couples as identified above is exhaustive. But the Commission finds that it is complete enough to recognize the magnitude of the benefits conferred as a result of the privilege to marry under the law.[6]

The applicant couples correctly contend that the [Health Department's] refusal to allow them to marry on the basis that they are members of the same sex deprives them of access to a multiplicity of rights and benefits that are contingent upon that status.[7]

I am writing in support of same-sex marriage. I am writing as a heterosexual Christian who takes his faith seriously. . . . If same-sex marriage is not permitted, I believe that homosexual couples should be accorded the same economic benefits as married heterosexual couples.[8]

Legal same-sex marriages would allow access to health care benefits via spousal or family plans and would greatly impact a couple's ability to remain outside of the government-funded health care system. That in itself would affirm the dignity and self-worth of the individuals involved.[9]

We are simply asking for the same privileges, rights, legal recognition and economic [taxes, medical insurance, etc.] benefits as enjoyed by heterosexual unions. Nothing more. Nothing less.[10]

As these examples from the Hawai'i debates reveal, the argument that same-sex marriage equalizes the distribution of economic benefits is commonly cited by supporters as a reason for acknowledging economic citizenship and protecting equal rights. The unarticulated genealogy of this argument is found in the decision made by labor unions during the Second World War to pursue private benefits guaranteed by the labor contract at the expense of national health care, old-age insurance, and the like. This labor strategy was a consequence of the declining radicalism of the unions of the CIO. As a collection of industrial unions, the CIO originally had hoped for a broad nationalization of social welfare policy that would have united the working classes. Tamed by the needs for uninterrupted wartime production, the bureaucratic favoritism of leadership over the rank and file, a conservative Congress suspicious of and hostile to social justice unionism, the growing power of corporations, and the weakening effects of the split in the house of labor between AFL and CIO, industrial unions opted for privatized workers' benefits later generalized to the family (Quadagno 1988, 157ff.). The consequence of these labor decisions have often been social and economic fragmentation. Thus, means-tested health insurance tends to freeze the advantage of nonmarginally employed workers, segregating them from poor and socially stigmatized social groups (such as unwed mothers) who are covered by "welfare" programs (Gordon 1990; Schram 1995; Skocpol 1990). An example of these divisions can be found in the War on Poverty of the 1960s, which primarily targeted the poor. As one study concludes,

> The political energies mustered for social reform in the 1960s and early 1970s were channeled into programs that did not function to draw together the constituencies separated by the social policy decisions of the 1930s, but instead worked to increase the *political* isolation of the poor, especially the black poor, from the working and middle classes. (Weir et al. 1988, 430; see also Quadagno 1994)

If the claim by same-sex marriage supporters that equalization of benefits guaranteed by marriage rights signifies equality of citizenship, then silence about these social divisions in their distribution is warranted as well as the historical role of unions in the creation of these patterns. Union accommodation to civil rights demands by workers resisting these historical inequities, the dictates of EEO policy, and the legal duty of fair representation have necessitated broad attention to contractual fairness and equality of benefits as a key ingredient to survival in light of these legal and social pressures (Burstein and Monaghan 1986; Youngdahl 1974).

Despite these imperatives, unions were conspicuously absent from early organizing in the marriage case. Once the Hawai'i Supreme Court overturned the 1990 circuit court ruling denying the issuance of marriage licenses to three same-sex couples in 1993, the plaintiffs, already heavily in debt to their lawyer, immediately needed money to exploit this historic opportunity. A fund-raiser was held in 1993, and finally the Marriage Project was organized to provide financial support for the plaintiffs and disseminate information to the community about the case. The Marriage Project raised about one hundred thousand dollars annually, mostly from gay- and lesbian-friendly networks; labor did not contribute, nor was it asked to support the plaintiffs, in part because the fund-raisers were unprepared and, according to one organizer, too "timid" to engage the controversy that such a request might produce.[11] Grassroots support grew without labor's involvement, sprouting organizations such as the Hawai'i Equal Rights to Marriage Project, the Alliance for Equal Rights, the Coalition for Equality and Diversity (which was coordinated by the state American Civil Liberties Union), and the Clergy Coalition. The Lambda Legal Defense Fund of New York, a powerhouse gay and lesbian public interest firm, fur-

nished a lawyer to support local counsel and promoted regional Freedom to Marry Coalitions around the nation in order to keep public
involvement high. Right-wing concern about the implications of the
case began more slowly. As conservatives were weak and poorly organized in Hawai'i, there were few local exhortations of opposition,
except within the Mormon and Catholic churches. This would change
as the political maneuvering surrounding the case began to provide a
more obvious set of opportunities to channel grassroots organizing
against civil rights.

As the Hawai'i house, prodded by its conservative Judiciary chairman, Terrence Tom, began to hold hearings on the case, voices supporting legislative or citizen intervention in the case were increasingly
heard. The 1994 act was passed to redefine marriage, the Commission
on Sexual Orientation and the Law was convened and upheld the *Baehr*
decision, the trial was held in 1996, again upholding the right to same-
sex marriage, and debates once again were started in the legislature,
finally producing the amendment language that was approved in
1998.[12]

Two aspects of this history of the marriage issue bear emphasis.
First, as studies of law and policy have repeatedly shown, court decisions are rarely taken in a political vacuum (Horowitz 1977; McCann
1994). Throughout the six-year-long political crisis that the *Baehr* case
initiated, there has been ample citizen involvement. From the writing
of amicus briefs to grassroots campaigning, testimony before legislatures and Congress, and public declarations of support, numerous
avenues of expression outside the courtroom have given this case a
highly charged and political character that "drowned out" most other
concerns (see fig. 3). Despite this attention only one labor union in
Hawai'i out of 118 made an early declaration of support for marriage
rights. Only a handful of other unions joined the bandwagon by the
time of the November vote, and a similar number quietly endorsed the
amendment campaign.

The second notable aspect of this history renders the sparse support
of labor even more surprising. Despite the novelty of same-sex marriage, the principle by which *Baehr* was decided has become part and
parcel of labor notions of fair play and due process: the right to be free
of gender discrimination. Additionally, the idea that was solidified in
public testimony and the findings of the Commission on Sexual Orientation and the Law, that the right to marriage has to be seen as a direct
economic benefit denied gay and lesbian couples, is also a traditional

DROWNED OUT

Fig. 3.   Editorial cartoon commenting on domination of the same-sex marriage issue in the fall 1998 campaign. (*Honolulu Star Bulletin*, 13 August 1998.)

issue of justice for unions: family benefits and their fair distribution. Labor's twentieth-century embrace of legal protection and civil rights as both "Magna Carta"[13] and a language of citizenship (reflected in John Sweeney's quotation opening this chapter) has striking parallels to the commitments of same-sex marriage proponents. In activist Barbara Cox's words, "Preventing same-sex couples from marrying treats us as second-class citizens. As long as this society refuses to legally recognize our relationships, gay men and lesbians cannot be equal members of the polity" (1997, 158). Acknowledging these common claims to equal citizenship voiced by workers, gays, and lesbians, we must again ask, where have the unions gone on the marriage question?

Hawai'i Calls: Explaining Why the Unions Do Not Hear

In this section I detail three structures of political language and argumentation—which I call discursive frames—that have surrounded the

Baehr decision. I see discursive frames as dominant structures of argumentation, oriented around a binary tension of competing ideas,
through which political and social action is constructed and made
meaningful (see also Johnston 1995; Zald 1996). Discursive frames matter because of the underlying nature of collective action in the post-
Fordist period. As plummeting union density and the rise of new forms
of collective action since the 1960s attest, the decline of the industrial
economy has produced what Klaus Eder (1992) has called a decoupling
of class and action, or an extinction of "once-natural" affinities between
similarly situated class actors. What has taken the place of traditional
class politics is a complex field of interaction increasingly mediated by
communication. For this reason, common interest and social attitudes
are often insufficient to motivate action or alliance. Agency today is
organized by discursive frames that provide meaning for signifiers
used by collective actors to visualize social boundaries and reproduce
identity, and permit agents to, in the seminal words of Erving Goffman,
"locate, perceive, identify and label" the characteristics of political and
social events (1974, 21).

Elaboration of Goffman's interpretive "frame analysis" by social
movement theorists has demonstrated the strategic and transforma-
tional capacities of individual and collective agents (Gamson 1988;
Snow and Benford 1988; Snow et al. 1986). Relevant frames may be
articulated by one party, or fixed through mutual conflict, but are just
as often borrowed from previous struggles where they have been
secreted within the local understandings, common sense, and over-
arching discourses (Johnston 1995). Discursive frames resonate deeply
with common cultural ideas, delimiting boundaries of action and identity, or because they expand that action in tactical ways, drawing in
allies or electoral majorities larger than the size of the pool of primary
identifiers might indicate (see Melucci 1989). I believe that it is the tactical reliance on discursive frames about "civil rights" in the struggle
over same-sex marriage that has made common cause between unions
and gay and lesbian groups so hard to produce.

These broad discursive frames are made all the more potent within
the heavily bureaucratic forms of "business unions" that eschew direct
action, democratic organization, and the like (Davis 1986; Moody 1988).
By creating membership through compulsory collection of dues and
satisfying the needs of members through selective incentives (Olson
1965), business unions have few mechanisms—and few needs—to

reproduce institutional ideologies of collective solidarity (Fantasia 1988; Marshall 1983). This is exacerbated by the changing nature of work in the postindustrial world. With more work being individualized as it is accomplished with personal computers, and with technology reducing the need for extensive crews of production workers, there are fewer opportunities or requirements for mutual trust between workers in many economic sectors. This may have important consequences for the types of relationships that are possible between union leadership and the rank and file. As trust is diminished among workers, there are fewer nonbureaucratic resources available for leaders to mobilize the rank and file.

These internal dynamics have important ramifications for civil rights struggles, as I show in this chapter. Despite an early failure to attract the commitment of many unions to the issue of same-sex marriage, Protect Our Constitution decided that unions were key to a victory over the amendment in 1998. As David Smith, communications director of the Human Rights Campaign—the POC's major contributor—recounted in an interview,

> Part of [our] strategy early on was—and this became even more important once it became clear the elected officials were going to bail on us—we needed to establish credible messengers to help deliver our message. Because the [civil rights] message was not as easily digested as Save Traditional Marriage's was, it required people that you trusted. If you were going to hear it and believe it, you needed to hear it from people that you trusted. This involved much constituency targeting. Union [members] are going to listen to their leaders, or at least other union members. . . . Unions have an ability to turn out their membership if they are committed to an issue.[14]

The success of labor's turnout was dependent on persuading leaders to support the issue, and on how well leaders could challenge workers to see same-sex marriage as a union concern. The state AFL-CIO came very close to a blanket endorsement of the POC position in August 1998, but then backed away when it could not reach consensus,[15] leaving the decision up to individual unions. I argue in this chapter that lacking vibrant democratic traditions and trust, even leadership committed to the civil rights campaign had a difficult time exploiting the dominant discursive frames to work in their interest and persuading their membership to vote along.

To substantiate this argument, I turn to a discussion of three discursive frames with relevance to labor unions and how their activation within the debate over same-sex marriage has inhibited union support for same-sex marriage. Each frame marks a contest over the role of "civil rights" in democratic practice and recapitulates aspects of the dominant discourses, identified in earlier chapters, that have propelled the marriage controversy. The first frame relates to the social production of norms for social change; the second is an argument about the economic cost of rights and intervention into market relationships; and the third is a political concern for the relationship between courts and electoral majorities. I call these frames activist/traditional civil rights; unlimited/scarce civil rights; and court/public democratic ideals.

Activist/Traditional Civil Rights

The supreme court opinion in *Baehr* acknowledged that there is no tradition of same-sex marriage in Hawai'i or elsewhere and, thus, that there is no right to same-sex marriage that can be extracted from common practice. Nonetheless, the court reasoned that deep legal traditions of antidiscrimination, bolstered by the state constitution, prevent the state from limiting the recipients of marriage licenses. This ambivalence about the legal meaning of tradition has been further played out within the political debates and subsequent legal arguments surrounding the case. As I show below, this discursive frame has had a direct impact on union commitments.

Perhaps the strongest tactical lines between opponents and proponents of same-sex marriage have been drawn with the rhetoric of "traditional marriage." For many conservatives in this debate, the tradition of heterosexual marriage is set against claims for civil rights by gays and lesbians that are said to be antagonistic to and even mock community values. As the leader of the largest coalition against same-sex marriage testified before one legislative committee, "It is clear that Hawai'i residents do not want to legalize same-sex marriage. It's time for the legislature to acknowledge this and put aside diversionary tactics, like specious civil rights arguments or twisting the equal rights amendment to achieve a purpose for which it was never intended."[16] Such a line drawn between "tradition" and "civil rights" is, for many conservatives, a barrier between valued ways of life, on the one side, and complicity in unwanted social change, on the other. "I am opposed to compromising traditional marriage in an attempt to validate the alternative lifestyle of homosexuality. . . . We would be sacrificing what we know is right and what we know isn't," testified one traditionalist.[17] Arguments for changing tradition can only be seen in this frame as alien. As another conservative testified, "The well-financed push to weaken traditional marriage is a result of queer theory and the radical agenda. . . . Please don't kill the American family."[18] Even the state's attorney argued that "same-sex couples can be denied marriage on the strength of our cultural and moral traditions."[19]

In an attempt to resuscitate the traditional values embedded in the concept of "civil rights," supporters of the *Baehr* decision testified to the "state's long-held traditions of diversity, tolerance, acceptance of different cultures and family relationships and a commitment to equality,"[20] to "traditional values and the principles of fairness and equity,"[21] and "Hawai'i's traditions of non-discrimination and fairness to all."[22] This attempt to broaden the meaning of traditional practice reproduces the discursive frame distinguishing activist civil rights and questions of what is right and civil from what is commonly practiced, even while it embraces a progressive view of marriage rights. Despite the fact that those seeking access to marriage are asking for a traditional sanction of their relationship, that they must ask, and that such sanction must be given by courts, seems to support the conservative theme that same-sex marriage is something that is imposed according to the logic rooted in abstract ideals rather than custom.

One might expect that unions would feel an affinity with the more activist tradition and seek to support the side arguing for "civil rights." After all, there is much in the tradition of American labor, and the Hawaiian experience with labor in particular, that values activism. With John Sweeney's accession to the helm of the AFL-CIO came a stated commitment to re-create the traditions of activism that energized the labor movement of the 1940s, and to renew traditions to increase labor's organizing options today (Gapasin and Yates 1997; Moody 1997a). Yet this discursive frame works against this call to progressivism by juxtaposing tradition against activism, a tension naturalized by the material context of labor's declining strength and its consuming efforts to hold on to what it once had, which displace struggles to expand its entitlements. When unions substitute bureaucratic modes of organization for democratic procedure (Offe and Wiesenthal 1980), activism is further removed from an understanding of fair play. In these ways, the frame resonates with workers who see the commitment to civil rights protections for gays and lesbians, especially outside of the workplace, not as a matter of simple justice—as when something unfairly taken away is later returned—but something to be measured by the yardstick of appropriate activism or even personal energy and commitment. The right to marriage, in this metric, becomes an issue that might be—and even should be—deferred to the future, even though it is present in legal time. This frame works against union assistance for these marriage politics by making the costs of support seem "exceptional," defeating the idea of common interests.

The constraining power of this frame was evident in my interviews with the leadership of major unions in Hawai'i. The executive director of the Hawai'i Governmental Employees Association, the largest public union in the state, was opposed to political involvement in the case. He talked about his commitment to fairness, choice, and equal treatment in regard to benefits for nontraditional partners, but drew the line at marriage. This was "not a good or timely idea," and, he averred, he had privately told the legislature this during their deliberations.[23] The head of the Hawai'i Carpenters Union echoed the HGEA president. He made the political distinction between marriage and extended benefits for gay and lesbian partners, suggesting that his union could support the latter but not the former. Marriage "went too far and asked too much." Since gay and lesbian groups had not asked his support on the issue, he felt his union should remain publicly uncommitted,[24] a position he retained even after Protect Our Constitution begged for his endorsement. As the amendment campaign heated up in 1998, the carpenters' newsletter presented a balanced article drawn from interviews with supporters of a civil rights perspective as well as those advocating "traditional" marriage. Yet, this presentation of the debate only served to reinforce the power of the activist/traditional discursive frame that discourages the perception that this was necessarily a *union* issue. The article concluded that

> The issue is pretty clear cut. It just seems complicated. Voters who feel strongly about traditional marriage and are definitely against same-sex marriage should mark "yes" on their ballots. Those who

don't have a firm opinion on the matter and who are worried about setting a dangerous precedent in terms of Legislative scape-goating should vote "no." Either way, the main thing is to vote.[25]

The University of Hawai'i Professional Assembly (UHPA) rejected this common frame that had discouraged involvement of other unions. One reason, perhaps, is that the leader of the Marriage Project, which had championed the *Baehr* case from the beginning, sat on the board, as did three other gays and lesbians. This "personalized" the issue, according to the union president, and brought the legal time frame of the *Baehr* case into realistic alignment with the frame of traditional civil rights commitments. UHPA was the first union—and for many years the only one—to endorse the same-sex marriage case. Rather than claiming that same-sex marriage was an open issue awaiting further decision making, UHPA's tactic was to argue that marriage, like other traditional equal protection issues, had been already decided. The union testified before the legislature that "gays and lesbians comprise less than 3% of the population of Hawai'i, but they took on the State of Hawai'i in court, and they won fair and square. . . . To now change the rules on gays and lesbians is simply unfair."[26]

The experience of the Hawai'i State Teachers Association (HSTA) demonstrates just what internal dynamics were required to commit unions to the fairness of marriage case. In 1997, the union's leader desired to move the organization toward declaring a public stance in support of the *Baehr* decision and against the political machinations designed to weaken or kill it. However, with her board increasingly influenced by conservatives (who have been supported by conservative groups organized initially in opposition to the marriage issue), she reluctantly concluded that "the members are not ready for this," as they could not agree that this was a proper or timely union issue.[27] She was replaced by another president in 1998 who had first considered the issue of same-sex marriage in her Methodist church four years earlier, when *Baehr* was first decided. Her personal skepticism about the idea of same-sex marriage began to melt when, in the course of a discussion group that she had been charged to facilitate by her pastor, she saw even the most homophobic members eventually join in a unanimous conclusion that same-sex marriage was just and an issue that the church should commit itself to. Deeply influenced by this experience of consciousness-raising, she decided to apply this model to the democratic process of political endorsements within the union. She immediately began a similar set of open discussions among the union board and the leaders of the twelve chapters concerning the same-sex marriage campaign.

These participants were charged to consider the question of whether same-sex marriage was a vital issue for teachers, and therefore, for their union. Confronting the campaign for a constitutional amendment that was beginning to heat up in the spring and summer of 1998, the union's president asked them, "If we don't take a position, what does it mean for our students?"[28] Over a period of two months, several leaders of the proamendment forces were invited to appear before the union officials with an equal number of leaders of Protect Our Constitution to talk about their respective positions. Addressing the issue of how same-sex marriage affected work conditions personalized the issue in a manner analogous to that experienced by the professors. The president's recollection of the proamendment forces makes this apparent. They tried to stress what teachers would be forced to teach in their classrooms if the amendment failed, an argument that was not taken seriously by the assembled union leadership. One partisan then made the argument that single-parent families would be deleterious to children, an outcome for which the board would have to hold itself complicit if it endorsed the antiamendment campaign. This argument caused one board member to weep and ask whether this meant that as a single parent herself she was a bad parent. According to the memory of the union's president, this outburst galvanized later discussions. The officials had little trouble agreeing that since they were responsible for teaching social studies and constitutional principles, their work was directly implicated by the amendment. But they also recognized that the divisiveness they had witnessed in the presentations was a critical issue for the union. One board member revealed that he was gay and that this was an important issue to him personally. An African American member who was not gay said that he empathized with those who wanted marriage rights and that he wanted solidarity on the board as a sign of support for *his* civil rights. Another woman admitted that she had lived with her present husband before marriage and that she feared the message that would result from the amendment's passage. The assembled leadership of the union voted overwhelmingly to endorse the antiamendment campaign.

The endorsement was couched into the language of civil rights. As the executive informed the leadership of the board's decision,

> The position to vote "NO" on the constitutional amendment was overwhelming. The Association has a strong commitment to human and civil rights. It is part of the Association's mission statement adopted by the HSTA Convention. It is also part of the proud union tradition in Hawai'i to believe that "injury to one is an injury to all." *The Association is not endorsing same sex marriage rather the Association is supporting human and civil rights.*[29]

In a mailing to its members, the union emphasized the fact that "HSTA has not taken a position on same-sex marriage." Instead, four reasons for voting no were adduced:

> Our Bill of Rights has always been used to protect the rights of people. If passed, this Constitutional amendment would be the first time in history that a constitution was amended to take away rights already afforded to its people. If we give away this right, it could set a dangerous precedent.
>
> The constitution should provide equal protection to all people in Hawai'i, and no one should be singled out for differential treatment.
>
> The amendment would give the legislature unprecedented power to overturn a Supreme Court decision. It violates the checks and balances of our system of government.
>
> Protecting human and civil rights is a basic tenet of HSTA's philosophy.[30]

Although the stress on civil rights was explicitly distinguished from the marriage issue itself, this argument nonetheless served to weaken the temporal disjunction promoted by the activist/traditional frame, constructing civil rights action as an immediate imperative of the union.

What succeeded for the board, particularly the democratic discussion process that revealed the connections among constitutional change, working environment, and the ethos of solidarity, did not extend to the rank and file. Immediately after the announcement of the union's endorsement of the same-sex marriage campaign, the leadership was publicly attacked by angry union members.[31] As one disgruntled teacher recapitulated the activist/traditional frame,

> As a teacher and member of the HSTA for nearly 30 years, I have usually supported the decisions made by its board of directors. But I cannot support its endorsement of a "no" vote on the traditional marriage amendment. How can HSTA state that "this would be the first time in history that a constitution was amended to take away rights that people already have?" Same-gender marriage has never been a constitutional right in the U.S. or Hawai'i, so how can it be taken away? The board should have remained neutral on this critical moral issue, and just provided unbiased information for teachers to make their own personal decisions.[32]

That HSTA, one of the state's most democratic unions, experienced such vehement dissension reveals the difficulty of bringing civil rights commitments to the fore. The president, chastened by the rank-and-file response, has expressed no more willingness to encourage the union to work on the same-sex marriage issue, or to take any further positions of this type.

Unlimited/Scarce Civil Rights

> Giving legal recognition to . . . same-gender relationships, whether by marriage or otherwise, will economically affect every resident of Hawai'i. After obtaining legal recognition, economic demands—enforced by the courts—will quickly follow. Taxes will have to be raised due to the increase in numbers making demands on the state for benefit entitlements. In the private sector, every worker in Hawaii will receive lower wages and benefits than would normally be available because part of company revenues will have to go to someone whose only connection with the company is that he or she has a "friend" that works there.[33]

If the activist/traditional civil rights frame erases the immediate pressure of the evolving court case from contemporary union commitments, a second frame reinforces the narrowing of union concern. This frame is constructed around the neoliberal discourses of political economy that have infused the same-sex marriage debates. From this perspective—as evinced by the excerpt from a letter to the editor above—civil rights are depicted to lie in a zero-sum relationship to one another and some, especially those "special rights" for gays and lesbians, are seen as excessive or "inflationary" in the rights economy, threatening to crowd out other more cherished rights and values.

The argument between those who see rights as expandable and ultimately beneficial to an economy and those who argue for their scarcity due to the limits of fiscal responsibility has direct consequences for union support. In the expanding postwar Fordist economy in which union wages regularly increased, fueling high levels of consumption and production, workers' rights could be neatly equated with the general interest. In this framework, those rights grew as economic health increased. The civil rights movement and the women's movement would follow in labor's wake through the 1960s and 1970s. However, once the economy ceased its expansion in the mid-1970s, labor experienced the tension between its demands and the profit expectations of the private sector, as well as the homologous concerns for fiscal solvency of the public sector. In the new political economy, workers' rights represent only a particular interest, and other rights claims make competing demands on a limited economic base. As Offe and Wiesenthal (1980) have pointed out, mature unions can resort to "opportunistic" strategies of survival that minimize the need for democratic collective action present early in their formation and that reaffirm the logic of the market (see also Moody 1988). In the years since Offe and Wiesenthal wrote, the market and the state have together demonstrated their commanding power to weaken American unions, which quickly learned to go along, often at the cost of principled support for democratic rights.

In Hawai'i, this trend has become most noticeable in the marriage case. Unions have borrowed heavily from neoliberal discourses about the scarcity of civil rights, contributing their voices to the chorus arguing for fiscal restraint. Private and state sector unions are frequently divided on macroeconomic strategy, especially the role of state budgets on economic health. However, in times of recession or economic downturn (as has been the case in Hawai'i since the early 1990s), both types of unions find themselves victims of cost-cutting. This has pushed them to develop similar positions on the economic value of rights. Many union leaders in Hawai'i argued in interviews that the cost of new benefits for gay and lesbian workers that would follow either legalized same-sex marriage or the recognition of domestic partnership status was too high to bear and would weaken labor's already precarious position by slowing the economy. Public union leadership voiced concerns about the state's ability to afford the cost of new benefits in the midst of chronic budget shortfalls. Private sector unions involved in the building trades indicated a similar reticence, arguing the imperative of awaiting the economic flood tide that will float all boats; the added cost of new beneficiaries was, in their minds, too much added ballast.

Activists within the state AFL-CIO who supported a firm civil rights commitment argued to unions that some economic language might be effectively turned to a civil rights advantage. Echoing a traditional CIO argument about the importance of inclusive contracts from the late 1930s, it was proposed that "the contract has to cover everyone" might be useful for persuading workers to acknowledge the constitutional imperatives of equal rights.[34] Yet many unions were stymied when it came to these arguments because of the power of neoliberal reinterpretations of contract. One local of the International Brotherhood of Electrical Workers whose leaders decided to join the anti-amendment coalition nonetheless found it impossible to argue to the rank and file that same-sex marriage was a legitimate union issue of benefits. The problem was not that workers were unwilling to see this as an economic issue, but that the discourse of justice was outdone by the rhetoric of scarcity compounded by lingering arguments that gays were vectors of human diseases such as AIDS. Since every member was responsible for some part of her medical premiums, benefits language became an impossible terrain for gathering support. The difficulty educating the rank and file within the union made the fear of skyrocketing costs impossible to counter, he argued.[35] In the end, the union issued no explanation for its endorsements, just a list of preferred positions and candidates.

Economic issues were also smuggled into the marriage campaign by unions inadvertently. For example, the Longshore and Warehouse Workers (ILWU) made an endorsement supporting the POC campaign in July 1998. With perhaps the strongest antidiscrimination legacy of any union in the country, the Hawai'i local nonetheless found itself unable to argue for same-sex marriage directly, as there was too much opposition among the membership. Instead, they followed the POC rhetoric that the important issue was a commitment to the U.S. Bill of Rights and the state constitution. This position aligned the union against the constitutional convention, as well. But here contradictions became evident. Electing not to address the same-sex amendment issue directly, the constitutional convention was attacked as an assault on "rights and freedoms" central to unions, Hawaiians, and others (see fig. 4). But it also depicted the convention as a costly mistake. One advertisement run in Maui and the island of Hawai'i by the union argued that "our constitution is working and doesn't need to be changed. Let's not waste any time and money to 'fix' something that's not 'broken.' "[36] Concern over wasting money reinforced the neoliberal idea that marriage rights were, also, unaffordable.

This scarcity rhetoric was critical for weakening support for domestic partnership legislation as well. Even after the RBA (which was examined in the previous chapter) was signed into law, many unions continued to thwart the law in its first few months, convinced by the growing clamor of business that it would cost too much. The force of this argument was evident in discussions about health benefit policies across the state. In their first meeting after the requirement to extend benefits took effect, union trustees for the Health Fund insurance pool accepted the legal requirement for inclusion of domestic partnerships but debated (without resolution) who should pay. Many argued that the added cost of beneficiary coverage should be absorbed by the workers requesting coverage and should not become a burden to the state. The teachers' union, HSTA, which offers an attractive private insurance plan, voted through its health trustees to exclude domestic partnerships because of the added cost. Those demanding such coverage were urged to rejoin state insurance coverage, instead.

Court/Public Democratic Ideals

Why have such obvious double standards that go against the grain of valued democratic traditions of solidarity been allowed to continue within Hawai'i's unions? Collective action within unions has rightly been seen as a delicate balance between democratic and bureaucratic elements, the former contributing to collective identity, trust, and militancy and the latter to the discipline necessary to make a threat of job action credible, controllable, and ultimately codifiable by contract (Kelly 1988; Offe and Wiesenthal 1980). The boundary between these dynamics has often been mediated by labor law that establishes the responsibilities of leadership and the rights of members. But this

Fig. 4.   ILWU advertisement opposed to constitutional amendment. (*Maui News* and *Hawai'i Tribune Herald,* 28 October 1998.)

boundary is also determined by internal custom, shared ethnic and religious values, and political necessities. This complex amalgam of bureaucratic and democratic forces was realigned by the sovereignty politics surrounding the marriage case. The discursive frame of whether courts or publics should have the final say in determining the ambit of civil rights protections challenged the sources of union authority and the goals of collective action.

The tension between courts and publics is raised in the marriage case, as we have seen, through the common argument that the courts have usurped traditional legislative prerogative, thereby necessitating the patriotic restoration of democratic sovereignty. These arguments have been used to support the claim that equal rights for gays and lesbians are "special rights" that impede the function and efficiency of democratic majorities. This idea has a special resonance for labor unions that have themselves been labeled as "special interest groups," seeking public rents without an equal exchange of public gains. Rather than making unions natural allies of other "special groups," however, many unions in Hawai'i tried to escape the contagion effect by backing away, becoming unwilling to challenge the neoliberal implications of this discursive frame. As the looming threat of the constitutional convention was felt, the fear that rights of all special interests could be curtailed made some unions sensitive to public opinion about what kind of democratic players they were going to be. For these unions, advocacy for same-sex marriage rights seemed to be shortsighted in the face of graver institutional threats.

As is apparent in the near-universal rejection of the constitutional convention, it is not that unions actually endorse the notion of unfettered democracy. Rather, the matter is one of political expediency as well as a concern for the internal political culture of the union. As long as law is open to challenge on grounds of majority rights, many unions were unwilling to act on any other principle. It is for this reason that the teachers' union, which had separated the provision of health benefits to domestic partnership families from families constituted through marriage, welcomed a legal challenge to their decision. "We have nothing to fear from litigation except clarity in this matter," the president acknowledged in an interview. Litigation would not only clarify the duties of leadership to members of the union who have domestic partners. It would also serve as a strong signal to the rank and file—who are themselves not immune to the backlash against the marriage case—that democracy cannot be opposed to equal protection arguments.

Indeed, legal uncertainty appears to be the very concern that killed an early opportunity for the teachers' union board of directors to consider a policy statement advocating same-sex marriage in 1996. The union's Youth and Human Civil Rights Committee had endorsed support for the *Baehr* case but, according to the committee's chairman, balked at submitting the resolution to the board for consideration when one lesbian member of the committee feared that a refusal to endorse the issue would fuel conservatives within the union and the public without, doing more harm than silence on the issue ever could.[37] Democratic commitments could not be heard clearly amid the uncertain status of legal authority.

Of course, the latent potential for democratic solidarity within unions to create support for civil rights and to counteract the rhetoric of democratic sovereignty against the marriage case can dissolve into the very terms of the court/democratic frame. The predominantly Filipino and Catholic Laborer's Union, for example, took no official position on same-sex marriage, "since [the] issue has no direct bearing on the Construction Industry and our union,"[38] but the union's business manager nonetheless seized the opportunity to frame the issue on behalf of the amendment forces.

> For the record, I am in favor of *traditional marriage*. I believe that this issue is about marriage, tradition and family. The institution of marriage is a core building block in our society and needs to be preserved for one man and one woman only. Despite what the pro–gay marriage side is saying, changing the Hawai'i Constitution is not about discriminating against a certain group, but rather a public policy question. Currently, the Circuit Court has already legalized same-sex marriage. However, same-sex marriages haven't been allowed to take place because the case is on appeal before our state's Supreme Court. State Legislators, in expectation that the Supreme Court will uphold the Circuit Court's decision, passed a bill calling for a constitutional amendment that would keep the decision of defining marriage with the people through their elected officials, not the courts. . . . On Nov. 3, 1998, I will be voting "Yes" to Question #2 on the ballot. . . . Remember, a "No"

vote *or* a blank ballot will give the state same-sex marriage. That is not a Hawaii I would like to see.[39]

How well common religious beliefs can serve to build solidarity between union leadership and the membership is not well understood, but it seemed to form a strong subtext in unions such as the Laborers. The Teamsters Local 996 leadership were persuaded by appeals by Protect Our Constitution in the summer of 1998 and agreed to lead their membership to support the antiamendment forces. In an attempt to weaken religious solidarity within their union, they argued for a vote based on the constitutional law of religious establishment.

You may have heard a political ad on the radio or TV recently. It stated that it was just "common sense" to amend the constitution to define marriage to their beliefs. It was "common sense" (at least to the white minority in South Africa) that blacks should not have the right to vote. It was "common sense" to some pre-war state governments that interracial marriages were wrong. Now some people are claiming that it's "common sense" to amend the constitution based on someone else's religious beliefs. . . . This country was founded on the principle that Church and State must be separate. No religious belief, no matter how popular, should ever be made into a law. The founding fathers knew that religious beliefs must remain a strictly personal matter—that way every citizen would be able to exercise their own beliefs—without the fear of persecution from those who think that they should believe in something else. VOTE NO ON AMENDING THE STATE CONSTITUTION.[40]

The attempt to build a civil rights consciousness was unsuccessful. One union official observed,

The discussions I had with members of some of our bargaining units indicated that the "Vote Yes" side had gotten their message across and the "Vote No" side had not. Almost every comment alluded to the negative feelings towards the gay marriage aspect of the Constitutional Amendment—virtually none acknowledged any danger of the broader constitutional concerns. The Union's official position as voiced [above] was almost universally condemned by those members who voiced an opinion.[41]

As nearly every union that tried to take a stand against the amendment learned, building successful arguments for civil rights amid the growing sovereignty politics so taxed internal democratic processes that valued individual participation and consciousness, ethnic and religious ties, and political involvement, all of which gained distinct meanings in light of the languages of tradition, democratic control, and economic scarcity surrounding the campaign. Without vibrant forms of democratic association that could once again teach vital lessons about equal rights and the accommodation of pluralistic differences, the older multiethnic traditions of Hawai'i's unions would fade away. Top-down attempts to persuade members to vote against the amendment on behalf of rights were, by the unions' own admission, as unsuccessful as they were institutionally incoherent.

Conclusions

The impediments to successful alliances between unions and gay and lesbian groups concerned with the marriage issue are many and broad. The discursive frames that constitute democratic debates make most unions wary of defending rights, even when those rights directly impact some of their members. Equal rights for gays and lesbians are seen by unions to reach too far, cost too much, and further isolate unions already vulnerable to low public opinion. What, then, can be learned from the few cases where an alliance was made and internal campaigns waged to support the political endorsement of civil rights?[42]

The University of Hawai'i Professional Assembly bucked the trend early for several reasons. First, it had an understanding of the marriage case almost from its inception because one of its active board members and chair of the political action committee was also a leader of one of the first community groups organized to raise support for the plaintiffs. According to Tom Ramsey, this threefold position allowed him to educate the then-union president, who came to slowly appreciate the justice in the position, and the union's responsibility for its gay and lesbian members, prior to the construction of the issue through predominantly public discursive frames. As the former president recollects, this cause soon became her personal passion.

This process is similar to that of the teachers' union (HSTA), which also had gay and lesbian activists who were involved early in the case, and a president committed to the issue. However, unlike the professors' union, there were no formal and few informal channels of communication between the board of directors and the special committee that was empowered to consider civil rights issues before 1998. By the time the committee had decided to bring their recommendation of support to the board—months after the professors had publicly announced their position—the stakes seemed too high, opposition on the board had already been voiced, and the issue languished. Not until a vigorous discussion among the leadership was reinitiated in 1998 did an endorsement pass.

Second, UHPA, like HSTA and the ILWU, had self-identifying lesbians and gays on the board at the time this issue came up for discussion. According to those on the boards, this personalized the issue to an important degree. Where discussions in the abstract can easily draw upon dominant discursive frames for reference, personal accounts of discrimination, reminders of common goals, and the recognition of diverse interests can break through the bonds of convention and formulate commitments to the new opportunities that are at hand. The strong support of leadership on behalf of the civil rights issue was also instrumental in these unions.

Third, the memberships of UHPA and HSTA—professors and teachers—take occupational pride in free thinking. This often leads to explosive debates between union leadership and some rank and file, especially on controversial political issues. Internal polls taken shortly before UHPA's decision to endorse same-sex marriage in 1995 (and reward political candidates with compatible positions), revealed that 25 percent of the faculty were strongly opposed to same-sex marriage, and another 24 percent were slightly opposed. That left only the barest of majorities who were in favor or unconcerned about the issue, a poor base of support for a politically risky endeavor. However, in this particular case outrage by those opposed was successfully deflected by another issue. The union leadership simultaneously voted to support a call for legalized casino gambling to bolster the economy, which they knew had even less support among the faculty. This other issue evoked a vehement set of responses from the membership, eclipsing same-sex marriage as a strong political litmus test.

In sum, the factors favoring UHPA's, HSTA's and ILWU's endorsement of same-sex marriage were both fortuitous and enabled by organizational design. Although these are just a handful of cases, they offer some insights into labor and gay and lesbian cooperation.

The value of common projects engaging both union and community interests, and the visibility of gays and lesbians within the union, stand in direct challenge to the discursive frames that tend to separate notions of gay and lesbian rights, identities, and even citizenship from those of other interested citizens and organizations. The "queering" of such boundaries through common endeavors may be essential for successful labor coalitions. Political theorist Shane Phelan captures this point with her notion of affinity politics.

> The problem for coalition politics is not, what do we share? but rather, what *might* we share as we develop our identities through the process of coalition? Coalition cannot be simply the strategic alignment of diverse groups over a single issue, nor can coalition mean finding the real unity behind our apparently diverse struggles. Our politics must be informed by affinity rather than identity, not simply because we are not all alike but because we each embody multiple, often conflicting, identities and locations. (1995, 345)

There is little to suggest that professional or public unions have any organizational advantage over other unions in the practice of this type of coalition building. An exciting body of new literature is challenging the idea that blue-collar attitudes evince increased hostility toward, or intolerance of gays and lesbians (Gluckman and Reed 1997; Raffo 1996), suggesting little difference in structural homophobia between unions. Sectorally powerful, blue-collar Canadian unions such as the Canadian Automobile Workers have demonstrated that a long-term commitment to fighting discrimination against lesbians and gays can lead to corporate provision of benefits to same-sex partners without incurring membership backlash.[43] That union uses an "affinity" language to acknowledge the importance of lesbian and gay rights to the membership.

> Lesbians, gay men and bisexuals are everywhere: they work beside us, they are active in our unions, they are our neighbours, they are church members, community activists, professionals, athletes, elected officers and politicians. They are our mothers, fathers, brothers, sisters, spouses and our friends. Over the last few years, the CAW has made some giant steps forward in the fight against homophobia in the communities and in the union as well

as in the workplaces. Some workplaces, through bargaining, have been able to obtain same sex spousal benefits and pensions. Since 1995, there have been workshops for same sex spouses on lesbian and gay issues at the CAW Human Rights Conferences, regionally and nationally, as well as at the Women's Conferences.[44]

In the United States, both public and private employers have voiced similar economic concerns about the increase in rights, militating against sectoral advantage when it comes to this issue. Nonetheless, the middle-class bias of many gay and lesbian organizations may increase the membership overlap with white-collar unions. Where strong democratic traditions (which can run in any union) permit dynamic coalitional politics between these organizations, then Phelan's vision can be realized.

Of course, legal cases often provide poor conditions for the development of these coalitions. Cases rarely progress as slowly as *Baehr* or offer as many political opportunities for intervention. And even where there is opportunity for political organizing, coalitions that spring up in response to the sudden surprise of controversial legal decisions may not have the breadth or timeliness to combat the dominant discursive frames articulated in media and by political opponents.

Isolated legal cases such as *Baehr* also place their own impediments to successful union coalitions. The hefty investments already made in rhetorical strategies surrounding the marriage issue make the tired tactics of reweighting the discursive frames unlikely to be successful either in changing the tenor of public debate, or in building the common identities between various groups that could provide a new foundation for politics. By failing to post a challenge to discursive frames, unions have placed themselves in a vulnerable position when these same neoliberal frames are used against generous public worker benefits and for the economic imperatives of privatization. As much as gays and lesbians have needed unions in the past few years, unions themselves now need committed allies.

Chapter 5

Hawaiian Wedding Song

The majority of Hawaii families oppose same sex marriage because it is a personal affront to the traditional family structure and values which have been a strong part of their rich history and culture. As you know our state motto declares, "The life of the land is perpetuated in righteousness."

> —Rosemary Garcideunas, state director
> of the Christian Coalition of Hawai'i, 1993

I was born of Chinese, Hawaiian, German ancestry in Hawaii and raised in an environment where traditional family values from these three backgrounds were nurtured and taught and became the basis of my being. This gave me a clear sense of purpose and direction as I charted the course of my life. My husband also was born and raised here in Hawaii and grew up loving the heritage of his kupuna [elders]. It naturally occurred that the common base of the structure of our marriage was greatly influenced by all that growing up in Hawaii Nei meant to us. The motto of Hawaii "Ua mau ke ea o ka aina i ka pono" to us was more than just a phrase to be repeated in ceremonies. To us it was a part of what being Hawaiian meant and we have since striven to teach that to our children, grandchildren and all the children of Hawaii. Presently as docents at the Iolani Palace we feel a great responsibility to preserve the traditional qualities our alii [royalty, ruling caste] strove to pass on to us . . . and above all, the institution of the family as the basic unit of society.

> —Amanda K. DuPont, "Citizen of
> the State of Hawaii," 1997

I would urge you to make the courageous and righteous move. Hawai'i has led the nation in the past. We were the first to grant women the "right to choose" and right now our health care system, with all the faults which we see, is being held up to the nation as a model. Let us be the first to grant "full citizenship" to all our people, regardless of their sexuality. We know that "The Life of the Land is Perpetuated in Righteousness"—UA MAU KE EA O KA AINA I KA PONO.

> —Danny Brown, 1993

In keeping with the motto of our great state, *Ua mau ae ea o ka aina I ka pono—the life of the land is perpetuated in righteousness*—let us as citizens of Hawaii do the correct thing—the *righteous* thing. If we lower the standards of life by committing the unrighteousness act of legalizing same-sex marriage, we will no longer have the spirit of *aloha,* but rather we will be known as the homosexual capital of the Pacific.

—Dr. W. E. Anderson, 1993

I strongly oppose same sex marriages. Our state motto is "Ua Mau Ke Ea O Ka Aina I Ka Pono (The life of the land is preserved, perpetuated, continues, is constant, and perseveres in righteousness.) Pono in Hawaiian means goodness, uprightness, morality, moral qualities, correct or proper, excellence, well-being, fitting, proper, right, in perfect order. Hawaii and its people will continue when there is "Pono" in the land, when we stand for "Pono" righteousness. "Unrighteousness" is that which is not good, not proper, not right, not in "perfect" order. Same Sex marriages would allow "unrighteousness" to infect Hawaii nei.

—Jeanne P. Haili, 1993

As these excerpts from the Hawai'i debates over same-sex marriage illustrate, the historical and rhetorical value of "traditional marriage" is supported by religious memory and by the construction of state sovereignty, both impressed upon the laws to retain and perpetuate "righteousness." To this end, the motto of Hawai'i, which hangs as a lei[1] around the state seal symbolizes for many the honor of this noble purpose. Yet memories that animate the meaning of the motto are selective readings of history that elongate time in order to anchor tradition, and meld together discrete political spaces in order to craft a seamless and unambiguous sovereign commitment: the state, as actor, is bound to do right for the life of the land.

While many are inspired by the motto, few can cite its genealogy. The words were originally said by Kauikeaouli, King Kamehameha III, in 1843 after the intercession of Admiral Thomas of England marked the end to the five-month government of British Lord George Paulet (Kuykendall 1938, 206–26). Paulet had seized power after threatening to turn the guns of his warship on Honolulu if the king did not hand over disputed land to the British consul, Richard Charlton. Kauikeaouli's pleas for aid were received by Thomas in Chile who returned to

Hawai'i and dismissed Paulet. Thomas remained to oversee the raising of the Hawaiian flag. In an otherwise unremembered thanksgiving service, the restored king uttered the words, "Ua mau ke ea o ka aina i ka pono" (Kuykendall 1938, 220 n. 47). Contemporary scholars of Hawaiian now translate this as "The sovereignty of the land continues once more through justice / as it should be."[2] This genealogy reveals a subtle but important distinction from the "official" English translation ("The life of the land is perpetuated in righteousness") that undermines its rhetorical deployment. The attribution to the democratic state of righteous or pious ends designated to restrain or broaden marriage rights and validate state sovereignty (as deployed in the contemporary debates) is, when measured by its original meaning, entirely post hoc. The sovereignty of which the king speaks is not performed through proper ends, but rather exists as a precondition for the state's very voice—and, not insignificantly, a Hawaiian voice at that.[3] Indeed, it is the very precariousness and marginality of that Hawaiian voice today that illustrates how sovereignty is often lost even while spoken in the resonant languages of legal rights or Christian ethics. The misreading of the motto therefore both affirms and negates the presence of this prior Hawaiian sovereignty, ambivalently picturing sovereignty on the one hand as a continuity within linear time, and, on the other, as a haunting copresence, "an insistence of the past in the present" (Perrin 1995, 56).

The disruption of sovereignty that this ambivalence creates opens important political opportunities for some—especially indigenous groups and sexual minorities—and complex discursive obligations for others as it "provides a way of understanding how easily the boundary that secures the cohesive limits of the Western nation may imperceptibly turn into a contentious *internal* liminality providing a place from which to speak both of, and as, the minority, . . . the marginal" (Bhabha 1994, 149). This chapter examines the attempts by many Hawaiian nationalists to recover a sovereign voice and explores how that postcolonial politics has become interwoven in the marriage case, deconstructing the very terms of the debate as marriage rights activists and conservative opponents are both left rhetorically unsettled by the insistence of the past.

The recent scholarly attention paid to the postcolonial—understood both as the period of decolonization after the Second World War and as the complex global and local social discourses and practices that

have undergirded this transformation—has been influenced by the
works of Edward Said, Frantz Fanon, Antonio Gramsci, Michel Foucault, and others (see Williams and Chrisman 1994). Said's concept of
"orientalism" directs attention to the "Western style for dominating,
restructuring, and having authority over the Orient" via the mutual reference of the West with its Oriental Other often romantically depicted
as ahistorical and timeless, homogeneous, tradition-bound, and femi-
nized (Coombe 1993, no. 3380, 252 n. 20). "European culture gained in
strength and identity by setting itself off against the Orient as a sort of
surrogate and even underground self" (Said 1979, 3ff.). Recent influential criticisms have taken Said to task for his constructivist assumptions
that the Orient cannot resist Orientalism except through the exercise of
Western discourses that ultimately fails to acknowledge "the transgressive potentiality of mutual dependency between Europe and its Others" (Darian-Smith 1996, 293; see also Merry 2000). Perrin understands
this mutuality as the cause of a general anxiety associated with the
demands of indigenous peoples who "appear to contest rather than
confirm a progressive [Western] narrative of modernity" and signaling
"the proximity of indigenous peoples not simply as a lack *of* modernity,
but as a lack *in* modernity" (1995, 66; emphasis added).

Postcolonial scholarship explores this anxious moment in order to
"intervene in those ideological discourses of modernity that attempt to
give a hegemonic 'normality' to the uneven development and the differential, often disadvantaged, histories of nations, races, communities,
peoples" (Bhabha 1994, 171). The success of this (scholarly and practical) intervention depends upon highlighting the local particularities—
lingering traces of this uneven development—that can reveal the particular and complex power relationships belied by the hegemonic
temporal generalities often associated with the "postcolonial" (McClintock 1992). These interventions disrupt origin myths that serve as the
source of the traditional, demonstrating that what is modern and what
is traditional is not, as yet, decided. Hence, the compelling, though
uncertain referent of the Hawai'i state motto.

Hawai'i scholars, influenced by the postcolonial tradition, have
recently shown that "traditional" marriage has had an ambivalent
meaning in Hawai'i, where numerous forms of family and a broad
spectrum of acceptable sexuality predate the arrival of the Christian
missionaries (around 1820) and the haole (foreign) warships. The contemporary claims for Hawaiian sovereignty voiced by some indige-

nous nationalists have acknowledged these pre-Christian roots and the kinship and property relations they supported, challenging church doctrine on sexuality and the meanings attributed to civil rights in the marriage debates. At the same time, the modern identities of "gay" and "lesbian" and the institutions promoting same-sex marriage are not indigenous, and the rush to same-sex marriage seems to some to invite a neocolonial invasion of outsiders wishing to avail themselves of this legal status. For these reasons, "traditional" and contemporary sexual identities—understood in their myriad and contradictory meanings—have increasingly become competitive subject positions from which the anticolonial struggles for Hawaiian sovereignty have been waged.

Complicating this picture further, the politics of sovereignty have operated on another level propelled by the marriage case. The demand for legislative sovereignty over courts by some activists attempting to overturn the high court's ruling in *Baehr v. Lewin* and for a constitutional convention to lessen the threat to conventional morality and property relations in the future (particularly, the court-sanctioned rights of Native Hawaiians to gather and practice traditional arts on private property) has posed a unique threat to Hawaiian culture and nationalist aspirations. Who speaks for the people—legislature, courts, or churches—and how Hawaiians can maintain their voice within this sovereign chorus became inextricable from issues of sexuality that have threatened their exclusion.

In an effort to excavate this complexity and map its enabling and constraining effects on political action, this chapter examines three actively contested sites in contemporary Hawai'i. The first is the discourse of Hawaiian rights/rites that occurred in the legal arguments of the *Baehr* case. Here, I look at the politics of history that this case has engaged, particularly the struggle over the significance and place of Christian values in political and legal discourse and Hawaiian activism, and the struggles over the meaning of such historical institutions as hānai family relationships and same-sex practices. The second site studied is the strategies and tactics of Hawaiian activists in light of the sovereignty politics surrounding the case. Through interviews with several prominent activists, whether and how issues of sexual politics are played out or subsumed under wider goals of the sovereignty movement, and how they interact with religious values, are explored. Additionally, this study of practical politics provides an opportunity to examine the tensions between the deconstructive impulses of some sexual activists challenging state authority over sexuality and property, and the constructivist tendencies of the indigenous rights movement committed to nationalism and local control. I examine how these competing theoretical and practical strategies have been modified in the present climate. Finally, I return to the discussion about coalition politics developed in the previous section. In this case, my primary interest is what the costs and benefits of cooperation have been for Hawaiian groups, and what an alternative sexual politics might gain.

History and Sovereignty

Before had England
even before had
     Jesus!
there was a voice
and the voice was
maoli.
          —ʻĪmaikalani Kalāhele, 1998

People like Genora [Dancel] and me are not the enemy of those who support the family values of love, commitment, and mutual care. We don't look like the Waltons, but families come in many varieties, particularly here in Hawaiʻi, where the practice of loving people of one's own sex was accepted for years and years before the white missionaries came. For this reason, we believe it is especially fitting that Hawaiʻi be the first state to stop discriminating against same-sex couples who seek to marry.
          —Ninia Baehr, original plaintiff in *Baehr v. Lewin*

The common meanings associated with the Hawaiʻi state motto demonstrate the ways in which a foreign ethics and a discourse of rights and law have come to be associated with the language of state sovereignty. It is through these discursive lenses that a timelessness and a solidity—"the life of the *land*"—appears to connect contemporary political struggles with the sovereign firmament. In this section I look particularly at the colonial and postcolonial meanings of legality in order to recover lost meanings of sovereignty and the politics that today attempts to bring these hidden dimensions back into the foreground.

Sally Merry has recently noted that the threats by the United States, France, and Britain to the strategically and economically attractive Hawaiian kingdom in the early nineteenth century were met with attempts to conform society, culture, and politics with colonial ideas of "civilization." In part, this can be seen as a capitulation to the powers and discourses of colonialism: global mechanisms of imperialism, capitalist expansion, the rise of modernity, and the *mission civilisatrice* (Merry 2000, chap. 1). From another angle, however, incorporating and redefining some aspects of this civilizing mission served as a form of resistance, a strategy of survival that could stave off threats to Hawaiian sovereignty. This imparted an ambivalent—and hegemonic—role to law as deference to Western legal norms became both sign of state legitimacy and agent of cultural change and oppression.

> The search for sovereignty in the nineteenth century depended on the creation of a society that appeared "civilized" to those European states whose recognition conferred sovereignty onto aspiring peoples. A fundamental part of this construction of a civilized society was the adoption of the rule of law, defined in European terms. Efforts to transform the family and sexuality by prosecuting adultery in Hawai'i reinforced efforts by the Hawaiian king and chiefs to mimic the forms of "civilized" society. Only by becoming a "civilized" people could they claim an autonomous space in the world of nations. Yet this required alterations in manners of eating, covering the body, naming, and engaging in sexual relations. As the Hawaiian *ali'i* sought to claim "civilized" status, they demanded cultural changes from the population, most notably a reshaping of the family and gender order. The creation of a bourgeois form of marriage required the energetic prosecution of adultery and fornication. (Merry 1998, 598)

The mimetic quality of Hawaiian law was at the center of an attempt to create a new common sense through processes of legal recategorization (Hirsch and Lazarus-Black 1994), submerging cultural practices in an effort not just to gain international standing and autonomy, but also domestic legitimacy and social harmony—pono—in the face of the violence, disease, and rapid depopulation brought by Western contact. Hula, surfing, and kite flying were made illegal or socially discouraged in favor of activities conforming with a more puritanical work ethic (Silva 1999). Hawaiian language was suppressed in favor of English. These cultural changes had consequence for governmentality.

For instance, restrictions on sexuality and family arrangements bound the ali'i tightly to the law and its legitimate social categories as these legal kapu (proscriptions) directly threatened their divine source of authority. One contemporary historian and Hawaiian linguist illustrates what was most imperiled:

> Through incest, the first Ali'i Nui [high chief], Hāloa, was born, and because Ali'i Nui are Akua [gods], incest is by definition a formula for creating divinity. . . . [I]ncest is then an Akua-like attribute. How do Ali'i Nui gain (and maintain) divine status? By behaving like Akua, no doubt. Hence, incest is not only for production of divinity, but the very act of incest is proof of divinity. No wonder the Ali'i Nui guarded incest so jealously and refused to allow the kaukau ali'i [lesser chiefs] and maka'āinana [commoners] that privilege. (Kame'eleihiwa 1992, 40)

Western legal categories also endangered the social basis of solidarity built from family relations whose propriety was antithetical to Christian norms, what Marshall Sahlins has called a political economy of love: "Sex was everything: rank, power, wealth, land, and the security of all these" (1985, 26). This sexual attraction was decidedly not puritanical.

> [P]unalua, literally "two springs," . . . referred to two lovers who shared one mate, either at the same time or one after the other. The situation might be two men sharing one woman . . . or it might be two women sharing one man. . . . Punalua was not only practiced by the Ali'i Nui but also by the maka'āinana. Punalua required that the partners of the same sex put jealousy aside and care for one another's children as their own. While a certain amount of jealousy was inescapable, nonetheless, envy between lovers was considered very bad form and subject to derision. Children from such a mating were often taken in hānai [adoption] and treated with every affection. (Kame'eleihiwa 1992, 44)

There is strong scholarly evidence that these indigenous relationships included same-sex pairings, known as aikāne (Kame'eleihiwa 1992, 47, 160–61; Malo and Emerson 1903). As Robert Morris has argued:

Aikāne marks persons of any gender in a homogamous relationship. . . . The traditional meaning of *aikāne* as a same-sex lover is crucial. From the first day of Captain Cook's arrival in Hawai'i through the formative years of the American and other foreign presence in Hawai'i, the *aikāne* of the chiefs *(ali'i)* of each island facilitated the foreigners' livelihoods, their use of land, their very existence. . . . Did the Hawaiians "marry?" Not in the sense or the ways mainland Americans usually associate with that term. . . . For most traditional Hawaiians, Justice Douglas's definition of "marriage" (which, significantly, omits the church, priest, and ceremony) would be perfectly apropos: "Marriage is a coming together for better or worse, hopefully enduring, and intimate to the degree of being sacred. It is an association that promotes a way of life, not causes; a harmony in living, not political faiths; a bilateral loyalty, not commercial or social projects" [citing *Griswold v. Connecticut*].4 This fairly describes the relationships between *aikāne* throughout Hawaiian culture and literature. (1996, 128)

The significant material and social consequences of these relationships is one reason for their persistence even after the imposition of Western legal categories. For example, Morris found that sodomy was rarely prosecuted in nineteenth-century Hawai'i despite its criminalization on the books by the mid–nineteenth century. Linguistic evidence and a cultural renaissance within Native Hawaiian communities celebrating traditional literature and hula—with its many gay kumu hula (ordained hula teachers)—attest to the accommodation of these familial forms to contemporary cultural practice and Hawaiian identity (Viotti 1999). While the law may provide a text in which to read—as did the *Bowers* Court—the "ancient roots"5 of a repressive sexual tradition, these Hawaiian relationships and enduring values can tell another story. As Morris argues, "The Hawaiian extended family *('ohana, kaka'i)* including the *aikāne* . . . deconstructs the modern notion that a relationship between a man and a woman must be a prerequisite or the only correct enactment of a 'marriage'" (1996, 138).

Nā Mamo O Hawai'i hoped to advance this deconstruction in the law through their intervention as amicus curiae at the trial phase of the *Baehr* litigation. Nā Mamo was formed in 1993 in response to the Hawai'i House Judiciary Committee hearings on the *Baehr* case by a group of Native Hawaiian lesbian and gay activists at the University of Hawai'i. The inspiration for the group had come from oral testimony offered at a committee hearing held on Kaua'i in 1993 by Native Hawaiian Christians who publicly interpreted the state motto to read "the life of the land shall be perpetuated in Christianity,"[6] and later by gay and lesbian activism in South Africa that led to the constitutional protection for sexual orientation in 1994.[7] In order to prevent "tokenization," Nā Mamo committed itself to addressing gender and sexual inequities in the context of nationalist and postcolonial struggles. As one activist recounted,

> The way that we've articulated things in the context of Nā Mamo is that homophobia, misogyny, and racism are similar institutional power moves that are interrelated and they are also interrelated with class. And sometimes one is used to affect the other. Homophobia and misogyny are really closely related. A lot of homophobia against men is because gay men are like women. And women are supposed to do whatever they are supposed to do and men are supposed to enjoy their privileges. And if they are not experiencing their privilege, then there is something wrong with them. There is all that tangle of thought about it. . . . What we were trying to fight against was the institutionalization of all of this. Institutionalization in the real broad sense, as groups of people exerting power over us. . . . [I]f we are working towards making life better for ourselves, we can see that there is homophobia here, or racism against Hawaiians or Asians here, and discrimination against poor people here. If we only address racism, and we knock that out, then the rich, male, straight Hawaiians will be the only ones no longer discriminated against.[8]

Nā Mamo's sexual politics were received with some controversy among Hawaiian nationalists, but the group drew internally upon an increasingly popular construction of Hawaiian tradition at the same time that it indicted colonial institutions for substituting their own timeless ideas of the traditional. Here is how Nā Mamo members somewhat bravely characterized their goals at a gathering of diverse Hawaiian activists in 1996 who were searching for common ground but were unfamiliar with, and skeptical of, the sexual aspects of nationalist struggle:

We are Hawai'i pono'ī—we belong to Hawai'i; our 'āina [land] permeates every part of us; our land is in our blood, our iwi [bones], our minds, and our na'au [gut]. The land is our kupuna, our ancestor, without whom we have no place. And our place is our link to our past, our history, and to our future well-being. Our language, cultural concepts, and traditions are all linked to our relationship with the 'āina. Our genealogies trace back to land forms.

Aloha 'āina, then, is a familial relationship that requires that we resist all efforts by the U.S. government, the State of Hawai'i or anyone else to further separate ANY of us Kanaka Maoli [Native Hawaiians] from our 'āina, which includes the waters, the oceans, and all natural and cultural resources.

Our freedom to use of our own 'āina is linked to the freedom to use our own bodies, to live our lives as we see fit, to live in 'ohana relationships that may be different from American ways of life, to build our communities, and to embrace our culture and traditions. Colonialism brought with it an ideology that tried to invalidate who we are as a people and the diverse ways in which we live on islands, in different moku and ahupua'a [traditional districts].[9] Our oral and literary traditions tell us that prior to colonialism, the Kanaka Maoli lived in an atmosphere of openness and diversity of sexual thought and behavior.[10]

I return to many of these themes of nationalism, memory, identity, and sexuality in the next section of this chapter. For now, I want to address how Nā Mamo used legal discourse to create a *Hawaiian* voice in the marriage case. Of particular interest to me is how sovereignty concerns articulated throughout the case on what we might see as a horizontal grid of inclusion and exclusion, of federalist relationships between Hawai'i and the national government, and of the sovereign tensions between a "democratic" legislature and "activist" courts, gained a new dimensionality by questioning the assumptions of traditional practice assumed to lie as a basis for legal authority. Indeed, the call for a democratic and inclusive sovereignty to limit judicial control over the *Baehr* case by its opponents—in the very words of the indigenous language of the motto—opens up the possibilities of the sovereignty discourses of the subaltern. As Wendy Brown has noted in another context,

Just when polite liberal (not to mention, correct leftist) discourse
ceased speaking of us as dykes, faggots, colored girls or natives,
we began speaking of ourselves this way. Refusing the invitation
to absorption, we insisted instead upon politicizing and working
into cultural critique the very constructions that a liberalism
increasingly exposed in its tacit operations of racial, sexual and
gender privilege was seeking to bring to a formal close. (1995b,
200)

In McClintock's engaging terminology of colonial discourse, the political assertion of this alterity—at least for Hawaiian nationalists—can be
seen as an attempt to defeat legal support for both *anachronistic space* in
which indigenous peoples exist in a permanently anterior time, and
panoptic time in which "history [is] consumed—at a glance—in a single
spectacle from a point of privileged invisibility" (1995, 37). How well
this works in the context of a struggle for civil rights and the nonindigenous identities of gay and lesbian bridged by Nā Mamo provides
much of the grist for this chapter.

As contemporary anthropological studies of courts and law in
colonial and postcolonial contexts have revealed, "Courts are 'complex
sites of resistance' in part because they have the potential to play prag-
matic, ideological, and symbolic roles in contestations over power
[and] by the fact that people use courts to contest multiple relations of
power, reworking understandings of gender, race, class, and other
hierarchies sometimes simultaneously" (Hirsch 1994, 210; see also
Merry 1991; Moore 1986). In colonial contexts, this is often facilitated by
dual legal systems that give credence to some (often manufactured or
modified) indigenous norms. Many postcolonial legal systems have
again unified their legal codes, but Hawai'i remains an exception. Law
in the colonial period was unitary. However, since 1978 the Hawai'i
Constitution has recognized an aspect of duality as a virtual part of historical legal practice. Article XII, section 7 reads, "The State reaffirms
and shall protect all rights, customarily and traditionally exercised for
subsistence, cultural and religious purposes and possessed by
ahupua'a [district] tenants who are descendants of native Hawaiians
who inhabited the Hawaiian Islands prior to 1778, subject to the right of
the State to regulate such rights." The Hawai'i Supreme Court has cited
this section in its recent ruling that "ancient" Hawaiian usage and custom such as rights to gather from the streams and forests persist along-

side "generally understood elements of the western doctrine of 'property.' . . . [T]he western concept of exclusivity is not universally applicable in Hawai'i.'"[11] Similarly, the Reciprocal Beneficiaries Act granted funeral leave for domestic partners on the same basis as family members whether by blood or "the Hawaiian 'hanai' custom."[12] Apart from this invitation to articulation and acceptance of traditional practice, Native Hawaiians have no federal recognition of their sovereign status, as do Native Americans, an issue to which I turn later in this chapter.

In light of this constitutional endowment, Nā Mamo's brief argued that Hawai'i's "unequivocal obligation to preserve and protect Hawaiian traditional and customary rights" extended beyond gathering rights to the state's argued interest "in promoting the raising of children by their biological parents and its disparate and discriminatory treatment of same-gender couples."[13] The target of the brief was the language of tradition that had been articulated by the state and its proponents as a sovereign issue with consequence for two political relationships. The first was the separation of power between the court and the legislature. The state argued that "by arrogating to itself the decision to alter fundamentally our culture's traditional and universal, understanding of what constitutes a marriage, the Circuit Court has skewed the process by which our democratic society evolves."[14] If courts are a threat to democratic integrity and its commitment to orderly "evolution," so are gays and lesbians who threaten the sovereign powers arrayed to protect society's weakest individuals and key institutions of methodical reproduction. Epitomizing this sentiment is this argument on behalf of the state from an amicus brief: "[B]iological parents are the persons most likely to be willing to invest their time in the care of their own child. Traditional marriage is no insurance against fate, but for thousands of years it successfully served society by providing strong protection for the great majority of children, women and families."[15] Both arguments uphold the nuclear family as institution, and as a metaphor for authority. As McClintock has relevantly observed in the context of colonial discourse,

> The power and importance of the family trope was twofold. First, the family offered an indispensable figure for sanctioning social hierarchy within a putative organic unity of interests. Because the subordination of woman to man and child to adult were deemed natural facts, other forms of social hierarchy could be depicted in

familial terms to guarantee social *difference* as a category of nature. The family image came to figure *hierarchy within unity* as an organic element of historical progress. . . . [S]econd, the family offered an invaluable trope for figuring *historical time*. Within the family metaphor, both social hierarchy . . . and historical change . . . could be portrayed as natural and inevitable, rather than as historically constructed and therefore subject to change. (1995, 45)

Bursting this colonialist perspectivism, Nā Mamo interjected recognized cultural sovereignty rights in order to disturb the history of familial uniformity and its metaphorical consequences for gays and lesbians. Three legal examples were used to show the possible diversity of domestic relations into which same-sex marriages could be seen as traditionally supportable. The first was the 'ohana (extended family), legally acknowledged by negligence laws in Hawai'i allowing suits for injury to family members related by affection rather than blood. Second, was the cultural practice of hānai (informal adoption) of child *or parent*, which is accepted in Hawai'i for purposes of inheritance and other probate matters, as well as employment law. Finally, Nā Mamo pointed to the Hawaiian tradition of "recognizing and tolerating" same-gender relationships.

[C]oncepts of "family" are broader and more flexible in Hawaiian culture than in traditional Western/Judeo-Christian culture. The *hanai* practice continues to be a vital part of Hawaiian culture and society today. In arguing that biological-parent families create the "best" environment for a child's development, the State denigrates and ignores centuries-long Hawaiian traditions of child-rearing. Finally, the State's disparate treatment of same-gender couples also conflicts with the tolerance and recognition given to same-gender relationships in Hawaiian custom and practice.[16]

Nā Mamo's arguments carried little textual weight with the courts that have not acknowledged the duty to respect Hawaiian traditions as an additional reason to adhere to equal protection doctrine in the marriage case.[17] Nonetheless, the reminder of historical, enduring, and legally recognized non-Western traditions began to resonate both within the Native Hawaiian nationalist community, and in the wider debates over the marriage amendment waged in letters to the newspapers and in political advertisements. "I'm confused," wrote one man.

> Proponents of the proposed constitutional amendment on the same-sex marriage issue tell me they're "defending the traditional family." But none of the pictures in their advertisements seem to look like anything I can recognize as a "traditional family." My dictionary defines "traditional" as "the way things have been done for a long time." In Hawaii, where an indigenous Polynesian people lived in isolation until a little more than 200 years ago, "traditional" here means "the way the Hawaiians did it for more than 2,000 years," not "the way it's been done for about the last 150 years or so." But do the pictures accompanying the ads show large groups of people married to one another despite the fact that several of them are brother and sister, or cousin and cousin? They do not. This despite the fact that polygamy and, for the *ali'i*, incest, were considered traditional.[18]

In response to similar arguments, Save Traditional Marriage '98 insisted,

> Don't let them fool you into legalizing homosexual marriage. This issue is about *one thing* and one thing only: *the definition of marriage.* That's it. Nothing more. It's *not* about Hawaiian rights. It's *not* about abortion. It's *not* about race. . . . It's *not* about anything else, whatsoever.[19]

Protestations proved the point, the attention ultimately working to Nā Mamo's interest in providing an important new site for reimagining Native sovereignty. This new imaginary provided an umbrella for non-Native gays and lesbians, too, by creating what Bravmann has called a "queer fiction of the past": performative narratives in which modern gay and lesbian identities are anchored by "temporary but compelling fabrications . . . remade through the actively inventive projects of political mobilization" (1997, 23).[20] One Nā Mamo activist described the political force of the cultural insight as "kind of like molten lava: it's creeping, you can't stop it."[21]

The spectacle of roiling lava spewing from Kīlauea has long provided a mainstay attraction for tourists to Hawai'i's "Big Island," but in this case the metaphor is apt to describe the fear that many conservatives voiced about same-sex marriage angering the volcanic goddess Pele and her economic appeal. As one citizen testified,

> Granting special privileges to same-sex couples will have lasting societal and economic consequences. Hawaii's economy and future prosperity are tied to the strength of our tourist industry in the world tourism market where image is everything. Families, a mainstay of the visitor industry, would likely chose [sic] other destinations if the Aloha state became known as the gay marriage state. Hawaii's image is too precious and its economy too fragile to be jeopardized by ill-conceived social experiments like same sex marriage.[22]

As another characterized the choice of image, "Do we want to be known as the "Aloha State" or as the 'mecca' [sic] for gays and lesbians?"[23] This commonly voiced alternative demands a choice between aloha (appropriated for the West) and the impieties practiced in the holy city of "the Infidel" in which sovereign control would decline inversely with moral decay. How distinct is this from ali'i interests in preserving Hawaiian autonomy in the early colonial period? The mimetic performance of "civilization" through law governing domestic relations still haunts the present, as it did in the nineteenth century of gunboats and missionaries, modulated now through the imperatives of political economy rather than international relations and diplomacy.

Can Molten Lava Make a Nation?

Nā Mamo posed questions about the legal status of tradition through its intervention, disrupting the binary nature of the discourses surrounding the case. The reminder of the colonial past with its deployment of law to promote "traditional" behavior confused the choice between abandoning the past or accommodating equal rights, between democratic sovereignty and legal tyranny, and between augmenting or blocking growth in the tourist markets, creating space into which new visions of sovereignty could be projected. How well did such a space further the nationalist goals of Kānaka Maoli (Native Hawaiians)?

The struggles for a Hawaiian nation are as old as the first Western contact: the killing of Captain James Cook in the Big Island in 1779 and Kamehameha's successful monarchical unification of the islands from 1795 to 1802. During the period of increasing haole control of the Hawaiian economy and government—especially from the time of the Māhele (1843), in which alienable Western property was established and sugar planted where once Hawaiians farmed, laws were imposed banning many cultural practices, the Hawaiian monarchy was over-thrown in 1893, and the islands annexed by the United States in 1898—the fight for a nation lived on, but with steadily decreasing resources and legitimacy. Twentieth-century struggles have included con-fronting increasing poverty, the presence of a large military complex that has controlled as much as 25 percent of the land on O'ahu and all of Kaho'olawe, and massive corporate tourism. As one activist scholar and nationalist explains the terrain facing Native Hawaiians, "Bur-dened with commodification of our culture and exploitation of our people, Hawaiians exist in an occupied country whose hostage people are forced to witness (and, for many, to participate in) our collective humiliation as tourist artifacts for the First World" (Trask 1993, 23).

Sparked by postcolonial movements, and inspired equally by indigenous cultural values and the history of Hawaiian resistance to this occupation, contemporary indigenous politics has driven toward self-determination through a discourse of "sovereignty." This articula-tion of sovereignty has, in part, been drawn from international law that has, even in the postcolonial period, tended to require conformity to liberal and statist norms that remain "deeply exclusionary in practice" (Otto 1996, 360; 1995). In this section of the chapter, I examine the domestic politics of sovereignty that formed around the same-sex mar-riage issue in order to examine the ways in which this discourse inter-acted with the other sovereignty discourses of the marriage case. I fol-low the general lead of subaltern studies,[24] which have suggested that contemporary governmentality tends to quell and subvert the voices of indigenous peoples (and, I would argue, sexual minorities) by regulat-ing permissible speech and narrowing acceptable interpretations (e.g., the advertisement in the previous section that is emphatic that the mar-riage case "is *not* about Hawaiian rights"). The discussion centers on the nation, as I think that conceptual territory brings both indigenous and dominant notions of sovereignty into (uneasy) contact and prob-lematizes the relationship of family form to political resistance.

Contemporary thought about the nation is indebted to Benedict

Anderson (1983), who has argued that nationalism is not a product of primordial ethnic identities, religion, or language, but is thoroughly modern. It is "imagined" through a temporal experience of a "homogeneous, empty time" reinforced by the cartographic quality of "print-capitalism" in which social and political identities are drawn from the similitude of journalistic consumption. While Anderson's presentation of the limited forms of European, American, and Russian nations is important for recognizing the similarities between these national experiences, it has raised particular problems for students of postcolonial nations. While these scholars are attuned to the ways contemporary postcolonial nations are, too, imagined, they have also explored the myriad subtle "local" differences that attempt to account for the silences imposed by dominant conceptual forms and challenge the "hegemonic 'normality' [given] to the uneven development and the differential, often disadvantaged, histories of nations, races, communities, peoples" (Bhabha 1994, 171). For Partha Chatterjee, "The most powerful as well as the most creative results of the nationalist imagination in Asia and Africa are posited not on an identity but rather on a *difference* with the 'modular' forms of the national society propagated by the modern West" (1993, 5).

Chatterjee and others have argued that these postcolonial alternatives have necessitated prying loose the laminated layers of sovereignty and political nationality, challenging the adhesive strictures of governmentality through theories that talk distinctly about community and state. The challenge is to examine the ways in which sovereignty can be articulated within cultural and spiritual forms that are modern, even though not Western. For Hoffman, removing sovereignty from its statist form—even within the West—requires finding alternative voices silenced by sovereign practices: "[T]he state is a contradictory institution which uses force to secure community so that it ultimately works to prevent rather than facilitate debate" (1998, 19). As Kelsey has shown in her study of Māori anticolonial politics, the New Zealand state reacted incredulously to any attempt to undermine the "indivisibility of sovereignty, the universality of 'one law for all,' and the homogeneity of one language, one culture, and one people in one nation. Outside of this there was only a state of nature" (1995, 182). This silencing of alternatives reinforces Anderson's oft-quoted argument that the temporal frame of the nation projects sovereignty as "fully, flatly, and evenly operative over each square centimeter of a legally demarcated territory" (1983, 25).

Like the related Māori struggles,[25] the surgent Native Hawaiian claims for sovereignty disrupt both this idea of the indivisibility of sovereignty and the arguments for traditional practice, creating a deep unease at the meaning of their recognitional demands.[26] Bhabha has characterized this as an anxiety essential to nationalism.

> Counter-narratives of the nation that continually evoke and erase its totalizing boundaries—both actual and conceptual—disturb those ideological maneuvers through which 'imagined communities' are given essentialist identities. For the political unity of the nation consists in a continual displacement of the anxiety of its irredeemably plural modern space—representing the nation's modern territoriality is turned into the archaic, atavistic temporality of Traditionalism. (1994, 149)

For some, this acknowledgment of unity at the cost of eliminating the spoor of this pluralism represents "the impossibility of the nation" (Fitzpatrick 1995a).

One aspect of this impossible tension stems from imagining the nation in terms of the rule of law. Law relies upon a mythology of universality, one that has affinity for—and practical potential within—the shape of the nation (Fitzpatrick 1992; 1995b, xv–xvi). At the same time, law is forced to express the particular.

> Universality and particularity are two faces of the same legal rationality, both "naturalizing" the overarching narratives of state authority as universally applicable, and at the same time identifying a particular nation-state and its capacities to define, enumerate and manage its subject-citizens. (Darian-Smith 1996, 296; see also Norrie 1996, 392ff.)

The acknowledgment of particularity is, in some sense, an acknowledgment of the uncivilized "other" that is not fit for recognition without the tautological characteristics that "count" for contemporary governmentality. Law also organizes these various aspects of governmentality and nationalism. One aspect with obvious relevance to this chapter is the family that, Balibar (1991) reminds us, has an important connection to conceiving the nation, since genealogical reproduction is critical to the reproduction of race and ethnicity in which the colonial nation is conceived. Balibar could have added that it is also nuclear and heterosexual families that are central to this imagination, the limits to which are categorically patrolled by governmentality and law (consider, in this regard, the parallel between the miscegenation cases and the concern over same-sex marriage (Koppelman 1994; Sunstein 1994a, 1994b; Valdes 1995, 1996), or Justice White's unreflective assumption that sodomy is strictly a homosexual crime in *Bowers v. Hardwick*) (Halley 1993). "The people is constituted out of various populations subject to a common law" (Balibar 1991, 94). For this reason, the nation appears not as ideal, but as the real because "one can be interpellated, as an individual, *in the name of* the collectivity whose name one bears. The naturalization of belonging and the sublimation of the ideal nation are two aspects of the same process" (Balibar 1991, 96).

To challenge the legal categories is, thus, to rely upon new imaginations, interpellations, and identities that renaturalize the world in order to recreate a sense of sovereign control over individual and collective destiny. As this is often entangled with legality, it is also a critical project designed to uncover the silences within the social life of the law (Coombe 1998, 473). It is here that the Hawaiian context is of particular interest. For the postcolonial law of Hawai'i has offered a constitutional invitation to discover and present "all rights, customarily and traditionally exercised." At the same time, flexible family and gender relations—conceived as "aloha"—have distinctive commodity value in the global political economy of tourism. Unlike the nationalist postcolonial subject position of Zimbabwe, in which homosexuality was identified with European cultural and political imperialism and its rejection with African authenticity (Stychin 1998, 62ff.), the Hawaiian colonization by "corporate tourism" preys upon images of a paradise of sexual access and delight "natural" to the "Native" and accessible to all (Buck 1993; Desmond 1997; Goss 1993; Kamahele 1992; Ross 1994, chap. 1; Trask 1993, 179–97). Hence, the near-universal appreciation of Hawai'i as a place of love, whose anthem, "The Hawaiian Wedding Song," is a global property. In contrast to Indian colonization in which woman—assumed by the British to be burdened by superstition and male labor demands—was the symbol of the unfree (Chatterjee 1993, 118), the myth of Hawai'i has been one of excessive freedom in familial and sexual matters that first needed to be curbed and later harnessed to the capitalist engine of tourism.

The political opposition to this myth is difficult to constitute because of the mismatch between the categories of colonial culture and law, and the nature of lived relations. The commodification of sexuality on the one hand and the diversity of lived familial relations on the other has made Hawaiians reticent to enter the debate over same-sex marriage. One Hawaiian clergyman, himself a supporter of same-sex marriage, thus understood his congregation's resistance to joining his opposition to the amendment:

> I think the problem with the terminology is same-sex marriage or sexuality. People get confused. Because I think for Hawaiians, it's not so much the sex—that's the Hollywood kind of sex—but . . . the relationship between two people that are close. We have people that live together, and [the debate makes] it sound like we have people who are having sex together. . . . Hawaiians [haven't] wanted to get involved in the [same-sex] battle. I think it's cultural. Hawaiians have a very—pure is the word that comes to mind—a very pure view of sexuality, and it hasn't been Victorianized. [Also] Hawaiians are very family people. And the extended family, that's where it's all centered. When you talk about the larger world and government, that's too big and complicated. The most we can do is protect ourselves, what little we have left and what little we're trying to regain and reclaim, and we have to pick our battles wisely.[27]

According to one Hawaiian Catholic priest, Native Hawaiians vote rarely and have refused to become drawn into same-sex debates because of a "colonized mind-set" acquired from two centuries of frustrating encounters with a political process unconcerned with Native issues, and an associated communal sensitivity that militates against "sticking out" for purposes of pluralist political agitation. Rather, Hawaiian spirituality—still intact despite the overlay of Christian concepts—provides a refuge for collective identity and fuels the indigenous sentiment for sovereignty.[28]

A Hawaiian Sovereignty

Nā Mamo's struggle to add Hawaiian support to the coalition to stop the amendment was forced to surmount this cultural restraint. They chose to work within the main nationalist organizations[29] that were increasingly fearful of the consequences of a constitutional convention that was also on the ballot. Unlike earlier attempts by Nā Mamo to build support for the litigation phase of the marriage case, Ka Lāhui Hawai'i, the largest organized nation of Native Hawaiians, did officially endorse the antiamendment campaign. In part this was due to a recognition of the links between a spiritual sense of sovereignty and a language of rights. The nation's Lieutenant governor, Keali'i Gora, explained this connection to me in the following fashion:

> The first element of sovereignty [according to] Ka Lāhui, is one that has a strong and abiding faith in the akua, God, because spiritually empty people do not make for a strong nation. Now, those Hawaiians that choose Christianity or those Hawaiians that wish to become Buddhists or traditional Hawaiians that wish to honor the ancestors of the past, we don't discriminate on any one of the akua that they choose. What we do say is that in Hawaiian culture we believe in . . . the multitude of ancestors, the multitude of God. If you want to add another Christian god it would be number 40,001. So that's fine, we don't have a problem with that . . . unless it threatens or impacts native rights and entitlements. . . . It is the respect [for] our ancestral ways and past that takes precedence because I don't just stand here an individual. I stand because I have a mother and father. They have a mother and father, and so forth. So we come with many generations that not only lay claim because of our antiquity of residence, but more so because we are here today to fight for what is right, morally, ethically, politically, culturally, which ever way—legally included—to embrace all of those thoughts.[30]

Legal rights, in this articulation, do not reach back to this ancestral depth but rather are presented as tactics temporarily suturing community support for Hawaiian sovereignty. Ka Lāhui's resolution in opposition to the amendment, passed two months prior to the election, accused the proponents of the amendment of applying the same hostility toward gays that had been perfected against "indigenous peoples, immigrants, people of color, poor people, women, environmentalists . . . and unionized workers" in the past. Threatened constitutional changes put Hawaiians in the same leaky outrigger canoe with gays since "a proposed Constitutional Amendment to limit marriage would allow the legislature to discriminate against a single group of people and thereby set a dangerous precedent which could negatively impact Native Hawaiians and other minorities."[31]

An ambivalence haunts these commitments. On the one hand, this language seems to articulate a pluralist civil rights space in which Native Hawaiian and gay rights are affirmed, and the rights of difference—equivalent with those of other minorities—are defended from the perspective that "this social space is infinitely partitionable and thus infinitely expandable" (Patton 1995, 230). On the other hand, the deference to civil rights is based on a pragmatism that Seidman reminds us is fundamentally a willingness to expose the connection between knowledge and power (1997, 257ff.). In this sense, Ka Lāhui embraces constitutional rights as instruments whose genealogy reveals the constellations of power that enforce the loss of Native Hawaiian sovereignty.

> J. G.-H. The [antiamendment] coalition Protect Our Constitution, as even the name suggests, argues that the constitution is for all, that it has to be defended. At the same time, this is the constitution that is postoverthrow, where sovereignty is still lodged in a state government that doesn't fully recognize the rights of Native Hawaiians nor their inherent sovereignty. Ka Lāhui has embraced POC. Is that problematic? Is protecting the constitution and defense of citizenship the wrong rhetoric to be using right now?
>
> Keali'i Gora. You're going to get many different answers from Hawaiian activists. What I could say is right now we need to protect and defend what we have now, because if you lose this, you have no rights. It will be even less than what you have now. So I'm not willing to take that risk at this present point in time, and I don't think that Ka Lāhui is willing to take that risk either. The right of citizenship—unfortunately we have been compelled to be American. Not by our doing, or by our ancestors' doings, but we have just been compelled. You are an American. At the same token here, we have our rights by the various articles in the constitution such as the freedom of speech, such as the freedom of religion, and the freedom to express our opinions. So those basic inalienable human political civil rights is something that we need to protect, and we're not willing to risk that.[32]

For another Ka Lāhui leader,

> Hawaiians are not only residents and citizens of Hawaii. They are
> the indigenous people. As such, Hawaiians have a special relation-
> ship with the state and federal governments that has been recog-
> nized by the Legislature and the federal courts through the estab-
> lishment of various agencies, such as the Office of Hawaiian
> Affairs and the Department of Hawaiian Home Lands, as well as
> the nearly two dozen existing federal programs earmarked for
> Hawaiians. In other words, Hawaiians occupy a special category
> of citizens. Because of their uniqueness as indigenous people, pref-
> erential programs for Hawaiians . . . are based on political rather
> than racial classifications. (Trask 1999, A11)[33]

The unique legal position of Native Hawaiians, revealed in their
status as a conquered people, is a product of the limits and excesses of
rights discourse as a bridge to nationalism. Unlike other governmental
discourses that construct difference on a pluralist frame of ethnic equality (Morris and Stuckey 1997, 143ff.), rights language is transformative
and revealing of another set of relationships.

> Indigenous peoples have neither been fully excluded nor have
> they been fully included. In a sense, their indigenousness is suffi-
> ciently "present" for them to be able to claim rights and suffi-
> ciently "absent" to make their claim to rights necessary. . . . [T]he
> double impulse to include and exclude indigenous peoples, to
> place them here or there, becomes apparent in the encounter
> between indigenous peoples and the nation. (Perrin 1995, 69)

This double impulse matters for nationalist politics as some aspects of
indigenous culture and discourse are permitted much more presence
than are others. The historical illegitimacy of indigenous family and
sexual forms made the arguments of Nā Mamo harder to hear, both
within and without Hawaiian sovereignty groups. And the open
avenue of coalition politics based on support for civil rights that regulate an economy of differences tended to lose much that was distinctive
about Hawaiian claims while it also submitted those claims to the
anti–civil rights sovereignty rhetoric of the "traditional marriage" supporters.

The success of Ka Lāhui's sophisticated analysis in encouraging Native Hawaiians to vote against the amendment appears limited. A statistical analysis of the influence of Hawaiian activists on the amendment vote in November 1998 reveals no significant suasion.[34] Perhaps this is because Ka Lāhui stood alone in their stance against the amendment. Other Native organizations rejected Ka Lāhui's position in part because they adhered to a special relationship with the state. The Office of Hawaiian Affairs, which oversees Native Hawaiian interests in some state lands, refused to take a position on the amendment while rejecting any constitutional move that might take Hawaiians "back to being a powerless minority in our own homeland,"[35] a language hardly conducive to alliance with other embattled and powerless minorities. Native Vote '98 cited wardship restricting the right of Hawaiians to sue the state, embattled gathering rights on private lands, lost revenue from ceded lands, and insufficient funding for Hawaiian language, health, and environmental issues as reasons for Native Hawaiians to register and vote against the call for a constitutional convention; no mention was made of the same-sex marriage amendment.[36] If the articulation of indigenous rights and the same-sex marriage vote led to anxiety on the part of proponents of the amendment because of the excess that indigenous rights signified, it was just as likely the anxiety over the insufficiency of such a linkage to many Hawaiian groups limited the influence of Ka Lāhui and Nā Mamo. To some Hawaiians, the mutual accusations of outsider influence in the amendment campaign—mainland churches to one side and mainland gay rights groups to the other—appeared as another aspect of neocolonialism requiring a safe distance from the entire issue. As one person framed it, "Once again, the missionaries, they'll come and solve all our problems."[37] The idea that civil rights commitments would promote a coalition supporting self-determination in light of this uncontested rhetoric of outsider meddling was difficult to sustain.

Love of the Land

The ambivalence between civil rights as a sign of citizenship and inclusion on the one hand, and a distinct historical relationship to the land and the overlying state that transcends civil rights on the other, demonstrates more than "the impossibility of the nation" in Fitzpatrick's sense but also the impossibility of postcolonial nationalism waged on a legal terrain of civil rights. Nonlegal alternatives to building support for same-sex marriage and opposition to the amendment were tried within the nationalist community to avoid just these problems. For many of these nationalists—including the leadership of Ka Lāhui, who supported the legal strategy—a sovereignty conceived of in modern spiritual terms could be tied to the Hawaiian ideals of aloha 'āina and mālama 'āina (love of country and care for the land). For one Nā Mamo activist, these commitments forced a working out of the nature of Hawaiian sexuality. In her evocative understanding, the division of private property during the Māhele of the nineteenth century had done more than dispossess the majority of Hawaiians from their land and lead to their colonization. It also created a "māhele of the body" in which sexual exploitation, and the reinterpretation of Hawaiian culture and familial norms by Christianity and, later, Hollywood and the tourist industry, created an internal colonization.

> When we divided up the land . . . what had to change, too, was our relationship, our personal relationship to it. And also the way that we were related to ourselves and our bodies. And one of the things that I began to realize is that the self becomes compartmentalized. Whereas traditionally one's whole body was—in terms of our relationships, our personality, our sexuality and spirituality—it was not divided, it was intact. And now it's divided us into little pieces. So there is spirituality which is when you go to church, and there's the sex in the foreground, and the sex in the bedroom and the intimate relationship with your partner, but if it's an intimate relationship with other people, [sex] is not part of that. . . . That to me is what the māhele of the body is all about, this kind of division. No longer are you whole.[38]

The ideals of mālama 'āina and aloha 'āina promise a return to wholeness unmediated by legal notions of property or constitutional promises of governmental stewardship.[39] Instead, as Nā Mamo had declared, the connection was direct: "Our genealogies trace back to land forms." The origin myth of Hawai'i and its people is recapitulated daily in the lovemaking between Papa, the verdant undulate mountains, and Wākea, the sky whose seminal rain pours its life lovingly within his foggy cloud-cap embrace.

Genealogies are perceived by Hawaiians as an unbroken chain that links those alive today to the primeval life forces—to the *mana* (spiritual power) that first emerged with the beginning of the world. Genealogies anchor Hawaiians to our place in the universe and give us the comforting illusion of continued existence. . . . Genealogies also brought Hawaiians psychological comfort in times of acute distress. The greatest distress began in 1778, upon contact with the Western world. . . . By the 1870s, Hawaiian religion and politics had made a very definite shift to Western models wherein genealogies seemed irrelevant. Nonetheless, Hawaiians continued to cling to our great genealogical debates as if the lineages of the *Ali'i Nui* were proof that the race still existed as a great nation. (Kame'eleihiwa 1992, 19, 20; see also Meyer 1998, 24)

That sense of nationalism can be recovered in the period of the māhele of the body through a revisiting of the specifically sexual aspects of this genealogy and physical geography, according to some activists.

When I think about the myth of Papa and Wākea . . . all of this is very sexual, lots of sexuality there, it's very intense, and also very spiritual. There is the birth of a child, the birth of the islands, the birth of the first kalo [taro] plant that is so significant to us Hawaiians. . . . It is important when people begin to embrace their history and the ways sexuality is a part of it. It's like we're reclaiming those sites, embracing it in a way that makes it powerful. Claiming that we're not crazy, this is real, this is what happens, and this is part of it. I think the issue of sexuality is part of that process. . . . The interesting thing about the constitutional amendment, too, is because there's a sexuality mixed in, a Native Hawaiian cultural tradition and lifestyle, you cannot separate them. . . . [A]ll of them are affected [by the amendment].[40]

The politics of the amendment provides a handy site in which to begin this cultural therapy by encouraging introspection and talk about the continuing place of sexuality in the culture despite the displacement of the land by other constitutional means.

The nationalist imagination is expressed in less spiritual and more practical relationships to the land by the Ahupua'a Action Alliance

(AAA), whose principle organizer's decision to speak out against the amendment was inspired by the organization's practical alternatives to legal notions of sovereignty. In her view, law is simply too abstract a notion in which to build support for Hawaiian nationalism.

> So we fix the constitution, and everything's going to get OK? Don't be ridiculous. At some level, we still have to interact with each other on a personal level. . . . [The AAA uses] the ahupua'a [traditional districts] as a model for community, not as a geographic model but as a personal model, and a cultural model, and in this model everybody is in. It's not an exclusive model. All you have to do really is be aware of where you are, and take some responsibility for where you are. Good space. So, while it's a Hawaiian model, it's not necessarily limited to Hawaiians. Its inclusive nature requires that the people who are in this particular geographic area come to some understanding about their relationship with the land they live on, and then some kind of responsibility for where they live. . . . If you can love this place, if you can mālama [take care of it], then what keeps you from loving each other, as neighbors, or as community members? And then, what's the criteria that you're going to use? Because you know, land makes no distinction. . . . That's the kind of model that we've been using, and the approach then to the issue of same-sex marriage for us is like every other approach. Are you not my neighbor, my son's teacher, my cousin, my kids? There's not any room for actually leaving somebody out.[41]

The AAA's reinvigoration of a traditional sovereign space through environmental restoration activities, historical awareness of the impact of colonialism on land use, and a social commitment to "let the land mediate" social differences in the undertaking of community projects reconfirms the wide varieties of family relationships in which precontact Hawaiian social reproduction took place. According to one Hawaiian nationalist and linguist, this celebration of the earth and its peoples again makes the provisioning of food sacred as it was in traditional culture, while refuting the Christian themes of earthly transcendence and sexual restraint.[42] In contrast to the arguments of amendment supporters, sovereignty is refigured on principles of inclusion in a modern common project of care and love for the land. Nonetheless, the paradox of this renaturalization of sovereignty stems from the very distance that it creates from postcolonial legal and political dynamics. The principle organizer of AAA recounted her own experience with amendment politics in the following manner:

> The idea of each of us as friends, as partners, or whatever, defining for ourselves how our relationship should look, is very powerful, and the kind of thing that I would support. But it is so common [in my community], it never occurred to me that we would have to support it. You know, I didn't think that we would have to talk about it, as something that we want to preserve.[43]

The tendency toward silence in the AAA about rights is perceived as an antagonism by one lesbian activist who likened it to the military policy of "Don't ask, don't tell."

> What is missing [from AAA] is that people say, "We accept you, you are a part of the ahupua'a, you are a part of our tie to the land, to resources, to all of that." Well, no, I am not, really. I am not. Because if that were true, then I could go up in front of the Alliance and say, "Where is our position on gay rights and lesbian rights and gay men of color?" So, I think that there isn't . . . the cultural acceptability of taking the next step. You know, we accept you, but we kind of don't. We accept you as long as you don't talk about it.[44]

Just as the politics of sovereignty propounded by amendment supporters precluded vigorous debate over the issue of Hawaiian rights/rites, the sovereign power of silence over altering forms of ordering creates high thresholds for interest and action in its postcolonial variants. When numerous relationships are already recognized in the citizenship of the ahupua'a, when does law make a significant difference?

Conclusion

The argument that the electorate must decide the fate of same-sex marriage before the supreme court can speak for the meaning of the constitution has opened up the possibility of powerful sovereign discourses in the marriage debates. What gives these alternative discourses their animating force is the haunting yet repressed recognition that a call to democratic sovereignty involves a suppressed alterity, a denial of history, meaning, and rights that implies an uncompleted and permanently fractured nation, while calling forth an active refusal of this imagination by those denied.

> In the very moment when modern liberal states fully realize their secularism, just as the mantle of abstract personhood is formally tendered to a whole panoply of those historically excluded from it by humanism's privileging of a single race, gender and organization of sexuality, the marginalized reject the rubric of humanist inclusion and turn, at least in part, against its very premises. Refusing to be neutralized, to render the differences inconsequential, to be depoliticized as "life-styles," "diversity" or "persons like any other," we have lately reformulated our historical exclusion as a matter of historically produced and politically rich *alterity*. (W. Brown 1995b, 200)

The politics of alterity is complicated in the Hawai'i debates. Gays and lesbians and their supporters in the marriage case have made demands to be legally recognized in the name of modern liberal secularism and middle-class values, ultimately to be respected and included as abstract citizens. They have professed a faith in progress as the ultimate vindication of the concept of equal rights and entitlement, articulated a concept of political space that is pluralist, flexible, and accommodating of any and all differences, and recognized—at times— the precontact sexual traditions of Native Hawaiians that they have called their own. Their demand for abstract recognition on these bases has frequently been drowned out by conservative activists alarmed by queer activism and fearful that the court-sanctioned same-sex marriage issue is "a foot in the door for homosexual activists to achieve their ultimate goal—societal acceptance of homosexuality on an equal basis as heterosexuality [and] 'radically reordering society's views of reality.'"[45] This rejection of equality goes to the heart of a new idea of political space, one where differences crowd out the legitimate—even nativist—interests of the majority and the dominant culture. Hawaiian nationalists, on the contrary, have not demanded citizenship on this liberal and middle class terrain, but instead have voiced a pre-Christian spirituality, sexuality, and family organization that is based in demands for control over land and assets seized illegally by an illegitimate state. Where the liberal demands for marriage rights/rites have inspired and drawn upon a theme of legal progress toward social inclusion and universalism through civil rights (which has served to oppose conservative concerns over radical temporal reordering), it has been Hawaiian nationalists, deeply concerned about sliding ever socially downward and backward, who have ultimately called for an end to the myths of universal inclusion.

Viewed from this tension over the temporal and mythological character of rights, perhaps the conservatives are correct in their insistence that the marriage case was never really about Hawaiian rights. Certainly, the difficulties that Hawaiian nationalists and same-sex marriage supporters experienced in finding common ground in the amendment campaign shows that they diverged not only in their faith in the power of legal norms, but also in their understanding of sovereignty. For supporters of same-sex marriage, the restrictive politics of sovereignty begun by conservatives was met with a complex notion of democracy in which equal rights played a compelling role in reimagining the *Baehr* case as a legitimate opportunity for national integration of gays and lesbians in particular, and all others deprived of their civil rights in general. For Hawaiians, the recovery of traditional tolerance for diverse sexual and family forms was an affirmation of the cultural basis of a sovereignty that could be used to further political power through the establishment of an economic base able to resist the degradation of the globalized tourist economy, a transformation that would ultimately remain unaffected by civil rights. In the words of one activist,

> When people start talking about the organization that's coming in and pouring in millions of dollars and trying to "save" traditional marriage, the marriage is really a smaller issue because what they're trying to build is a wealthy Hawai'i for them at the expense of us Hawaiians. So shame on them, because we know what they're doing. It's not like we've been lost in the shuffle here. We have many Hawaiians who are lawyers, doctors, and are very knowledgeable in many different fields. So when it comes to this particular issue, we have to pick a strong stance and literally say we are going to enunciate a solid and resounding "No" to this constitutional amendment. It will impact and threaten and literally

diminish or even eliminate the native trust assets, which we are not willing to risk.[46]

Hawaiian nationalists perceive less chance to gain inclusion in this wealthy Hawai'i from broadened marriage rights and a commitment to middle-class ideals than they do from a political self-determination that leaves many middle class edgy and uncertain. And yet, while these disparate ends destabilize the alignment of Native Hawaiian and civil rights groups, both have been discursively forced together by the politics of sovereignty as foreseen by Na Māmo. Both indigenous and civil rights groups serve as self-referential signs regulating the fears that motivated the wildly popular conservative reaction against the *Baehr* case by disrupting these orientalizing discourses. Hawaiian hānai traditions as well as a cultural tolerance for same-sex desires and families demonstrated that not all heterosexuals think the same way about marriage. When this was allowed to intrude in the debates, it forced to mind the original suppression of the Hawaiian people and the tenuous and illegal basis of any claim of nonindigenous sovereignty in the islands. Because the conservative rejection of same-sex marriage is mimetic of the first attempt at sovereign control and hegemony by the missionaries, gays and lesbians stand in for the Hawaiians of the early nineteenth century. They are the "savages" requiring a new political evangelization, a purging of the excesses of rights pursued in the courts. Through these associations, domestic policy returns as the central sign of the civilized nation, even more central than Christianity ever could be. Indeed, Christianity emerges in this conservative discourse as a simple tradition in need of the protection of rights rather than the basis of rights.[47]

If indigenous, lesbian, and gay claims are entangled—less through their cooperation in legal mobilization than through their potential for disruption of the "supposedly universal forms of the modern regime of power" inherent in the sovereign imagination (Chatterjee 1993, 13)—then a coordinated politics of some sort should prove to be mutually beneficial. But what might that look like? The lessons in this subaltern politics surrounding the marriage fight are likely bidirectional. From Native Hawaiian struggles, progressive civil rights advocates may learn to be cautious of the silences about the historical nature of sovereignty preserved in rights discourse, and to be wary of assumptions of progress embedded in struggles for equal rights that leave indigenous peoples without a voice and houseless in their own homeland. And from advocates for equal rights to marriage, Hawaiian nationalists might learn that the discourse of sovereignty absent an explicit critique of the heterosexual family forms in which its imagination is historically embedded remains exclusionary and is likely to submerge some of the very tools needed to recover indigenous culture and to challenge subordination through commodification in the tourist economy.

An important question for both groups to pursue now is what might be at stake in anchoring the national imagination neither to rights nor restoration, but to a revised history of sexual openness and tolerance. Where diverse family forms are recognized to be both culturally appropriate and essential to indigenous genealogies, and where the acceptance of sexual diversity is understood to be an element of aloha and of pono, then challenges to a conservative construction of sovereignty can act to limit zero-sum alternatives in which one group's gains is necessarily another's loss, prompting new forms of cooperation and new strategies of action. This is a politics akin to Bravmann's (1997) queer fictions of the past in which history is engaged in ways that foster community. But while it need not draw its inspiration from legal discourse in Hawai'i, neither can it avoid engagement with the politics of law that has grown up around the marriage issue.

Chapter 6

Global Wedding Bells

My vote is not intended to be judgmental and hurtful. It's simply I don't believe it's . . . in the best interest of the state [of Alaska] to have . . . homosexual marriages sanctioned, and to the best of my knowledge [to be] the only state in the nation and probably the only nation in the world [to recognize same-sex marriage].

—Alaska state representative Scott Ogan, 1998

Forget the lies and the outside influences. Consider the possibility that Alaska might be the first in the United States to write discrimination into our Constitution.

—Liz Brown, 1998

If we didn't do what we did, we would have been the first state to have same-sex marriages, and then we would have been blamed by opponents for not doing enough. You're darned if you do and you're darned if you don't.

—Terrance Tom, former Hawai'i House
Judiciary Committee chair, 1999

Since Hawaii would be the first state to set up . . . a [domestic partnership] contract, we don't know how it will affect us. It is precedent setting and should be discussed at length and be voted on by the general public. . . . I feel that *my* civil rights are being violated because I have not had the time to study the information or the right to vote on this issue.

—Barbara Chung, 1996

The officers and members of the Kauai Filipino Women's Club strongly OPPOSE SAME-SEX MARRIAGE. We do not want our beautiful Aloha State to be the first place in history to approve and endorse "same-sex marriage."

—Anabel Portugal, president, KFWC, 1997

Hawaii is fertile soil for equality. Everybody's a minority. Because civil rights are deeply rooted here, we were the first to legalize a woman's right to choose and the Equal Rights Amendment. A "no" vote sustains that tradition of civil rights for all citizens.

—Jan-Michelle Sawyer, 1998

The dangers and rectitude that devolve from being the first jurisdiction to recognize same-sex marriage open a vast horizon from which to triangulate a sovereign position. In one direction stretch the shoals of economic ruin and the mirage of fabulous gain that reward or punish being first. In another lie the beckoning twin peaks of autonomy and social collapse, the promise or pain of exposure. In a third direction, the tranquil seas of reason are threatened by the turbulent tsunami of irrationality. In another, the faintly shimmering images of a timeless past are easily occluded by the modern construction on the legal skyline. Guiding the sovereign sensibility is the compass of analogy. Analogy provides the acceptable links between the chains of signification binding varied members of the polity to a common reference point of generalized citizenship. It also offers a connection between past and present, joining political struggles into a common heritage of democracy, and the legal imperatives to treat like cases alike in a timeless commitment to justice. But analogy is—as the quotes above reveal—decidedly ambivalent, useful not only for drawing limits to the sovereign imaginary, but also for extending it and keeping the horizon at bay.

Analogies had always been a part of the demands for same-sex marriage. Whether the claims were made that privacy for same-sex couples was analogous to those constitutional rights secured by opposite-sex couples,[1] or the arguments that lesbian and gay families were families *tout court*, or that lesbians and gays had analogous identities and sexual practices to precontact Hawaiians that entitled them to respect, the analogies to others were crucial to their claims. When the Hawai'i Supreme Court ruled in *Baehr v. Lewin* that discrimination against same-sex couples was akin to discrimination on account of race, it set up an inevitable confrontation with the power and limits of analogy in the political struggles over the court's legal reasoning. The boundaries of this reasoning are often imagined on what Warner has called a "liberal-national frame of citizenship [within which] there is an important common ground to be grasped between identity movements" (1993, xix). In this chapter, I seek to show how this frame is articulated (often by majorities rejecting common ground) and expanded beyond this national imaginary. I examine this analogical reasoning in two interlocked dimensions: the analogies between the political and legal identities of civil rights groups, and the analogies between the community of nations in which legal identities are seen to be lodged. Connecting the two, I argue, is the politics of sovereignty.

A Sovereign Conceit

The Hawai'i Supreme Court's argument in *Baehr* that denial of marriage licenses against same-sex couples is akin to unconstitutional racial discrimination against mixed-race marriages opened to constitutional scrutiny the social construction of legal categories. By citing the antimiscegenation precedent of *Loving v. Virginia*, the court analogized discrimination against same-sex marriage to the perpetuation of white supremacy, which was dependent, as Chief Justice Warren had then noted, on policies designed to keep the white race uncontaminated through intermarriage. Although Virginia had argued that their policies were nondiscriminatory since, after all, neither blacks nor whites could equally marry outside of their race, Warren's opinion acknowledges that it is the policy of segregation and the explicit social hierarchies that it draws that in effect *define* race, not some anterior, naturalized notion of the races.[2] The analogy to same-sex marriage that the Hawai'i court drew was through gender. The fact that neither women nor men could equally marry someone of their own gender remains discriminatory not just because the gender of the parties requesting a license is scrutinized, but for another reason implied, though never explicitly stated in the opinion. As Sunstein has constructed this reasoning:

It is indeed true that some people are black, in the sense that they have African-American ancestors, and others white, in the sense that they do not. Very plausibly, this is no less true, or less "factual," than the division of humanity into men and women. The question is what society does with these facts. It is possible to think that the prohibition on same-sex marriages, as part of the social and legal insistence on "two kinds," is as deeply connected with male supremacy as the prohibition on racial intermarriage is connected with White Supremacy. Perhaps same-sex marriages are banned because of what they do to—because of how they unsettle—gender categories. Perhaps same-sex marriages are banned because they complicate traditional gender thinking, showing that the division of human beings into two simple kinds is part of sex-role stereotyping, however true it is that women and men are "different." [Legally, t]he ban has everything to do with constitutionally unacceptable stereotypes about the appropriate roles of men and women. (1994a, 20–21; see also Koppelman 1988, 1994)

The unsettling of gender categories in the law acknowledges the complexity of gender construction by recognizing its cultural "conflation" with sexual orientation and with biological sex (Valdes 1995, 338ff.; 1996). Yet, despite the Hawai'i court's finding that gender be treated with the same, maximal level of scrutiny afforded discrimination on account of race, the analogy to *Loving*, however deep, still distinguishes gender from race as a discrete legal category.

Recent scholarship that has criticized legal categories from the perspective of emerging forms of identity has broadened the social theory that lies embedded in the *Loving* reasoning. If the distinction between racial or gender categories has the potential to create and reinforce social hierarchies, so does the distinction among legal categories of race, gender, class, and the like. As Angela Harris has suggested, the legal imagination is often bound to an essentialist understanding of identity that, in the case of gender, furthers the sovereign privileges of silencing difference. Mainstream and even some feminist legal theory relies upon

> the notion that a unitary, "essential" women's experience can be isolated and described independently of race, class, sexual orientation, and other realities of experience. The result of this tendency toward gender essentialism . . . is not only that some voices are silenced in order to privilege others . . . but that the voices that are silenced turn out to be the same voices silenced by the mainstream legal voice of "We the People"—among them, the voices of black women. (1990, 585)

Critical race theory has its intellectual origins in the efforts to transcend essentialist and single-axis jurisprudence, opening new discursive spaces for those, such as black women, who are silenced by cross-cutting juridical categories (Crenshaw 1995; Delgado 1995). The imagination of discrete identity categories in the law is a reflection of the idea that identities are fixed and immutable rather than contingent and fluid, creating a hidden normative field. As Stychin understands this, "[E]ach category becomes a distinction from the norm, for which protection is appropriate. The norm though remains in place, permanently fixed, immutable, and 'undeconstructed.' The categories of prohibited discrimination represent mere deviations" (1995a, 52). The particular experiences of black women, for example, lie unseen in the law that takes the patriarchal, cultural assumption of maleness as the norm of blackness, and racial assumptions of whiteness as the norm in gender. That this disadvantage is not purely additive forms the core insight behind critical race theory. As Crenshaw suggests,

> Black women are sometimes excluded from feminist theory and antiracist policy discourse because both are predicated on a discrete set of experiences that often does not accurately reflect the interaction of race and gender. These problems of exclusion cannot be solved simply by including Black women within an already established analytical structure. Because the intersectional experience is greater than the sum of racism and sexism, any analysis that does not take intersectionality into account cannot sufficiently address the particular manner in which Black women are subordinated. (1989, 140)

"Intersectionality" thus serves as a critical intervention to uncover the experiences of marginalized individuals by recognizing both the multiplicity of normative determinants of identity and the various discourses intersecting at their putative locations.

Intersectionality in particular and the critical race project generally have been recently criticized for their own reductionism, failing to account for sexual orientation (Eaton 1995; Eskridge 1996, 980; Hutchinson 1999; Kwan 1997; Valdes 1998), class (Karst 1995, 318ff.; Robson 1995) and other systems of social oppression (Colker 1996). In addition, progressive criticisms of intersectionality attempting to amplify its antisubordination stance have pointed out that the theory itself—while acknowledging the complexity of social identity and mechanisms of oppression—loses explanatory traction as categories multiply, and as other categories relinquish their meaning through social processes of assimilation (especially with regard to race), or political processes of deconstruction (e.g., queer politics, bisexual identity). Without some accounting for "multidimensionality" (Hutchinson 1997) and "cosynthesis" (Kwan 1997) of social identities, critical interventions can themselves re-create social marginalization at the analytical level by shaping new quasi-essentialist categories such as "black women" or by simplifying social relations in binary terms of black/white as the central paradigm of race. For this reason, the emerging "LatCrit" scholarship, which attempts to avoid essentialist accounts of Latina/o[3] experience, favors the particular and contextual aspects of subordination and its relationship to categories of jurisprudence, over the generalized and abstract. For LatCrit theorists, the mutual implications of language, religion, family life and sexuality, internationalism, race, poverty, and the like have all become important interrelated yet hierarchically unprivileged points of analysis in an effort to produce critical knowledge, advance social transformation, expand and connect antisubordination struggles, and cultivate progressive coalitions (Valdes 1997, 1093–94; see also Gomez 1998; Iglesias and Valdes 1998; Montoya 1998).

These theoretical advances problematize our understanding of the analogies that have emerged in the arguments over same-sex marriage. By privileging the contextual, historical, and multidimensional aspects of identity categories, this scholarship questions the sovereign privileges of silence about differences that permit an integration into "We the People." For example, "race" emerges as a protected class of inclusion (and so becomes an illicit mark of exclusion from citizenship) only because it is not acknowledged to be layered with, and indeed, to depend upon, other constructions of class, sexual orientation, or gender that could divert the historical memories linked to the legal recognition of color and permit differences to unravel "categorial" (Kropp 1997) and essentialist logic. This essentialism becomes useful for popular constructions of sovereignty. It prevents fragmentation of majority identities by suppressing the relevance of social dynamics that interfere with legal logic or by encouraging disidentification with other groups whose analogical reasoning for inclusion seems unjustified or purely imaginary.

This appeal to sovereign privilege and essentialist logic is evident in this legislative testimony from an African American woman in Hawai'i who was opposed to the reasoning supporting same-sex marriage:

> As an African-American, I find serious flaws in [the report of the Commission on Sexual Orientation and the Law regarding] Equal Protection and the Loving Case. The effort of the Commission to link the experiences of African-Americans to same gender couples is absolutely appalling! When was a homosexual last denied an opportunity to attend a university of their choosing, to vote, to live in a specific community or neighborhood of their choice, to use

public rest rooms, to drink from a public water fountain, to ride on the front of a bus, to drive freely through any neighborhood without harassment by the very individuals sworn to protect these freedoms? When I went to college, less than twenty years ago, I was followed in stores, chased by individuals in cars, I was afraid to walk around campus after dark, my car windshield was broken twice, even more grave, a young African-American was murdered and thrown out the back of a truck in clear view of on-looking citizens who refused to cooperate with the police. All this occurring for the simple reason of skin color. These basic "inalienable rights" are and have always been afforded to other citizens to include gay and heterosexuals alike with the exception of African-Americans. So, Mr. Commissioner to link the Equal Protection and the Loving vs Virginia case is offensive and a slap in the face of all African-Americans.[4]

As this testimony makes clear, race is almost effortlessly coded as heterosexual, appealing to the sanctioned memories of historical acceptance, and, implicitly, the dominant social norms established by the sovereign. The African American body made visible in this testimony links historical violence and suffering to the tropes of citizenship laid down in civil rights law while occluding the issues of sexual violence that have also been a part of the historical experience of race (see Richards 1999, 34ff.; Roediger 1991). As Jefferson has aptly noted in this regard, "Invisibility and hyper-visibility compliment each other . . . [and] serve the same purpose—the legitimation of dominant cultural control" (1998, 264).

Of course, the sovereign conceit of essentialism is a multifaceted game. Not only does it cement majoritarian identities, but it also is a useful fiction for social movements requiring some bounded identity for the purposes of mobilization (Bravmann 1997; Gamson 1996). Ignoring difference comes at a cost, however. Valdes notes, in the case of sexual orientation, that

ignoring race and ethnicity in sexual orientation law and scholarship effectively codes "sexual orientation" as white and "race" or "ethnicity" as heterosexual, a coding that is factually inaccurate. This coding in turn erects an equally false dichotomy between "sexual orientation" and "race" or "ethnicity" in social and legal

conceptions or perceptions of the persons and groups implicated
by anti-subordination struggles linked to this trio of constructs.
(1997a, 1321)

False dichotomies help explain why suspicion between civil rights
groups is not uncommon. Hutchinson argues that

> despite the persistence and virulence of heterosexist oppression,
> white gays and lesbians remain socially advantaged in a racially
> hierarchical society that privileges whiteness. By treating black
> subjugation or other forms of racial domination as the same as
> white gay oppression, the analogies mask the reality that social
> and economic power is racially distributed. As a result, many peo-
> ple of color have rightfully criticized the deployment of the analo-
> gies in gay and lesbian political discourse. (1999, 44; see also
> Brandt 1999)

This criticism is also resonant within "essentialized" groups when economic, gender, and race differences are masked to the point that goals
and strategies fail to be sufficiently generalized (Jefferson 1998; Robson
1995).

The work of critical race theorists, LatCrit scholars, and others has
demonstrated that the value of essentialized categories for the politics
of sovereignty cannot be contained without the maintenance of particular silences and rhetorical investment in the invisibility of multidimensional realities of social oppression and hierarchy. The cultural and
political work necessary to maintain these sovereign fictions and control the meaning of analogies operates on many planes. One dimension
is the international. Sovereignty has always imagined itself as a sovereignty among equivalent sovereignties, a set of synchronic relationships in which respect, honor, and duty condition and constrain
national authority. In this chapter, I look to the particular tension
between liberal-national sovereignty claims propounded by civil rights
activists and sovereignty articulated upon the subtleties of a governmentality concerned with social and economic security in the international sphere. In particular, I examine the myths of citizenship constructed from soldiers in the defense of national sovereignty, and the
economic norms regulating the peacetime competitive relationship of
sovereigns with other sovereigns. This set of international relationships

stabilizes the types of analogies deployed in the global debates over same-sex marriage. How this stabilization limits or expands the gains of lesbians and gays is the question that I explore.

Heroic Democrats and Republican Myths

Based upon polling and focus group research conducted in the spring of 1998, Protect Our Constitution—the main coalition opposing the amendment prohibiting marriage rights—decided to avoid a campaign that would directly address same-sex marriage or gay and lesbian lives and love. POC found that while a majority (77 percent) of uninformed respondents agreed that "homosexual Americans deserve the same rights and privileges as heterosexual Americans," only 36 percent would agree that there was a right to same-sex marriage. In comparison with other ethnic groups, support for gays, gay rights, and same-sex marriage was disappointingly low (see table 1). Focus group discussions had suggested that analogies to other minority groups whose rights were held in higher esteem would be most effective as a campaign tactic. However, a stumbling block was found in the common belief that lesbians and gays lived a lifestyle created by choice and defined solely by their behavior. As one participant put it, "Well, you made the comparison about should we take away the rights from Asian people. To me that's really different because you have absolutely no choice in your race, absolutely none at all." Another said, "I can see a major difference with inter-racial marriage. Your children see inter-racial marriage they won't turn black but they might turn homosexual."[5]

The belief that gays and lesbians are defined as a class by their behavior made their representation problematic for same-sex marriage advocates, even through analogy. Sexual orientation did not compare with race and ethnic identity for purposes of civil rights for two reasons. First, the identification of gays and lesbians with their behavioral choices—whether perceived as sinful or not—suggested that their public claims for redress rested upon a duplicity that violated republican images of the citizen. Warner has argued that the culture of republicanism is a "structuring metalanguage" that historically reinforced the ability of print media to create a public—it is, in fact, the genealogical origin of *publication*. "It was in the culture of republicanism, with its categories of disinterested virtue and supervision, that a rhetoric of print

TABLE 1.   Hawaiian Attitudes on Rights of Persons of Different Ethnicities and Sexual Orientations May 1998 (*N* = 681)

	Agree Strongly (%)	Agree (%)	Disagree (%)	Disagree Strongly (%)
Asian-Americans deserve the same rights and privileges as Caucasian-Americans	78	20	1	0
African-Americans deserve the same rights and privileges as Caucasian-Americans	76	21	2	1
Jewish Americans deserve the same rights and privileges as Caucasian-Americans	76	22	2	0
Homosexual Americans deserve the same rights and privileges as heterosexual Americans	50	27	13	9
Asians should have the right to marry Caucasians	74	24	2	0
Caucasians should have the right to marry African-Americans	73	26	1	0
Christians should have the right to marry Jews	70	27	2	1
A man should have the right to marry another man	20	16	22	41
A woman should have the right to marry another woman	20	16	22	41

Source: Qmark Research and Polling, and Human Rights Campaign.
Note: Because of rounding, rows may not total 100 percent.

consumption became authoritative, a way of understanding the publicness of publication" (Warner 1992, 380). This persistent rhetoric posits the virtue of transparency: in their public representations, citizens should seem to be as they are in private (Berlant 1997). It also supports a public ethic of abstract love. As Phelan has noted,

> Republican love . . . is a love simultaneously personal and abstract, in which others are loved as citizens, but not as individuals. Citizens are not loved by other citizens because of their personal virtues or qualities, but because they are fellow citizens. The primary love is for one's country; love of one's fellow citizens flows, as it were, in a circuit from citizen to country to citizen. (1999, 63)

According to Warner, the abstraction that grounds this semiological circuit "provides a privilege for unmarked identities: the male, the white, the middle class, the normal" (1992, 383). While others (women, people of color) can be included on the basis of a naturalized connection between their private condition of difference and their public representation, integration into the sovereign is particularly difficult in the case of gays and lesbians. Claiming public protection on the basis of private lives highlights the centrality of a love that is concrete and romantic rather than abstract, raising the potential for conflict.[6] Although this potential antagonism was literally domesticated in the history of heterosexual relations, same-sex recognition poses acute problems for republican sensibility.

> Acknowledging queer love would . . . endanger the polity through the reintroduction of particular love. If love between men is possible, it threatens the polity just as romantic love for women did. Love between men, however, cannot be dealt with by isolating the potential object of affection and contest; since such love may ignite from any man who opens himself to it, the opening itself must be squashed. This can be ensured (never successfully) only by seeking out and removing those who manifest the possibility of opening to other men. (Phelan 1999, 74)

The need to police the intrusion of homosexuality into the homosocial realm of citizenship is not limited to marriage but poses representational problems all through the campaigns over marriage rights.

A second reason that representations of gay and lesbian love and lives are difficult for civil rights advocates devolves from the behavioral definitions of the legal class. Precisely because same-sex behavior is diverse, it poses a representational paradox. On the one hand, diversity demonstrates that same-sex partnerships are not one of a kind and therefore are undeserving of protection, unlike race and ethnicity, which can be represented discretely as facts of nature or historical happenstance. On the other hand, the representation of diversity makes same-sex relationships meld into the everyday situations, diverse cultures, and economic classes in which they are embedded and from which lesbians and gays have articulated their "coming out." While this representational alternative accounts for the rhetoric of fear attributed to coming out as a violation of numerous sovereign privileges, it also can be discursively channeled into the image of lesbians and gays as everyday neighbors and family. This paradox operated as a representational constraint for both sides of the debates. Promarriage forces decided to avoid the representation of diversity that might weaken their claim to a legally significant categorical discrimination, while proamendment forces wanted to avoid any sense that lesbians and gays made up a significant presence anchored across social strata in Hawai'i.

The strategic consequence of these representational problems was a mixed set of campaign images. Save Traditional Marriage '98, the largest proamendment coalition, represented same-sex marriage largely through the icons of white, gay men, dressed in mainland attire. Avoiding lesbian images, same-sex marriage was thus shown in its form most transgressive to republican imagery and most foreign to the values that could assimilate these relationships as recognizably local and acceptable. STM also capitalized upon the general markers of whiteness and maleness, and with them, the assumption of middle-class economic privilege (Robson 1995, 7ff.) in order to weaken the claims that gays needed civil rights protection (fig. 5). Protect Our Constitution chose to avoid direct representation of lesbians and gays. This opened them up to a line of attack for violating republican notions of openness and transparency. The lack of representation fortified STM's claim that POC was duping the people. The phrases "Don't let them fool you into legalizing homosexual marriage" and "Don't be fooled into legalizing homosexual marriage" were prominently written above the exhortation to "Vote YES on the Marriage Question" in nearly every printed advertisement. Others had prominent subthemes of gay trickery, as in the text of figure 5: "They're trying to deceive you" and the punning promise that STM "can set you straight."

In order to authenticate its claims and combat STM's representational strategy, POC chose a campaign of analogies. In particular, it relied upon the painful case of internment of Americans of Japanese ancestry (AJAs in local parlance) during the Second World War to intimate the exclusion of gays and lesbians that the amendment would create (see figure 6; gays, lesbians, and marriage are never mentioned). Its research polls had suggested that the public—especially AJAs, who make up about one-third of the population and who vote heavily—was most convinced by one analogous argument: "In Hawai'i, many of our

Make sure you know what you're voting for.

In most political campaigns, it's considered a bad thing to mention the opposition. But in this case the opposition is the bad thing.

They're trying to deceive you.

They claim to be about protecting your civil rights, but in reality they're just afraid to address the real issue: preserving traditional marriage. That's because polls show that more than 70% of Hawaii's voters are opposed to homosexual marriage.

But we can set you straight: traditional marriage versus homosexual marriage. That's what it's all about.

So if in your heart, you feel that marriage should only be between one man and one woman– then vote YES in the general election on November 3rd. It's just common sense.

☑YES
VOTE TRADITIONAL MARRIAGE

Paid for by Save Traditional Marriage '98. / P.O. Box 27683 Honolulu, Hawai'i 96827 / (808) 623-2312

Fig. 5.   Advertisement in favor of constitutional amendment, placed by Save Traditional Marriage '98. (*Honolulu Advertiser*, 30 September 1998, A11.)

parents and grandparents fought long and hard for equal rights and tolerance. They saw their rights denied and their families interned in camps. We should not turn back the clock on everything they fought so hard to achieve."[7]

Citing the internment of AJAs during the Second World War and the laws that once prevented Asians and other nonwhites from marrying Caucasians, the local chapter of the Japanese American Citizens League (JACL), with full support from the national parent organiza-

It must not happen again. To anyone ever.

Well-meaning people once decided it was perfectly fine to discriminate. Just this one time, and only against one small minority.

That's not prejudice, they said. It's necessary to save our traditional way of life.

So they suspended the constitutional rights of 120,000 American citizens.

The Honolulu Chapter of the Japanese American Citizens League says we must never again make any group an exception to our constitutional rights. Ever.

JAPANESE AMERICAN CITIZENS LEAGUE

Vote NO ☑
on the Constitutional Amendment on November 3rd.

Paid for by Japanese American Citizens League, Honolulu Chapter; P.O. Box 1291, Honolulu, Hawaii 96807 and Protect Our Constitution/Human Rights Campaign, 870 Kapahulu Avenue #110, Honolulu, Hawaii 96816

Fig. 6.   Advertisement opposed to constitutional amendment, placed by Japanese American Citizens League. (*Honolulu Advertiser*, 9 October 1998, A14.)

tion, became the first nongay or lesbian organization to endorse the *Baehr* plaintiffs, acting early in 1994. In testimony before the Hawai'i house in 1997, the JACL again argued against a proposed antimarriage amendment by invoking the painful memories of wartime internment, which had a profound impact in Hawai'i.

> Distinguishing a particular group of people for special treatment under law invokes memories of the internment of 120,000 Americans of Japanese Ancestry during World War II. Continuing to deny rights and benefits to a class of citizens violates Hawai'i's traditional spirit of tolerance, acceptance, and *aloha*.[8]

Echoing its arguments on behalf of the plaintiffs in an amicus brief filed in the *Loving* case years before, the JACL explicitly invoked the antimiscegenation analogy in its argument to the *Baehr* trial court that the State of Hawai'i had relied upon little more than "crude stereotypes."[9] In line with its testimony to the Hawai'i senate, the JACL brief concluded that the social history of Hawai'i's intermarriage[10] had demonstrated the state's

> rich tradition of racial acceptance. The diversity of our ethnic population enables Pacific Islanders, Indians, Caucasians, Asians, Hispanics, African Americans and others harmoniously to co-exist. It is apparent that interracial marriage—once stigmatized and irrationally condemned—has been replaced by a united social fabric of racial and ethnic accord. Notwithstanding the fact that our great state has dispelled the myth of interracial marriages, the State continues to hurl similar arguments that same-sex marriages would have deplorable effects on our community and its children. This Court should not turn back the clock on social justice by denying the right to marriage to persons based on sex, in the same way marriages were at one time denied to persons based on race.[11]

The myth of Hawai'i's "rich tradition of racial acceptance" (see also Lind 1943; Kotani 1985; Takaki 1983) has a particular genealogy in the postwar rehabilitation of AJA status. Victimized by the wartime edicts that interned few but restricted many under the rules of martial law,[12] AJAs saw the opportunity to restore their citizenship claims through their participation in the European war in a manner analogous to the experiences of African Americans, whose contribution to the Civil War accumulated the debt of citizenship (Donald 1995; Richards 1999, 133). Unable to enlist, AJAs appealed to the government for a chance to prove their loyalty. The opportunity was granted. Formed into two all-AJA battle groups—the 442nd regimental combat team and the One Hundredth infantry battalion, with their "go for broke" slogan representing the heavy personal and community stakes at issue—seventy-five young men, many from Hawai'i, fought with valor to became the most highly decorated American soldiers of the Second World War. As Mackey has argued, their treatment in the military, especially the near-legendary "rescue of the lost battalion" in which eight hundred AJA soldiers died to save the lives of 211 Texans surrounded by German forces, taught a hard lesson with lasting political implications.

> When the Nisei volunteered for service in the war, they went in with the idea of "proving themselves." That the world was split along racial lines, between "white" and "non-white," occurred to them only in the context of their own prejudices, but it was never applied to Humankind. When they volunteered, they were in fact "proving themselves" for *what they were*, as not only equal but better. The discovery that their actions were dominated by the dichotomy between the "white man" and [themselves] did not occur to [them] until [they were] shown that one life of the "white man" was worth two of theirs. (1995, 133)

Combined with the 442nd's storied involvement in the liberation of Dachau, an event that explicitly contrasted the pluralist American effort against the racist and anti-Semitic violence of the Nazi regime, the returning AJA soldier was able to represent for many in Hawai'i the solidarity of the oppressed while making a due claim for denied citizenship. As Senator Daniel Inouye, veteran soldier and the first AJA elected to Congress from Hawai'i, recalled,

> We had played a small but vital part in the great war, and now that it was won we were not about to go back to the plantation. We wanted our place in the sun, the right to participate in decisions that affected us. Day after day, rally after rally, we hammered home the point that there must be no more second-class citizens in the Hawai'i of tomorrow. (Quoted in Mackey 1995, 190)

The heroic accolades earned by Senator Inouye (who lost his right arm in the war) and other AJA veterans were parlayed into a new constellation of power in Hawai'i. In 1954, the AJA community led by the veterans joined with other dispossessed ethnic groups to overthrow the Republican majority run by haole (white) elites, displace the socialist labor leadership that had emerged in the organization of the sugar plantation workers (Kent 1983, 122ff), and establish the liberal Democratic party as the central political organization ever since. The Democratic party that thoroughly dominates the legislature and has controlled the governorship since 1962 (shortly after statehood) historically depended on the AJA vote and drew much its leadership from the AJA community.[13]

Resting on the meaning of soldiers to citizenship (see Elshtain 1995), the myth of racial solidarity that was counterposed to the ethnic divisiveness that existed prior to Democratic control and statehood (a theme borrowed from the socialists) is nonetheless purchased at a particular cost: the cultural elevation of the masculine. Ferguson and Turnbull argue that this construction of masculinity in Hawai'i sutures the liberal emphasis on individual rights to the republican virtue of citizenship, an intersection that can be read upon the altered bodies of ethnic/military heroes such as Inouye.

> Inouye's dismemberment was a key to membership in the national political elite, transforming his racial and class alienness into masculine belonging. . . . Race is temporarily suspended, masculinity is achieved, and entry into the arena of patriarchal power is secured. (Ferguson and Turnbull 1999, 161)

Still Hawai'i's senior senator, Inouye's tenure is a powerful sign of the endurance of this masculine myth of political power and authority.

The meaning of this masculinity as proof of citizenship has uncertain ramifications for lesbians and gays. This is seen most clearly in the public ambivalence of Senator Inouye over marriage rights. Although he has a long history of championing civil rights issues for Native Americans, Hawaiians, Asians, and other people of color, and despite being one of only fourteen senators to vote against DOMA, Inouye did not endorse the POC campaign and was so noncommittal about the same-sex marriage issue that he was publicly thanked by STM on election day for being "opposed to the legalization of same-sex marriage."[14] Although POC did rely upon Major General Togawa—another AJA veteran—as a spokesman, STM responded with an advertising campaign that played up both the state's founding mythology of the AJA citizen-soldier and the uncertain status of gays (and lesbians), who are denied the right to prove their citizenship openly in the military. With twenty-two AJA male combat veterans fronting the state capitol, mustered two ranks deep in aloha shirt regalia, the caption read, "Because we served our Country during many wars, as military veterans we know a thing or two about protecting the constitution. Those pushing homosexual marriage pretend the constitution is threatened by a YES vote. *It isn't*" (fig. 7).

The republican ideal of masculinity and sacrifice, and the AJA claim of racial unity that ensued under their heroic leadership, in effect subordinates gays (and by association, lesbians) within the myth of AJA universal struggle. By calling upon civic duties in the form of military service, rather than the violation of rights that were also embedded deeply within the civic mythology of AJA soldiers, STM had converted the liberal argument for tolerance into the republican basis for exclusion. Represented as a phalanx of retired soldiers by STM, the image of AJA veterans standing shoulder to shoulder, uniformed in aloha-wear, conjures Sedgwick's (1985; 1990, 87–88) notion of the homosocial that acknowledges same-sex desire and marks it as the basis of republican citizenship, at the same time that it delimits its transgressive potentiality through norms of heterosexuality and homophobia as well as through the light of publicity that denies there is anything to hide. As Dumm has noted, "The intense discontinuity between the homosocial and the homosexual is born of . . . desire for security through superiority" (1994, 53). This gender performance not only makes invisible the gay male body whose own desires are forced to remain in the political closet. It also obscures the role of women whose value as citizens, by implication, remains within the privatized roles of "mothers of soldiers." Lesbian sexuality, as a consequence, is nearly completely concealed.

The mustering of soldier-heroes to debate the meaning of analogies permitted the proamendment forces to argue the lack of corpus delicti: where was same-sex marriage? At the level of "common sense" such a debate—no matter that it was two-sided—was used to argue the absurdity and deceptiveness of the civil rights position. One influential

Because we served our Country during many wars

Top Row (left to right): Tomosue Abo, US Army; Tokuo Kaneshige, 442nd RCT; Adney Komatsu, MIS; Walter Yim, Hawaii National Guard; James Takane, US Army; Frank Suzuki, 442nd RCT; Louis Molina, US Marines; Troy Bettencourt, US Army 100-442; Raymond Santana, US Air Force; Fred Holck, US Army, 2nd Infantry.

Bottom Row (left to right): Hiromi Abo, US Army; Kotaro Kaizumi, US Army, Artillery IX Corps; Jack Miyamoto, 442nd RCT; Susumu Arima, 442nd RCT; Harry Kanekos, US Army, VFW James Kuroiwa, US Army 100-442; Howard Okada, US Army Pacific Aubert Annee, US Army; Roy Iwamoto, MIS, Roger Ancheta, US Air Force; James Tsuya, US Army; Richard Hayashida, US Army

...as military veterans we know a thing or two about protecting the constitution.

Those pushing homosexual marriage pretend the constitution is threatened by a YES vote.
It isn't. A YES vote simply preserves traditional marriage between one man and one woman
— the way it has always been.

That's why we're voting YES on the Marriage Question.

Don't be fooled into legalizing homosexual marriage.

Please join us in voting YES.
It's just common sense.

Fig. 7. Advertisement in favor of constitutional amendment, placed by Japanese-American veterans. (*Honolulu Advertiser,* 30 October 1998, A22.)

religious figure in the proamendment forces articulated this "every-man" position in the following manner.

> I'm not a big theologian. I was a surfer. I came to Hawai'i as a surfer. I'm a pretty grassroots kind of guy. Jesus helped fisherman. He also helped surfers. I'm not that theologically inclined, and I'll admit it. But I know the Bible. I know what it says. . . . If you look at what the other side is doing as far as to draw people on their side, they're not just simply giving the issue. It's so convoluted. If you're Hawaiian, or if you're Japanese, you're going to be losing your rights and you may be interned again. What does that have to do with anything?[15]

This problem of an obstinate common sense was not lost on some in the gay and lesbian community, either. As one Native Hawaiian lesbian complained,

> I have a hard time explaining it to some [friends and family]. What does the internment camp have to do with marriage? . . . I was uptight trying to explain it because . . . it was very heady and con-ceptually elegant, but not very simple. Not very simple to under-stand. And it didn't speak to me. I felt, you know, we are not sim-pletons here anymore. We are not backward, we are not stupid, but you know that was a very difficult—conceptually—campaign to be around. . . . Many people with good hearts, good intentions, and bright minds couldn't follow that campaign.[16]

Despite its remove, the debate was not pointless to its proponents. The constant reiteration of AJA suffering and AJA heroism in the campaign points to the myths that link liberal rights through analogy to republi-can virtues. As an articulation of the limits of the sovereign, it thus points outward, beyond Hawai'i, to the horizon of international rela-tions where valor, honor, and true male heroism is bred and where the social division on the basis of ethnicity, race, and class is remade through the fraternalism of soldiers, the field of international alliance, and legitimate, manly competition.

In bringing this distant horizon home to the debate, the image of the AJA soldier exacerbated concerns about Hawai'i's being first to legalize same-sex marriage. DOMA was a warning shot across the bow of the Hawai'i ship of state that had veered too close to protected waters, and the State of Hawai'i's intervention in the Vermont case[17] along with the November vote to strike down the *Baehr* decision were means of retreating out of respect for a national civic duty. Even after the election, citizenship could be imagined within the myth of a fight for tolerance that had implications far beyond the borders of Hawai'i. This was made apparent in April 1999, when several victorious activists of the Hawai'i campaign sent a letter to all registered voters in Vermont, which was then hearing its own challenge to its exclusionary marriage statutes. Citing a "common civic crisis," the authors argued that their concern for Vermont was designed to help restore a domestic order in which "we citizens" could once again emerge with the proper virtues and linked horizons.[18]

> Vermont and Hawai'i are different in many ways. We are in the tropics; you are in the rugged mountains of the Northeast. We have the most racially and religiously diverse population of the United States; you have the most homogenous. You were the first state to join the Union after the original thirteen colonies; we were the last.
>
> Despite these differences, we share much in common. Our states are small in land area and population. Our states are both rich in natural beauty and our peoples are sensitive to environmental concerns. We are accepting of others as individuals and place a high value on matters of fairness and compassion, just as your citizens do.
>
> We also share a common civic crisis. . . .
>
> Because we citizens of Hawai'i have been there already, we want to share with you some of what we have seen and experienced over the past seven years concerning this issue. We offer our perspective in the spirit of aloha as a gift of friendship in the hope that you will be both informed and aware as you face this issue in Vermont. The stakes are very high. The decisions made in Vermont will impact the entire nation and the world.

That impact was projected, in part, as an economic reminder of the value of any location in a globalized economy.

In Hawai'i this was promoted as a boon for tourism. "Think of thousands of homosexual couples coming to a gay Las Vegas to Marry." More cautious citizens imagined the tens of thousands who would choose not to come. Vermont's own tourism industry and its proximity to Boston, New York and Montreal should raise similar concerns.

Much as the AJA soldiers had restored their honor despite prejudice and cruelty, the letter assumed the resolution of the civic crisis would again include a fight with the internal enemy of intolerance. However, prejudice was projected in an inverted fashion, with civil rights supporters the main purveyors of intolerance.

We found that folks on both sides of this issue shared some common values and rules. Many individuals with deeply held beliefs but opposite views were able to discuss and share in ways that honored our Hawaiian culture of tolerance. Both sides began their campaigns with passion, determination and most important— civility. This was not to last.

As the pro-same-sex marriage strategy emerged, we saw a strong reliance on the tactics of repeating misinformation until it was accepted as fact, ignoring inconvenient realities, and demonizing the opposition. Any person or group standing up for traditional marriage was accused of being "homophobic" and "discriminatory." Those who based their views on their religious beliefs were the most viciously attacked. Our Roman Catholic, Mormon and conservative Protestant communities, whom we value for their histories of charity and compassion, were consistently characterized as "hate-filled bigots." . . . Moderation was not tolerated, people who had supported previous "gay rights" initiatives became enemies of the cause if they found "gay marriage" to be a step too far for them to support. Some who publicly supported traditional marriage lost their jobs—some had their businesses boycotted or harassed.

The press largely supported the "same-sex marriage" groups adopting their views and repeating their misinformation. This greatly handicapped us. We are encouraged to report that the power of the people prevailed over the power of the press. The citizens who stood publicly for the value of traditional marriage evidenced courage in the face of adversity.

The militaristic idea of "courage in the face of adversity," reinforced by the predominance of the soldier analogy in the campaign, demonstrates how central was the fraternity of sovereigns, both national and international, called upon to regulate the essentialized identities articulated in the debates. The image of (white, haole) gay men favored by STM came to stand as a common enemy, silenced by the soldiers mustered by the antiamendment forces as much as the soldiers regimented by STM. Diverse issues that could have emerged in the campaign, especially those central to many lesbians and feminists, were understated or ignored in the hand-to-hand combat of male proxies. As honor rose and fell in the campaign, one lesbian feminist activist searching for a reason to make common cause was unrequited. According to her reflections a year later, all too evident in the tenor of the campaign was a perhaps unintentional middle-class, white, gay male agenda.

> Not a bad one, but not very innovative, not very well informed, not [inclusive of] the issues of equity, of poverty, of insurance reform, or all the issues that really have been at the forefront of women's rights agendas. To me, access to health care, to good health care and to that kind of thing, should not be linked to marriage anyway. Why it has anything to do with my liberation as a lesbian, I am not so sure.[19]

If lesbians and feminist issues of marriage were ignored in the campaign, the successful co-optation of the meaning of AJA soldiers that had sustained the myth of Hawai'i's tradition of ethnic inclusion also showed the political exhaustion of the male imagery that had sustained a progressive coalition within the Democratic party. Confronted by same-sex marriage, the party's prominent politicians—once buoyed by the image of AJA valor—fell silent.

International Horizons

> One [i.e., AJA internment] is really something set in race. The other [i.e., same-sex marriage] is a lifestyle and the sanctioning of that lifestyle. No other jurisdiction in the world has sanctioned same-sex marriage. It is really not the same issue.
> —Stan Koki, Republican candidate for
> lieutenant governor, October 1998

The analogies that modulate social disadvantages into claims for citizenship are dependent upon republican forms that compel civic duties and require respect for social and economic forces that could endanger the security of the sovereign. Reading sovereignty as a purely local discourse is therefore inadequate in the face of global economic interests and the respect of other sovereigns on which republican duties are projected and civil rights analogies proved. The concern about whether the recognition of lesbian and gay marriage rights is sui generis and unprecedented, or commensurable with the experiences of other minorities granted civil rights, is therefore as much a concern about whether the recognition of marriage is a first on the horizontal grid of sovereignty, as the quote above suggests. Being first may be a prerogative of sovereignty, but it is no necessary virtue.

Worldwide, legal recognition of many aspects of same-sex partnerships is expanding (see table 2), and social movements addressing all sides of these developments have operated in national and subnational spaces with attentiveness toward these broader developments. In the American cases, the consciousness of other sovereigns and their experiences with a global concern over lesbian and gay rights and same-sex partnerships is scattered widely throughout the legal materials and the public debates surrounding them. International expansions of civil rights for gays and for gay couples substantiate the argument among supporters that the time is right for action on same-sex marriage by linking social progress to legal development and finding adequate precedent in these extrajurisdictional venues. Consider this argument by the plaintiffs in the Vermont same-sex marriage case:

> Legal recognition of same-sex relationships is developing concurrently around the world. The Netherlands, Denmark, Greenland, Finland, Iceland, Norway and Sweden offer same-sex couples all of the rights of legal marriage except for certain protections relating to children and church weddings. . . . In 1996 . . . Hungary legalized common law marriage between partners of the same-sex. . . . In short, legal recognition of marriages between same gender partners would not be as unprecedented as [the State of Vermont] suggest[s].[20]

Even legal efforts to quell same-sex marriage rights can be rhetorically transmogrified into progressive pressure for civil rights expansion. Again, as the Vermont plaintiffs argued to their state supreme court,

Recent court decisions in Alaska and Hawaii, along with international developments in marriage, presage the inevitability of recognition of marriages between same-sex partners throughout this country and the world. Even the federal Defense of Marriage Act anticipates that some states *will* end discrimination in marriage.[21]

TABLE 2.   Recognition of Gay and Lesbian Relationships in Selected Countries

Country	Adoption by Same-Sex Partners	Registered Partnership/ Common Law Recognition	First Anti-discrimination Legislation	Equal Age of Consent	Decriminalization of Same-Sex Acts
Australia		1999[a]	1984[b]		1982[a]
Austria					1971
Belgium				1985	1792
Canada	1995[c]	1999	1977[d]		1968
Denmark	1999	1989	1987	1976	1930
Finland			1995	1998	1971
France			1985	1982	1791
Germany			1992/98	1994	1969
Greece				1951	1951
Hungary		1996			
Iceland		1996	1996	1992	
Ireland			1989	1993	1993
Italy				1889	1889
Luxembourg			1997	1992	1792
Netherlands		1998	1992	1971	1810
New Zealand			1994		
Norway		1993	1981	1972	1972
Portugal					1945
Russia				1997	1993
Slovenia			1995	1977	1977
South Africa		1998	1993		
Spain		1998/99	1995	1988 (1822)	1822
Sweden		1995	1987	1978	1944
Switzerland			1999	1992	1942
U.K.					1982

Source: Adapted from Waaldijk 1999 with permission.

Note: Unlike Waaldijk, I imply no argument about the progressive development of rights with the ordering of this table.

[a]New South Wales

[b]South Australia.

[c]Ontario.

[d]Quebec.

For others, international developments deflect the concern about being the first jurisdiction to recognize same-sex partnership toward the dangers from historical judgment at being last. As one activist testified in Hawai'i,

> In the world today, the national assemblies of Brazil, the Nether-lands, France and Finland are currently debating and deciding the issue. Iceland, Sweden, Norway, Hungary, Denmark and Green-land have bestowed some sort of legal relationship upon which their same-gendered couples enjoy varying degrees of inclusion. Proposals have been submitted to the Parliaments of Italy and Bel-gium. Discussions on marriage-like arrangements are now taking place in Lithuania. Municipalities and territories within the United States, Spain, Italy, France, Belgium and Australia allow for lim-ited domestic partnerships. The Supreme Court of New Zealand is about to hear that nation's first test of their marriage laws. The leg-islatures in Canada and Australia are watching the outcome of the legal wranglings here. South Africa's new constitution expressedly [sic] forbids discrimination based upon sexual orientation. . . . Ladies and Gentlemen of this committee: You stand poised at the door to include the next group of citizens full protection and inclu-sion within realm of the law [sic]. You also stand poised to close that door. In twenty or thirty years, we, as a nation, will look back and wonder what all the commotion was about, and your actions today will frame how you are remembered in that struggle for equality.[22]

Future remembrance is linked to forms of historical judgment about the past in these debates as well. As a published letter framed this concern just days before the amendment vote in Hawai'i,

> I grew up in postwar Germany, a country burdened by an enor-mous sense of collective horror and guilt as the magnitude of Hitler's policy of discrimination became known. Worse, I grew up in an environment of deep national shame. This is not an experi-ence I would want for Hawaii, whose traditional culture has always been inclusive. Hawaii must vote "No" on the constitu-tional amendment.[23]

The avoidance of "national shame" in this argument situates Hawai'i's sovereign choices before the scrutiny of the world while raising to respectability its traditional cultural roots.

For others unwilling to accept this inclusive meaning of tradition, the important fact of international comparison is that marriage has been an incontrovertible limit to the recognition of lesbian and gay rights. As the Alaska legislature emphasized in a brief to the state's supreme court in the *Brause* case, "No nation of the world permits same-sex marriage today. None."[24] Hawai'i's attorney general made a similar argument to the court following the 1996 trial in which the state argued that same-sex marriage would create conflict for children. It cited the laws of Scandinavian countries that allow domestic partnership but deny the adoption of children or restrict joint custody in order to "give more value to marriage."[25] Articulating marriage as a distinct right, not analogous to other civil rights, permits international debates over same-sex marriage to be read in terms commensurate with those of the local venue.

> Hawaii voters should note that lawmakers in France, one of the most permissive societies on earth, thwarted the proposal to give legal status to unmarried couples. . . . Many members of the French Parliament . . . said the bill was an embarrassment and dismissed the measure. . . . Community groups feared it implied approval of gay marriages. . . . We need to be equally alarmed as the people of France and *not* approve same-sex marriages.[26]

In the argument that sauce for *l'oie* is sauce for the gander, the international realm continues to haunt the local. The expressed notion in this letter that French policy was an "embarrassment" floats to consciousness the centrality of international respect to the sovereign imagination.

Although limits to adoption have been a feature in Scandinavian recognition of same-sex partnerships prior to 1999, making contrasts to Denmark and Sweden commonplace in the rhetoric of opponents of same-sex marriage, the Vermont plaintiffs turned these legal deficiencies to their advantage by citing the state's past history of ignoring this international limit.

> As the State has noted, the Scandinavian countries that do extend marital rights to same-sex couples (Sweden, Denmark, and Nor-

way) withhold access to adoption and reproductive technology from such couples. . . . Given that Vermont already protects the procreative and parenting rights of same-sex couples, this limitation on the marriage rights of same-sex couples in the Scandinavian countries is inapposite.[27]

The argument to neutralize the marital exceptions through Vermont case law supported other claims in the plaintiffs' briefs that the Vermont court would not be acting to uphold marriage rights without precedent because of the recognition of same-sex partnership in Scandinavian law. Indeed, the Vermont Supreme Court agreed with the plaintiffs, even though the outcome of this analogy was ultimately an obstruction to their aims. In the final ruling of *Baker v. Vermont,* the court held that because Vermont's legislature had removed legal barriers to adoption by same-sex couples, the state's contentions that marriage should be reserved for heterosexuals because of the unique relationship between biological parents and children, and the claim that Vermont shared "a long history of official intolerance" of same-sex relationships, were "patently without substance."[28] At the same time, the court held that the relief sought by the plaintiffs was not necessarily marriage. Making reference to (but, explicitly refusing an endorsement of) Hawai'i's proposed comprehensive domestic partnership act,[29] and those of Denmark, Norway, and others, the court held,

> Plaintiffs are entitled under [the common benefits clause] of the Vermont Constitution to obtain the same benefits and protections afforded by Vermont law to married opposite-sex couples. We do not purport to infringe upon the prerogatives of the Legislature to craft an appropriate means of addressing this constitutional mandate, other than to note that the record here refers to a number of potentially constitutional statutory schemes from other jurisdictions. These include what are typically referred to as "domestic partnership" or "registered partnership" acts, which generally establish an alternative legal status to marriage for same-sex couples.[30]

For Justice Denise Johnson, concurring with the finding but dissenting from the remedy, the majority "declines to give [the plaintiffs] any relief other than an exhortation to the Legislature to deal with the problem."[31] Only marriage could provide "prompt and complete relief" to the plaintiffs and render a legal decision untainted by the "political caldron"[32] of the legislature.

Avoiding the political caldron that was stirred in Hawai'i, Alaska, and elsewhere throughout the United States since the *Baehr* decision is, for the *Baker* majority, a task "significantly insulated from [a] reality"[33] that intrudes across state boundaries and permeates political sovereignty. Here, the *Baker* majority opinion can be read as an institutionally sensitive account of the limits of courts to affect social policy, and specifically as a latter-day judicial revaluation of the "separate but equal" policy rejected by the activist Warren Court forty-five years before in *Brown*. From this perspective, the majority's explicit invocation of the Scandinavian solution demonstrates the ways in which the political imperative of judicial restraint is legitimated and stabilized by an internationalist account. By projecting the problem of a porous sovereign, the court simultaneously imagines a particular form of governmentality: a universalist technology informed by the failures of the Hawai'i and Alaska courts and the successes of European experiments, capable of resolving political demands without need for sovereignty embedded in local constitutional authority and civil rights law.

Judicial reliance on the exigencies of international sovereignty entails a particular form of forgetting. The contingency of social context and legal experience that informs the sovereignty of a particular people to "be first" in their legal rights appears flattened and diffuse as nations are made to appear spatially distinct and historically synchronous in global space with compatible technologies of social rule that take the "first" out of legal innovation and make policy respectable. Two aspects of social history are lost in this articulation. The first is the suppressed idea that every country, every jurisdiction, retains a similar consciousness of the synchronous, horizontal field of international relations that limit demands on the sovereign from "below." The second is related to the first. The demands on the sovereign by particular subnational groups—here, of lesbians and gay men—are simply dissolved in the national imaginary. These forgotten aspects of international analogy raise particularly stubborn and important questions of the adequacy of comparative analysis, apparent in an examination of the Scandinavian cases.

"Registered partnership" was first established in Denmark in 1989 and later spread to Norway (1993), Sweden (1995), and Iceland (1996).

Registered partnership has been considered by some to be a working separate-but-equal alternative to same-sex marriage, evidence that "the sky hasn't fallen" (Spedale 1998) and proof that public hostility can reach consensus. As the Hawai'i Commission on Sexual Orientation and the Law framed it in their advocacy for comprehensive domestic partnership, "when Denmark passed a national domestic partnership law the majority of the people were against it, but now the law is generally accepted."[34] Under the terms of the Danish Act of Registration of Partnership, "the registration of a partnership shall have the same legal effects as the contracting of marriage,"[35] and "the provisions of Danish law pertaining to marriage and spouses shall apply similarly to registered partnership and registered partners,"[36] subject to several exceptions. Those exceptions include a lack of pension rights for registered partners, no provision for adoption rights or joint custody of a child of one of the partners, and an exemption from recognition in international law as well as the requirement, specific to registered partnerships and not marriage, that one partner be a Danish citizen.

The limit drawn on the inclusion of children in registered families was a particular compromise to avoid heated conflict with the Danish Lutheran Church, which was opposed to same-sex marriage (Sloan 1997, 206ff.). Scandinavian attitudes toward adoption are different from American attitudes for reasons not reducible to Christian morality, however. Because foster families are subsidized by well-endowed Scandinavian welfare states, there is little need for the legal fiction of adoption, which, in the case of the United States, is prized for reprivatizing the costs of children no longer cohabiting with their natural parents (Maxwell, Mattijseen, and Smith 1999). The long tradition of extensive social rights in these countries makes it less likely that particular rights will be interpreted on an economic grid, one with significant international consequences. Nonetheless, if the national political economy disfavors Scandinavian adoption, the failure to extend this arrangement to lesbian and gay partnerships becomes an even more significant symbol of exclusion (Sloan 1997).

The case of immigration restrictions is decidedly different. There can be little economic reason to disallow registered partnership for non-Danish couples, and this restriction is not imposed on opposite-sex couples who wish a Danish marriage. The provision of the law that limits the rights of same-sex partnerships under international treaty likewise values concerns about international legitimacy over the purely internal rights accorded Danish citizens. The exclusions from parity with the laws of marriage have significant meaning for lesbians and gays, very few of whom have actually opted for registration (table 3)—a condition not unlike that in Hawai'i under the RBA. Evidence from the Netherlands, which initiated a Scandinavian-style registered partnership status in 1998, suggests that 80 percent of registrants would have chosen marriage if it had been available and 62 percent would convert to married status when full rights were offered. The most frequent reasons given for these desires were "full equality" and the idea that "Marriage has more significance" (Scherf 1999, reported in Waaldijk 1999). As Waaldijk (1999) has noted, the popularity of registered partnership among opposite-sex couples in the Netherlands suggests that significant differences between the statuses are perceived. Partly in response to demands for equality, Dutch law was changed to

TABLE 3.   Registered Partners in Europe

Country (population in millions)	Period	Total	Female-Female	Male-Male	Male-Female
Denmark (5.3)[a]	10/89–12/90	746	173	573	
	1992	218	87	171	
	1994	197	92	105	
	1996	199	93	106	
	1998	197	113	84	
Total		2,372	874	1,498	
Norway (4.4)[b]	8/93–12/94	294	91	203	
	1996	127	47	80	
	1997	118	43	75	
Total		674	232	442	
Sweden (8.8)[b]	1995	333	84	249	
	1997	131	52	79	
	1998	125	46	79	
Total		749	241	508	
Iceland (0.27)[a]	7/96–12/97	33	17	16	
	1998	12	7	5	
Total		45	24	21	
Netherlands (15.7)[b]	1/98–3/99	5,217	1,487	1,860	1,870

Source: Adapted from Waaldijk 1999 with permission.
[a]Population in 1997.
[b]Population in 1998.

recognize same-sex marriage, including rights to adoption or "joint-authority" over any children in 2001. The World's first legal marriages between same-sex couples were performed in Amsterdam at the stroke of midnight on March 31.

Canada serves as another reminder of the power of international sovereignty and the ways in which rights of lesbians and gays are diminished under the gaze of other nations. Despite a dynamic politics surrounding a set of key court cases on same-sex partnerships across the country, Canada has played a somewhat subdued role in the American debates, perhaps not surprising considering the rather small shadow cast by Canada across the insular American cultural landscape. Nonetheless, the loss of Canadian tourism was frequently depicted by opponents as the cost of same-sex marriage in Hawai'i, reinforcing the notion that the eyes of international judgment were fixed on the state and its people.[37] Only the Vermont plaintiffs used the Canadian experience to bolster their claims for extended rights. Citing *Rosenberg v. Canada*, a case in which the Ontario Court of Appeal struck down a law providing tax benefits to private pension plans restricting survivor benefits to spouses of the opposite sex, the plaintiffs quoted an argument from the case that was accepted by Justice Johnson in her concurrence and dissent:

> [G]roups that have historically been the target of discrimination cannot be expected to wait patiently for the protection of their human dignity and equal rights while governments move toward reform one step at a time. If the infringement of the rights and freedoms of these groups is permitted to persist while governments fail to purse equality diligently, then the guarantees of the [Canadian] *Charter* [of Rights and Freedoms] will be reduced to little more than empty words.[38]

Even though Canadian courts may have leaped two steps at a time, same-sex marriage still seems elusive. These limits are instructive to those seeking handy analogies to American lesbian and gay hopes.

Canadian struggles for lesbian and gay rights were furthered in the 1970s by attempts to establish protection for sexual orientation in provincial and national human rights codes that define and prohibit discrimination in public and private sectors. While early court cases were unsuccessful in securing benefits for same-sex partners and establishing protections against employment discrimination for lesbians and gays,[39] coalitions of lesbian, gay, feminist, civil libertarian, union, disabled, and other groups organized and struggled successfully for antidiscrimination language protecting sexual orientation in Ontario in the mid-1980s and in other provinces in the early 1990s.[40] The advent of the Canadian Charter of Rights and Freedoms in 1982, especially section 15, which guarantees "equality before and under the law"[41] and which came into effect in 1985, propelled a concerted effort at litigation targeting governmental legislation deemed discriminatory. In a series of cases throughout the 1990s backed by New Democratic Party (NDP) governments in British Columbia and Ontario, "litigation organizations" began to attack dominant and exclusionary statutory notions of family or spouse in the courts with growing degrees of success.

For example, in *Egan v. Canada* (1995),[42] two men living together since 1948 who were denied spousal Old Age Security benefits because they were not an opposite-sex couple sought relief under section 15 of the Charter. The court ruled that their treatment was discrimination since sexual orientation—while not explicitly included in the Charter— was an "analogous ground" to those enumerated grounds prohibited by section 15. Nonetheless, the court found this discrimination to be constitutional.[43] In *Vriend v. Alberta* (1998),[44] the court "read in"[45] to the Alberta human rights legislation protection for sexual orientation after the province—the last in Canada to resist—refused to amend its statutes in light of section 15 case law, leaving a professor who was fired solely on account of being gay without provincial recourse. Finally, in the decade's most impressive victory for gay rights, *M. v. H.* (1999),[46] the Canadian Supreme Court addressed the case of a lesbian who sued her former partner for support and an equitable division of property. The court held that the exclusion of same-sex cohabitants from the protections of the Ontario Family Law Act that regulates claims for spousal support of opposite-sex couples violated the Charter. Under *M. v. H*, the definition of spouse, and statutes addressing the rights of spouses both married and in common law, must now be read in to include same-sex couples.

M. v. H. promoted a dramatic rewriting of the law of equal protection. The day following the decision, the province of British Columbia introduced omnibus legislation to recognize same-sex spouses, and several weeks later the provincial parliament of Quebec *unanimously* acted to amend thirty-nine statutes and regulations in order to recognize same-sex partnerships. Other provinces acted to consider similar action. Despite the justices' arguments that the holding in *M. v. H.* "does not challenge traditional conceptions of marriage"[47] and "has nothing to do with marriage *per se*,"[48] the Canadian parliament was not so sure. Less than three weeks after the decision, the House of Commons adopted a resolution 216 to 55 that "Marriage is and should remain the union of one man and one woman to the exclusion of all others, and that Parliament will take all necessary steps to preserve this definition of marriage in Canada."[49] Unlike the amendments in Hawai'i and Alaska on which this resolution could have been modeled, attitudes in the Canadian public did not reflect this legislative sentiment. Fifty-three percent of Canadians, and as much as 61 percent in Quebec, supported same-sex marriage in a survey taken days after the spousal-equality decision was announced.[50] The courts appear to have had ample opportunity to secure popular support for a broader decision.

In addition to walling itself from the marriage debates, the *M. v. H.* holding was purchased at a second cost from the perspective of gay rights advocates. Spousal equality litigation had long enjoyed support from Canadian unions, which—unlike in Hawai'i—helped articulate the issues in these cases as matters of benefits to be bargained with employers (Findlay 1997; Gavigan 1999, 142ff.; Herman 1990, 809; Hunt 1999; Peterson 1999; Rayside 1998, 151). As one plaintiff recalled,

> Within unions, the support for [sexual orientation protection] has been strong. Unionists understand the old credo that "an injury to one is an injury to all." They understand that you cannot negotiate a *collective agreement* and leave out a significant percentage of your bargaining unit. Before anyone else, both the national office of the Canadian Union of Public Employees and my Local 1996 provided me with invaluable financial and moral support. Working people know that the so-called "fringe benefits" are no longer "fringe." In fact, they represent an increasing percentage of the shrinking wage. It was my experience that, with only a little bit of coaxing, unionized people understood denying the lesbian and gay worker family or spousal benefits represented a different job rate for equivalent jobs, and undermined solidarity. In short, it threatened everyone.[51]

Union support in British Columbia and in Ontario, especially in conjunction with majorities of the NDP, promoted early antidiscrimination legislation in those provinces (Casswell 1999; Rayside 1998). Yet, as Boyd (1996, 1999), C. Young (1997), Stychin (1995b), and others have recently argued, the articulation of same-sex equality as benefits raises important questions about who bears these costs that can limit its political utility. Rather than resonating as a claim for political equality, spousal benefits are often "privatized" within the family by powerful materialist discourses. This privatization infuses the majority opinions in the *M. v. H.* decision, which measure the value of same-sex spousal recognition by its function of "alleviating the burden on the public purse to provide for dependent spouses," a "pressing and substantial" objective.[52] By legitimating same-sex spousal recognition for reducing costs to society, Boyd has argued that the claim of sovereign inclusion that they purport actually reproduces hierarchy and normalization in the discursive light of social and economic security.

> [T]he incorporation of lesbians and gay men within family law may be as much about the domestication of deviant sexualities within a safe, useful and recognisable framework than about the transformatory confounding of normative sexualities. . . . For instance, in *M. v. H.*, although heteronormativity *was* . . . challenged, the ways that the legal arguments had to be formulated meant that the potentially disruptive lesbian subject was absorbed back into familiar roles and, to a large extent, her disruptive potential was displaced. In many ways the dominant relations of production and ruling were reproduced by . . . equality arguments: the role of the family in absorbing social costs of dependency and social reproduction was explicitly reinforced. (1999, 378, 381)

Without acknowledging what Boyd calls the "complex intersections between family, sexuality, poverty and capitalism" (381), spousal rights are a partial victory, and "full equality" an unlikely consequence of legal action.

The "domestication of deviant sexualities" because of threats to the public purse in the Canadian political context can be taken from another angle to reflect a globalization of economic insecurity and the importance of the international horizon to what might appear from the outside as purely autonomous concerns. Costs to the Canadian state resulting from individual impoverishment that stems from the dissolution of family relationships put the state at a competitive disadvantage with other capitalist states. Balanced against the costs of sovereign rights, the governmentalized concern about the place of Canada in the international political economy subordinates the recognition represented by equal rights to the recognition due between sovereigns. As a metric of what is possible to achieve with legal recognition, Canada and Scandinavia are in sovereign positions little different than what might be experienced by Hawai'i or Vermont. As analogies, therefore, perhaps these nations' experiences with rights for same-sex partners work well. But they will also work as a limit to union whose basis in social discourses rather than liberal sovereignty remains too often unacknowledged.

Conclusion

The use of analogy to promote same-sex marriage for gays and lesbians is designed to flatten the perception of difference, a cognitive leap perceived to be necessary to think the unity of the sovereign. Yet, as the campaign in Hawai'i and elsewhere demonstrates, the common sense of analogy is dependent upon exclusive, essentialized, and historicized comparisons made authoritative by distant horizons drawn from the discourse of sovereignty's own concern for "equal respect" of one sovereign in the eyes of others (a fraternity of sovereigns circularly premised upon gender and race hierarchies implicit in the very idea of fraternity—see Cooper 1998, 33ff.). Difference and conflict reemerge when the international/interjurisdictional relations that are called upon to stabilize this complex chain of signifiers are interrupted by social discourses raising the competitive uncertainties of a globalized political economy and the hierarchies inherent in military security. These discourses have cemented historical, essentialized categories rather than challenged them, yielding for gays and lesbians no more than the old pre–civil rights equation between separate facilities and equal treatment.

Analogy works mainly by bracketing relevant conflict, and for civil rights struggles this poses a keen paradox. Butler argues that

> the problem of unity or, more modestly, of solidarity cannot be resolved through the transcendence or obliteration of this field, and certainly not through the vain promise of retrieving a unity wrought through exclusions, one that reinstitutes subordination as

the condition of its own possibility. The only possible unity will not be the synthesis of a set of conflicts, but will be a *mode of sustaining conflict in politically productive ways,* a practice of contestation that demands that these movements articulate their goals under the pressure of each other without therefore exactly becoming each other. (1998, 37)

Butler's admonition to forsake analogy for an embrace of political and social difference as the only basis for unity underscores the losses of a campaign in which gays, when visible at all, were caricatured and homogenized rather than allowed to speak in their diversity.

These exclusions had significant effects in the postcolonial Hawai'i context. As a Hawaiian lesbian professor recounted a year following the amendment campaign,

It has been thirty years, but my parents still think I am a lesbian like all haole lesbians are on TV, you know. But this is the thing that keeps repeating over and over again in my work with gay men of color: our families think that we are white. You know, you can't think you are a lesbian and not be white. So you are either a betrayal to your race or you are an oreo or you are doing something weird. But you are not what we know to be our daughter. . . . Gay is constructed as white, and the campaign looked so white. I think the idea [that] gay equals male, equals white, equals middle class . . . is a problem for a lot of our families here. So constructing a campaign around what looks primarily like a white, gay-male, mainlandized agenda can't just fit into what everybody wanted. The missed opportunity was not doing more of a cultural spin that emphasized what is right, what is pono [just, legitimate] about the initiative, what is pono about life here. We should really think about what is right. And what is right is you don't denigrate your family members. You don't talk stink about people. . . . And you don't use religion to foment hate here. . . . So I feel that what happened on the POC side was not really taking the opportunity of just showing people in relationships, all of us.[53]

Postcolonial relations—whether understood as haole identities serving as signs for the diversity of cultural life, or as the gaze of international relations that created local self-consciousness—failed to be opened to scrutiny in the careful avoidance of social and family diversity. However, these features of contemporary life in Hawai'i continue to hold a significant potential for resuming the kinds of social conflict that Butler sees as being politically productive.

One missed opportunity was perhaps to seek analogies on new terms borrowed from the internationalism that emerged throughout the campaign. Certainly, the unique race relations of contemporary Hawai'i and the overlay of Christian gender and family relations explored in the previous chapter indicate that alternative constructions of identity and social conflict can be generated from deconstructing traditional identities through sensitivity to international historical events. While that did not prove to be politically successful, other analogies are suggested by the campaign. Perhaps most ignored has been alienage, which brings the international horizon close to home and which resonates deeply in a heavily immigrant culture. If the international horizon and the concern over "being first" is rhetorically deployed to stabilize essentialist identities, then alienage emerges as an interesting choice for demonstrating the need for legally protecting socially constructed, hence nonimmutable, identities. Added to a long national commitment to legal protections for religious practices and norms (both of which have lurked not far behind the stage of public culture in which same-sex marriage has been dramatized), analogies take on a very different hue.

A recent case from Oregon, *Tanner v. OHSU* (1998),[54] ordered health benefits be offered to same-sex partners of state employees on just this analogical basis. Rather than defining protection on the rationale of immutability—an essentialization that ignores historical and social constructions of race and gender—the Oregon Court of Appeals based its decision on precedent that protected individual choice as an expression of rights to conscience and moral freedom. The court wrote in its opinion,

> Both alienage and religious affiliation may be changed almost at will. For that matter, given modern medical technology, so also may gender. We therefore understand from [precedent] that the focus of suspect class definition is not necessarily the immutability of the common, class-defining characteristics, but instead the fact that such characteristics are historically regarded as defining distinct, socially-recognized groups that have been the subject of

adverse social or political stereotyping or prejudice. . . . Plaintiffs are members of a suspect class. Sexual orientation, like gender, race, alienage, and religious affiliation is widely regarded as defining a distinct, socially recognized group of citizens, and certainly it is beyond dispute that homosexuals in our society have been and continue to be the subject of adverse social and political stereotyping and prejudice.[55]

Seeing analogy in the protected legal categories that preserve freedoms of conscience may permit greater room for gays and lesbians to make claims for sovereign inclusion.[56] Linking inclusion to alienage demonstrates that liberal notions of equal treatment due the members of other sovereigns are as much a part of the international gaze as are limits to union. Further, the *Tanner* court's willingness to ground inclusion on the basis of adverse stereotyping rejects transhistorical categories for the local histories of social conflict faced by lesbians, gays, and others. However, even this alternative sovereign strategy continues to rely upon the national imaginary. Whether a globalized consciousness means rights must now be grounded in transnational appeals remains an unavoidable question.

Chapter 7

Conclusion—
the Mourning After

The struggle over same-sex marriage is a prism that splits citizenship and sovereignty. No longer seen in the white light and shadow of juridical relations, the demands for formal recognition on the basis of private lives has refracted citizenship into its many governmentalized components—the discursive spectrum of the new sovereign. Debates over same-sex marriage have revealed the privilege of citizenship to be as much about civil rights as it is about economic surplus, national security, the values of civilization, and the construction of temporality (tradition) and of space (the nation). In efforts to expose or rebuild these boundaries, citizenship has been articulated in its overlapping and countervailing civil, political, social, cultural, sexual, and intimate dimensions.

The exposure and manipulation of these myriad dimensions of citizenship has made for a new common sense. If this has precluded same-sex marriage in Hawai'i and Alaska, it is just as evident in civil union legislation now in place in Vermont. As midnight ushered in the month of July 2000, Kathleen Peterson and Carolyn Conrad exchanged vows and became the first same-sex couple to be recognized under the new civil union law in Vermont, followed shortly by couples from Massachusetts and elsewhere, demonstrating the appeal for some of this new legislation. Although these pioneers gained national media attention for their novel legal status, incurring some antagonism by those throughout Vermont and the rest of the country who were opposed to this experiment,[1] their status was neither subject to recognition by other states, nor relevant to the federal government's tax, immigration, or entitlement, policies as marriage would have been. The legal compromise that was proposed by the legislature in response to the *Baker* case, supported by the governor despite reelection threats,

upheld in a last-minute court battle pushed by eleven disgruntled legislators and several others seeking an injunction against the execution
of the law, had all the political hallmarks of a progressive civil rights
victory; and, indeed, there were many novel gains that were won. But
in significant ways, civil union remains ironically on the terrain of the
antimarriage activists. It recognizes same-sex relationships as something unique but lesser, entitled to fewer benefits than marriage. In this
regard, it seeks to reduce the power and context of state action, to
decrease the political ambit in which citizenship is imagined, and to
pull out of the political caldron the atavistic rabbit of separate-but-
equal social policy.

The limitations of Vermont's civil union legislation as well as the
failures in Hawai'i and Alaska to realize same-sex marriage telegraph
that the discourse of sovereignty, in its many revealed dimensions, is
more than a simple marker for the ambivalence between majority rule
and individual right by which James Madison first characterized
American political culture. The politics of sovereignty is no longer an
unreflective sign for the state and its institutional configuration (if it
ever really was), but is now discursively implicated in the construction
of the limits of state power itself. Moving one dimension beyond the
Madisonian dilemma, the debate over the state is more than simply an
institutional choice between majority rule (legislatures) and individual
right (courts), but what the fundamental relationship between society
and state will look like and how this interaction will be regulated. The
emerging common sense values a state that is limited in its ambit, ironically thought to accomplish more when it does less. The juridical con-
traction of the state has left many late-twentieth-century notions of civil
rights beyond reach, stranding such groups as lesbians and gays whose
citizenship claims are redeemed—if at all—at the cost of legitimating
this larger retrenchment.

The politics of sovereignty perhaps makes engagement with the
myriad revealed dimensions of citizenship inescapable for lesbians,
gays, and their supporters today, which raises central questions about
progressive politics and legal mobilization. Some of these questions are
foundational to the sociolegal disciplines, for example, whether winning in the courts makes a significant difference in social attitudes and
personal liberties; how rights languages are made malleable and mobilized by various groups; and whether the declaration of legal right

enhances progressive political possibilities. Nonetheless, these familiar questions do not always go far enough. Using law as the independent variable against which to measure social change forces us to dichoto-mize law and society in ways that can substitute analytical categories for political and historical developments. This rather liberal division misses, for example, several illiberal features of law that this book has explored in the previous chapters: for example, the particular means by which sovereignty is no longer invested in the juridical moment; the ways in which law is partially valorized and resisted (or *demobilized*), depending on the social identity of the legal subject; and the manner in which courts have been displaced by numerous other loci of constitu-tional authority. In addition, law has emerged in illiberal ways in the same-sex marriage debates as a sign of popular authority, as a marker of civilization appropriate to competition within a neoliberal world econ-omy, and as a badge of respect for other sovereigns and the anxiety related to legally "going first" and possibly out of turn. Traditional soci-olegal questions may tend to play down these new contexts in which rights operate, overly privileging the structural consequences of legal rights: their abilities to obfuscate social gains or to leverage solidarity.

Work on legal mobilization—which has had an important influ-ence on this book—has downplayed these structural concerns by high-lighting how central social, cultural, and organizational contexts are to the meaning and efficacy of rights (Herman 1994; McCann 1994; Milner 1986). Yet mobilization studies have often only weakly comprehended how rights are resisted and how broad structural changes in social and political context transform meaning about rights. Bringing this context forward demands attention to the paradoxical qualities of rights mobi-lization and demobilization. One paradox is that while rights claims are articulated as a prepolitical demand—a plea for inclusion into a politi-cal community so that politics can begin anew—rights claims require a political underpinning on which to be heard. As Wendy Brown has argued, rights are always attendant upon "the historically and cultur-ally specific ground of the demand for them" (1995a, 12) making them hardly the depoliticizing force their subjects argue on their behalf. In the case of same-sex marriage, this paradox has had important tactical consequences for civil rights supporters who have had to contend with vast majorities assembled on the basis that their rights detract from the social and cultural benefits of the democratic community. Politicizing

rights as foundational to citizenship increasingly demands more concrete claims about fiscal and cultural security as sovereignty is no
longer seen as a purely juridical category.

A second paradox is one of subject formation: rights are productive in that they create expectations, interests, and identities, as well as
constrain opportunities, but they can also lead to identities and interests that outpace them. This is not only true of traditional subjects of
civil rights, but also of majorities whose identities are formed in opposition to civil rights. Rights preserve some measure of self-sovereign
autonomy but also discipline the subject and create novel avenues of
resistance. For lesbians and gays this has produced debates over the
very meaning and importance of marriage as an institution compatible
with distinct community values at the same time that it has encouraged
mobilization to seek this novel right as a sign of and guarantor of civic
inclusion. In Vermont, the institutionalization of civil unions has also
raised questions about how well the universal premise of rights serves
to guarantee the recognition of and continued mobilization for citizenship. Majorities, too, are disciplined by their own opposition to further
civil rights as their claims for sovereign control over social policy innovations often revert to identities as the truly oppressed and most in
need of rights protections. This inversion of privilege binds majorities
to the neoliberal perspective of scarcity and zero-sum liberties.

On the basis of these paradoxes, Foucault has cryptically gestured
toward the importance of a new form of right, one that acknowledges that

> sovereignty and disciplinary mechanisms are two absolutely inte-
> gral constituents of the general mechanism of power in our society.
> If one wants to look for a non-disciplinary form of power, or
> rather, to struggle against disciplines and disciplinary power, it is
> not towards the ancient right of sovereignty that one should turn,
> but towards the possibility of a new form of right, one which must
> indeed be antidisciplinarian, but at the same time liberated from
> the principle of sovereignty. (Foucault 1980b, 108)

What this right might look like is an open question, one certainly not
yet apparent in the tactics and strategies of civil rights supporters and
their detractors. Yet, overcoming the ancient right of sovereignty seems
to be simultaneously a necessary, and perhaps already impossible,
task. Sovereignty has been both solidly reinstituted in the contempo-

rary governmentality and simultaneously transformed in ways that make it less likely to uncritically encompass all rights demands. Perhaps Foucault's hope for liberation from sovereignty must be won through a different set of sociolegal questions and tactics that take new forms of sovereignty seriously, while striving to develop something politically fresh.

In these concluding pages I want to pursue this hunch and ask a set of slightly different questions inflected from the perspectives of sovereignty and governmentality raised in the previous chapters. If new languages of sovereignty and the identities that have coalesced around them have characterized the opposition to rights enacting same-sex marriage, is it possible to embed rights in this new sovereignty? That is, can these majorities opposed to same-sex marriage and gay rights be held accountable to those whose demands for citizenship have provoked this sovereign formation? What arguments might make a political difference? Are there new forms of citizenship and political identity that can escape the pull of an antirights sovereignty?

A New Context for Rights?

Domestic partnership seems an enticing place to begin such an analysis. In Hawai'i and Vermont, the struggles for marriage rights have not achieved the original goals of the plaintiffs and their supporters. Yet domestic partnership legislation has emerged from this litigation, either as a weakened by-product of political maneuvering (Hawai'i) or as a declared right in the form of civil union (Vermont). Is domestic partnership a duty of majorities opposed to marriage, and can it be compelled from those opposed to gay rights? For many same-sex marriage advocates in Hawai'i, this has been acknowledged as the consolation prize for years of struggle for same-sex marriage. Securing this reward has been a consequence, first, of the discursive reality of same-sex marriage, regardless of the political tally of support. For some gay rights activists in Hawai'i, this discursive reality was reinforced as much by DOMA and the local politics of opposition—both of which acknowledged the likelihood of extended marriage rights—as it was by *Baehr*. As several activists recounted in interviews,

> In the late 1980s, when I first brought up [the goal of domestic partnership and same-sex marriage], no politicians thought about it.

But other people had been thinking about it, but it was always just a marginal consideration. Whereas now I think the whole idea that gay relationships be recognized is a real threat in everybody's mind if they are opposed, and a real potential in everybody's mind if they're for it. That's a big difference.[2]

[Despite the anti-*Baehr* amendment,] we're better off. Not immediately. This is a pretty whipped [gay, activist] community. It's hard to organize right now. . . . We haven't really recovered yet. . . . The reason why I think we're better off is because I think that, like [plaintiff's attorney] Dan Foley points out, there really now is a whole lexicon for this issue. We now talk about same-sex marriage.[3]

Talk about same-sex marriage both constitutes sovereign communities and inconveniences majorities who at least temporarily must relinquish their privilege of silence. The aftermath, according to some activists, is a politically productive sense of guilt.

The weird thing is the [gay and lesbian] community is in many ways better off. Legally we're worse off, because now there's a constitutional fence around us. But, in fact, because of the way we conducted this campaign, a lot of middle-of-the-road liberal people who stood on the sidelines were deeply embarrassed. They're deeply embarrassed by this. And so, for example, we just had a major vote by the Episcopal Church of Hawai'i . . . [to the effect that] gays and lesbians are due full participation in all aspects of church life. That wouldn't have happened a year ago. And so I think that the reservoir of guilt and shame is now working its way through certain levels of society.[4]

For some activists, playing off the guilt and shame can be leveraged to secure domestic partnership and to induce the support of reluctant political allies.

The last two times I've been into [U.S. Representative Neil Abercrombie's] office he talked forever. I went there last March. My boyfriend at the time and I were in there, and he talked to us for two and a half hours. This last time I went in [with a fellow activist] she said, "That man is so guilty he can't stand it." That's a good thing. We were just talking about hate crimes. He starts talking about marriage. We weren't there to talk about marriage. But we listened to him. He just said, we need to do this and that. [She] just put it out and said, "We don't want domestic partnership. We want marriage because it just represents full equality." He listened.[5]

Discourse about gays and lesbians initiated by same-sex marriage litigation is seen by some activists as politically beneficial not just because of the psychopolitical restoration of bad conscience, but also for the ways that the salve of domestic partnership undermines the defense of traditional marriage. As one activist framed this position,

> From a strategic point of view, religiously conservative people . . . take stands that intrinsically damage their social position. The conservative wing of the Catholic Church fought the domestic partnership law [Hawai'i's Reciprocal Beneficiaries Act] tooth and nail. And they dragged it out for probably a year and a half. . . . For all the maneuvering they did and the twisting and turning, they ended up making the new domestic partnership available to heterosexual couples. . . . So exactly the thing they don't want—alternatives to marriage for heterosexuals—is what they created by their opposition, by refusing to give marriage to gay people. Exactly what they didn't want, which is alternative forms of marriage, different standards for marriage, alternative models for the relationships between men and women, they managed to make available. . . . I mean, you couldn't have created an outcome more desirable to modifying, weakening, or transforming [society], and they've done it themselves. They did it by refusing to allow traditional marriage to be granted to gay people.[6]

If this paradox ultimately weakens the sovereign position while giving gays and lesbians some of what they ask for, this sovereign insecurity also fuels a fear of a broadly amplified politics that will redouble the efforts in Hawai'i and Alaska at the national level. As this same activist cautioned, "I think Hawai'i has now shown us that the religious Right is quite capable of amending the U.S. Constitution. Amending the Constitution is actually easier; it's not a vote of the people, it's a vote of the legislature. And those people are too fearful to be cautious."

It is this very fear of a nationwide mobilization against gay rights, one perfecting strategies deployed in state contests in order to modify the national Constitution, that points toward the progressive limits of rights demanded from this new sovereign. Although domestic partnership might still be a possible outcome of constitutional limits to same-sex marriage, this consolation prize could no longer be seen as a temporary rest stop along the linear path toward full equality; it would erect, instead, the more permanent edifice of "separate but equal" status. Anticipating these limits, some activists in Hawai'i see the need to pursue a policy less focused on sexual citizenship. Instead, strategies that envision delinking marriage from public policy—what some have called individualization (Waaldijk quoted in Donovan, Heaphy, and Weeks 1999)—permits greater attention to the provision of social benefits and stronger association with other social movements, while avoiding the hierarchies implicit in the family. Yet the individualization approach cannot stand outside the sovereign terrain, especially where that landscape is altered by the infusion of neoliberal discourses into sovereign identities, a governmentality that has made entitlements to social benefits commensurate with civil rights and devalued both for perceptions of limited governmental resources and heightened economic competition.

Claiming the Neoliberal Commons

The neoliberal dimension to governmentalized rights revealed in this study of same-sex marriage politics has important implications for debates over the specificity of lesbian and gay rights. Nancy Fraser's (1997) argument that gays and lesbians require recognition as a remedy for cultural injustice, but not economic redistribution, has created an industry of scholarly thought on the place of the economic in struggles over gay rights. Fraser's point is not that lesbians and gays do not suffer material disadvantage; rather, the source of their disadvantage is fundamentally cultural.

> Sexuality . . . is a mode of social differentiation whose roots do not lie in the political economy because homosexuals are distributed throughout the entire class structure of capitalist society, occupy no distinctive position in the division of labor, and do not constitute an exploited class. Rather, their mode of collectivity is that of

a despised sexuality, rooted in the cultural-valuational structure of society. From this perspective, the injustice they suffer is quintessentially a matter of recognition. Gays and lesbians suffer from heterosexism: the authoritative construction of norms that privilege heterosexuality. Along with this goes homophobia: the cultural devaluation of homosexuality. Their sexuality thus disparaged, homosexuals are subject to shaming, harassment, discrimination, and violence, while being denied legal rights and equal protections—all fundamentally denials of recognition. To be sure, gays and lesbians also suffer serious economic injustices; they can be summarily dismissed from paid work and are denied family-based social-welfare benefits. But far from being rooted directly in the economic structure, these derive instead from an unjust cultural-valuational structure. The remedy for the injustice, consequently, is recognition, not redistribution. (Fraser 1997, 18)

Important responses have been made to this assertion by Judith Butler (1998), Susan Boyd (1999), Iris Young (1997), and Anne Phillips (1997), arguing that the redistribution/recognition dualism has misleading political implications.

Butler, for example, has argued that the material/cultural binary is hierarchical, privileging the material while relegating gay and lesbian issues to the ghetto of the "merely cultural." The family, in her analysis, is both the locus of gender reproduction and a central concern for the capitalist economy.

[C]ontra Fraser, struggles to transform the social field of sexuality do not become central to political economy to the extent that they can be directly tied to questions of unpaid and exploited labour, but also because they cannot be understood without an expansion of the "economic" sphere itself to include both the reproduction of goods as well as the social reproduction of persons. (1998, 40)

Following Althusser, Butler locates the family as a material apparatus of the capitalist mode of production and political struggles over the exclusion of lesbians and gays as "a specific operation of the sexual and gendered distribution of legal and economic entitlements" (41).

The politics of sovereignty surrounding same-sex marriage suggests that Fraser's analytical distinction between recognition and redis-

tribution is too simple a key to help unlock strategic options for lesbians and gays. Fraser has amplified her point in arguing that "the
principle opponents of gay and lesbian rights today are not multinational corporations, but religious and cultural conservatives, whose
obsession is status, not profits" (1998, 146). As this study of same-sex
marriage has shown, it is conservatives who have repeatedly turned to
neoliberal arguments, supported by states and by corporations worried
about the fiscal impact of civil rights, in order to build broad political
majorities and restrict the benefits of citizenship through heterosexual
visions of the family. While Fraser's point that economic inequality
must be addressed in the interest of social justice has validity, the
obsession with profits of those seeking status in the opposition to gay
rights suggests that it is at this very site that arguments about redistribution are necessary.

Butler, too, falls short from the vantage of this political controversy. Although she is right that economic distribution and cultural
recognition are deeply enmeshed, this entanglement is not a necessary
consequence of the mode of production. This abstraction of the political
economy is, as with Fraser, too simple to account for the dynamics of
neoliberal reform. Neoliberal arguments are successful today because
they help make sense of the particular forms of dislocation and insecurity brought about by the transitions away from industrial capitalism
and toward a governmentality accounting for a political economy
embracing the vagaries of an unregulated transnational production.
Opposition to lesbian and gay rights can be seen, then, less as a factor
in the mode of production and more as an aspect of the various modes
of consumption (Aglietta 1979) vying for dominance, and their particular consequences for political and legal authority.

The important point here is that the historical terrain of capitalism
is not fixed and that struggles over political inclusion might be enabled
by an engagement with capitalist institutions as well as governmentalized discourses of citizenship. If the demand for marriage can no longer
be voiced as a simple liberal claim for equality and justice (as it perhaps
once was in the miscegenation controversy), but has now become a necessary struggle to redefine the meaning of marriage within an idiom of
scarcity and a subjectivity of responsible and entrepreneurial citizenship, then progressives may have much to borrow from transformative—though not necessarily revolutionary—discourses of political
economy. These discourses allow the powerful and valid argument of

the traditionalists—that the economy as presently constituted does create scarcity impinging on public and private institutions alike—to be acknowledged and then transcended. The nuclear family so valued by conservatives is tied historically to the period of industrial Fordism in the 1930s and 1940s in which regularized work habits and increasing productivity were seen to be enhanced by stable families that could contain preindustrial urges and enhance consumption (Gramsci 1971; Nicholson 1997). Progressive post-Fordist economic metaphors and narratives now seek to embrace a new vision of the postcentrality of work (because of diminished opportunities), new forms of flexible workplace relations including the loss or marginalization of contract, and newly crafted ideas of appropriately supportive workers associations in order to escape the resentment associated with the zero-sum rights logic of the politics of scarcity (Lipietz 1994; Rathke and Rogers 1996; Rifkin 1995; Rogers 1995).

Allies of this vision can articulate a new functional and moral discourse for families and social institutions that exploits some potential contradictions between sovereignty and economy in contemporary governmentality. At the heart of that vision stands the commitment to neoliberal economic citizenship endowing the economic subject with rights to flexibly craft relationships for purposes of production, consumption, reproduction, and affection. As postindustrial corporations borrow new identities for employees and loyal consumers alike grounded in the ideology of "family" (Casey 1995), so too progressives might exploit such articulations and assert them against the discourse of scarcity. Legal rights and public prosperity can potentially be fused in such an articulation, while flexibility can resist the dangers to some (especially queer) identities from limiting acceptable social forms to legalized models. At the same time, such a move might offer an antidote to the common sovereign analogy between gay "lifestyle" and the anarchy of hyperindividualism by demonstrating other models of care and acceptable forms of love. Discursively, this may succeed to reincorporate sexual minorities into common ideas of citizenship, or at the very least, promote change by "reconstituting . . . the affiliations of 'ordinary people'" (Bower 1994, 1030), through a lessening of antagonism to the rights claims of gays and lesbians.

This strategy of engagement with economic discourses does not seek an alternative to republican notions of responsible and restrained citizenship; rather, it acknowledges that the liberal citizen asserting

natural and human rights and due an abstract equality has little political appeal today. This alternative strategy must also presume that,
along with the declining salience of abstract rights amid a surging sovereignty politics, there will be few "natural" allies on which to count for
support. This study has shown how neoliberal and neocolonial discourses have been deployed to impede political association among lesbians and gays, labor, indigenous, and corporate groups by weakening
the appeal of civil rights and social justice. And yet, progressive attention to issues of economic justice and more public discussion of the economic good of marriage and family diversity that might reestablish an
alliance are also likely to underscore the class and gender particularities often obscured by the claim that marriage rights provide the key to
full citizenship, thus exacerbating new tensions. As Wendy Brown sees
this problem, once the fiction of middle-class "normalcy" is abandoned, political leverage is also weakened.

> If there is one class which articulates and even politicizes itself in
> late modern US life, it is that which gives itself the name of the
> "middle class." . . . [T]his is not a reactionary identity in the sense,
> for example, that "White" or "straight" are in contemporary polit-
> ical discourse. Rather it is an articulation by the figure of the class
> which represents, indeed depends upon, the naturalization rather
> than the politicization of capitalism, the denial of capitalism's
> power effects in ordering social life, and the representation of the
> idea of capitalism to provide the good life for all. Poised between
> the rich and poor, feeling itself to be protected from the encroach-
> ments of neither, the phantasmatic middle class signifies the nat-
> ural and the good between, on the one side, the decadent or the
> corrupt and on the other, the aberrant or the decaying. It is a con-
> servative identity in the sense that it semiotically recurs to a phan-
> tasmatic past, an idyllic, unfettered and uncorrupted historical
> moment (implicitly located around 1955) when life was good
> again—housing was affordable, men supported families on single
> incomes, drugs were confined to urban ghettoes. But it is not a
> reactionary identity in the sense of reacting to an insurgent politi-
> cized identity from below: rather it precisely embodies the ideal to
> which non-class identities refer for proof of their exclusion or
> injury: homosexuals who lack the protections of marriage, guaran-

tees of child custody or job security, and freedom from harassment. . . . Without recourse to the White, masculine, middle class
ideal, politicized identities would forfeit a good deal of their claims
to injury and exclusion, their claims to the political significance of
their difference. (1995b, 206–7)

The abandonment of middle-class injury might lessen the claims that
can be made upon new sovereigns by making it tactically less appealing and points up the problem that any given identity risks the dangers
of normalization through its politicization. The rights of citizenship are
likely to emerge as partial, class-bound, and particular. Same-sex marriage may still be attractive as a goal, but likely one of many tactics
designed to strengthen the position of working-class lesbians and gays,
of homosexuals of color, and the like.

This prismatic fragmentation of the political subject and the
simultaneous recognition that there is unlikely to be one universal
policy goal such as same-sex marriage that can recombine the spectrum of citizenship claims suggests the potential for a different model
for legal mobilization than that experienced in Hawai'i. Shane Phelan's notion of a politics of affinity (introduced in chapter 4) that seeks
to replace an ethnic model of identity politics with a willingness to
organize in overlapping and sometimes contradictory dimensions,
that acknowledges the inherent limitations of "unity," and that can
promote rather than quell discourse about difference illustrates this
type of strategy. While affinity politics need not turn away from
rights, it seeks to move beyond coalition by respecting boundaries
only when they are politicized. Thus, rather than asking labor unions
for support and seeking commitments from Native Hawaiian groups
for a vote on the amendment, affinity politics might orient campaigns
toward a development of common identities not colonized by governmentalized notions of rights, citizenship, "labor issues," or "sovereignty issues." The payoff of such alternative strategies is, perhaps,
not immediate; it is unlikely to have made a significant difference in
the Hawai'i campaign if only because the organization of forces in
favor of same-sex marriage was defensive, and fought on the
timetable proposed by their opponents. Nonetheless, the possibility
of lingering affinities after the election that can engage the new sovereign majorities would be enhanced.

Citizenship beyond Sovereignty

The reliance on affinity politics to engage with, rather than subsume, social hierarchies and differences in the struggle over sexual citizenship takes aim at the exclusionary boundaries and silences redrawn by a politics of sovereignty. The mobilization against same-sex marriage has constituted a public sphere in which the values of reason and republican restraint have been contrasted with irrationality, especially the inappropriate, uncontrollable, and uneconomical passions signaled by lesbians and gays who ask for equal marriage rights. The resulting spatial distinction between public and private realms is as much a sexual divide as a gender division, not just limiting appropriate topics for the public sphere and the private sphere to heteronormative forms of expression, but also differentiating between active and passive citizenship that maps a valued duty to civic reason and rights to dependency and passion. In the attempt to banish inappropriate civil rights demands and repair the privacy of the closet, this sovereign discourse has also drawn a broad horizon for its authority, seeking its recognition not just among the assent of "the people," but also in the international community where sovereigns mutually recognize each other.

These various spatial valences that make citizenship an exclusionary discourse can be undone, Carl Stychin suggests, by a sexual politics that seeks to allow rights and citizenship to "retain an unruly edge" (1999, 13). One manner in which this is accomplished is to take seriously the international spaces of sovereign recognition. Stychin has shown that in the case of the European Union, the public demand for social rights challenges the valences of the active/passive and public/private dichotomies, as it is the bearer of European social rights who actively asserts a broader context of belonging than the limits of national sovereignty would otherwise permit. At the same time that the assertion of citizenship claims by gays and lesbians seeking a broader basis for equal protection in the European context extends beyond traditional boundaries, it also revalues the private sphere as a separate space enhancing distinctive political identities and practices.

The present study of same-sex marriage augments this work by showing that the neoliberal concern about global competition that has been used to draw the limits to union continues to boost the significance of international civil rights developments for local liberties even without formal institutions recognizing pan-national forms of citizenship. International affinities are therefore significant; a single recognition of same-sex marriage might alter the insecurity of sovereigns going first, to the competitive disadvantage of being last. In the American context, economic citizenship holds the potential to work against forms of exclusion, retaining its unruly edge. In Hawai'i, so might a citizenship articulated on the basis of cultural self-determination in which Native Hawaiian spaces provide opportunities not just to revalue heteronormative sexuality, but also to recognize the dependency inherent in economic citizenship in a tourist economy.

The fragmentation of political spaces and of citizenship discourses does not eliminate the disciplinarity attendant upon the public sphere. Demands for same-sex marriage are, to some unavoidable degree, demands for a normalization of social relations—demands that could as easily become a right to marriage as they could devolve to a normalized institution of "separate but equal" legal relations, as they have in Vermont, or a failure of any significant legal status, as occurred in Hawai'i. To provoke meaningful change, citizenship discourse has no choice but to move inexorably against such normalizing moments and seek new tactics, new affinities, and new uses for rights language in the process. What the politics of marriage has joined together, continually must be torn asunder.

Foucault has suggested that the family provided the original model for modern governance based on a relaxation of sovereign control and the deployment of "social" mechanisms of power that are discursively organized with an economic concern for populations and political economy. Today, the family has reemerged as the focus of a new sovereignty in which "family values" provide the hub around which revolve a panoply of political, cultural, and economic issues: abortion, sex education, and prayer in the schools, gay rights, media decency, lowered social spending. The rule of law and the authority of court-ordered protections for civil rights can no longer slip easily beneath this encrustation of the social to pry it out of the way. Because this new sovereignty has drawn its boundaries with its own neoliberal and republican vision of civil rights—as an aggrieved majority deserving protection from the courts, as the guardians of economic and moral security threatened by excess rights, as the venerator of "true" civil rights in opposition to falsity and duplicity—it is increasingly difficult to assert liberal claims on law as the protector of discrete and insular minorities. The lessons of Alaska, Hawai'i, Vermont, and elsewhere are not lost upon those who value these social and economic ends. Whether they can now be seized by progressives is the historical question.

Notes

Chapter 1

1. *Baehr v. Lewin*, 74 Haw. 530 (1993). The case became *Baehr v. Miike*, reflecting the changing names of the directors of the state department of health.

2. 28 USC 1738C (1996).

3. The Alaska amendment, also passed with 69 percent approval, overturned *Brause v. Bureau of Vital Statistics*, Alaska 3AN 95–6562 Civ. (1998), which recognized a right to same-sex marriage based upon an equal right to privacy that sustained the liberty to choose one's life partner. That amendment read, "No provision of this constitution may be interpreted to require the state to recognize or permit marriage between individuals of the same sex." I address the *Brause* decision at greater length later in the chapter.

4. The original plaintiffs were Ninia Baehr and her partner, Genora Dancel; Tammy Rodrigues and her partner, Antoinette Pregil, and Pat Lagon and his partner, Joseph Melillo.

5. U.S. Constitution, Article 4, section 1.

6. See *Singer v. Hara*, 11 Wash. App. 247 (1974); *Jones v. Hallahan*, 501 S.W.2d 588 (1973) (Court of Appeals of Kentucky).

7. Act of June 22, 1994, No. 217, section 1 (p. 526), 1994 Haw. Sess. Laws. Act 217.

8. *Brause v. Bureau of Vital Statistics*, J. Peter Michalski.

9. Alaska's Proposition 2 added a sentence to the state constitution: "To be valid or recognized in this state, a marriage may exist only between one man and one woman." The language of the amendment was fought out in a protracted court battle led by the plaintiffs who ultimately succeeded in striking a second sentence from the ballot measure. That sentence would have added, "No provision of this constitution may be interpreted to require the State to recognize or permit marriage between individuals of the same sex." The supreme court ruled that that language might be construed in the future to "seriously interfere with important rights." See *Bess v. Ulmer*, S-08811/s-08812/S-08821, Alaska Supreme Court, 18 September 1998, esp. at 6–7.

10. Chittenden (Vt.) Superior Court, S1009–97CnC (1997), J. Linda Levitt.

11. The Hawai'i Supreme Court ruled, in effect, that the amendment took the state's statute limiting marriage to couples of the opposite sex outside of the purview of the constitution's equal protection clause, depriving the plaintiffs of a remedy and mooting the case. Untouched by this final ruling was the ques-

tion of whether other forms of relief short of marriage were compelled by the equal protection arguments of *Baehr* upheld in the trial. *Baehr v. Miike,* 910 P2d 112 (Haw 1996), remanded and reversed (994 P2d 566 (Haw 1999)).

12. *Baker v. Vermont* 744 A2d 864 (Vt. 1999), 886.

13. See ibid., at 43.

14. In 1998, the Missouri Supreme Court overturned the state's 1996 ban, leaving thirty-two states with statutes or constitutional language restricting marriage to opposite-sex couples as of the first half of 2000.

15. Gordon B. Hinckley, president of the Church of Jesus Christ of Latter Day Saints, speaking at the 169th Annual General Conference, 2 October 1999, AP Wire Services.

16. Ronald S. Carlson, letter to the *Honolulu Star Bulletin,* 6 December 1996. This sentiment was supported by the State of Hawai'i in its continuing opposition to the legal protection for same-sex marriage. In a brief filed with the state supreme court in 1997, the attorney general wrote, "Quite simply, the People of Hawai'i continue to refuse to affirmatively sanction and approve homosexual marriages, and thus to achieve an equal footing with the heterosexual marriages that have always been the bedrock of civilization." State of Hawai'i Reply Brief, appeal from the final judgment of *Baehr v. Miike* before the Hawai'i Supreme Court, Civil Case 91-1394–05, filed 16 June 1997.

17. Written testimony of Marga Stubblefield submitted to the Hawai'i House Judiciary Committee Hearing on Same-Sex Marriage, 21 January 1997, Honolulu.

18. *Loving v. Virginia,* Chief Justice Warren, 388 U.S. 1, 12 (1967). *Loving* ruled antimiscegenation laws unconstitutional, an analogy that has been drawn by the Hawai'i courts and other scholars and activists as appropriate for the case of same-sex marriage. I address this analogy later in the chapter.

19. Sodomy statutes, which were once ubiquitous in the United States, have been rapidly repealed or struck down. Since 1962, twenty-five states have abolished their sodomy statutes. Courts in seven states have had their statutes struck down by their high courts since 1980. Four states (Georgia, Maryland, Montana, and Tennessee) have declared their statutes unconstitutional since Hawai'i's same-sex marriage case was announced. The Georgia case struck down the statute that was upheld as a state prerogative by the Supreme Court in *Bowers v. Hardwick,* 478 U.S. 186 (1986), which I address later in this chapter. Five states continue to apply sodomy charges to same-sex acts (Arkansas, Kansas, Missouri, Oklahoma, and Texas). Sodomy laws, ostensibly applicable to same-sex or opposite-sex partners, remain on the books in Alabama, Arizona, Florida, Idaho, Louisiana, Michigan, Massachusetts, Minnesota, Mississippi, North Carolina, Puerto Rico, South Carolina, Utah, and Virginia (where it remains punishable by twenty years imprisonment).

20. Popular articulations of this *kulterkampf* include Bennett 1993; Schmidt 1997; Sowell 1984, 1998, 1999. See also the critical assessments of Herman 1997; Patton 1998; Valdes 1998, 1426ff. A judicial perspective can be found in Justice Scalia's dissent in *Romer v. Evans,* 517 U.S. 620 (1996), 134 L.Ed. 2d 855 at 868 (1996).

21. The names of groups opposed to same-sex marriage proclaim the imperative of this new sovereignty unmediated and undelayed by governmental institutions such as legislatures or courts: Take it to the People in Vermont and Hawai'i's Future Today and Save Traditional Marriage '98 in Hawai'i.

22. Consider these famous words from the Declaration of Independence, "We hold these truths to be self-evident, that all men are created equal, that they are endowed by their Creator with certain unalienable Rights, that among these are Life, Liberty and the pursuit of Happiness.—That to secure these rights, Governments are instituted among Men, deriving their just powers from the consent of the governed . . . "

23. See *Reitman v. Mulkey,* 387 U.S. 369 (1967) and *Hunter v. Erickson,* 393 U.S. 385, which struck down these popular reactions against civil rights laws in California and Akron, Ohio, respectively. See also the discussion by Keen and Goldberg (1998, 111–13).

24. This unusual constellation of national sovereign power seems rather extraordinary in light of contemporary attempts to contain other perceived minority threats. Consider, by example, how the use of anti-immigrant sentiment—supporting national sovereign power—has been used to reinforce nativist and anti-Latino/a policies such as document checks and English-only legislation.

25. Yang (1999) shows an increasing support for antidiscrimination protection for lesbians and gays (employment, housing), acceptance of gays and lesbians in the military, and for marriage during the 1990s (which nonetheless remains very weak, approximately one-half the amount of support for other antidiscrimination measures). However, he also finds increasing partisan polarization over the issue of lesbian and gay rights, and no growth in the majority sentiment disapproving of homosexuality. Support for lesbian and gay rights is still low when compared to support for racial minorities and women.

26. Donzelot explains this notion of the social in his genealogy of the family: the social "appear[s] to be rather the set of means which allow social life to escape material pressures and politico-moral uncertainties; the entire range of methods which make the members of a society relatively safe from the effects of economic fluctuations by providing a certain security—which give their existence possibilities of relations that are flexible enough, and internal stakes that are convincing enough, to avert the dislocation that divergences of interests and beliefs would entail" (1979, xxvi). See also, on the use of the social in contemporary governmentality, Burchell 1996; O'Malley 1996; and Rose and Miller 1992. This book extends these arguments by reconsidering the important place of the sovereign in contemporary governance.

27. Constable (1993), Fitzpatrick (1999), Dillon (1995), and others have shown that Foucault was strikingly ambivalent about law and sovereignty. Although he is famously noted for suggesting that sovereignty is an inadequate basis for theory ("in political thought and analysis, we still have not cut off the head of the king" [1980a, 88–89]), at the same time he saw that with governmentality "the problem of sovereignty is made more acute than ever" (1991,

101). However much sovereignty is distinguished from law, Fitzpatrick has argued that there remains a theoretical interconnection: "Law as state law and law as governmentality are simply [not] the same. There is, rather, a relation of apposition between them. The constituent limits of each come from their mutual inviolability, from a certain mutual opposition in the face of their similarity to each other. The element of alterity between them is set in the opposed character of each being a condition for the distinct identity and operation of the other. Each takes on that which operatively remains of the other but is incompatible with the other's self-presentation as pervasive. . . . In their alternation, the relation between state law and governmentality becomes one of mutual dependence in which they are integral to each other yet necessarily opposed. One constituently limits the other to a distinct space yet sustains a claim of that other to be unlimited" (1999, n.p.). In this book, I further the exploration of this interrelationship. My goal is to restore our recognition of the importance of sovereignty without losing its interconnections to the vastly complex political world we inhabit.

28. The words are those of Justice Harlan Fiske Stone's famous fourth footnote in *Carolene Products*, 304 U.S. at 152 n. 4, whose argument was adapted by Ely (1980), Chief Justice Earl Warren, and others.

29. Justice Brennan did argue unsuccessfully for treating gays and lesbians under the heightened scrutiny doctrine, giving some idea of how that might look. In a dissent from a denial of a writ of certiorari in 1985 he wrote, "[H]omosexuals constitute a significant and insular minority of this country's population. Because of the immediate and severe opprobrium often manifested against homosexuals once so identified publicly, members of this group are particularly powerless to pursue their rights openly in the political arena. Moreover, homosexuals have historically been the object of pernicious and sustained hostility, and it is fair to say that discrimination against homosexuals is likely . . . to reflect deep-seated prejudice rather than . . . rationality." *Rowland v. Mad River Local School District*, 470 U.S. 1009, 1014 (1985).

30. Nonetheless, Justice Blackmun speculated in *Hardwick* that equal protection questions about the state of Georgia's refusal to prosecute heterosexuals for sodomy might be relevant even "without having to reach the more controversial question whether homosexuals are a suspect class" (203).

31. For example, the justices wrote, "Proscriptions against [homosexual] conduct have ancient roots" (*Bowers v. Hardwick*, 191; J. White); "Condemnation of those practices is firmly rooted in Judeao-Christian [*sic*] moral and ethical standards" (196; C.J. Burger); "To hold that the act of homosexual sodomy is somehow protected as a fundamental right would be to cast aside millennia of moral teaching" (197; C.J. Burger).

32. Justice Antonin Scalia, dissent, *Romer v. Evans*, 517 U.S. 620, 642 (1996).

33. 163 U.S. 537 (1896).

34. 60 U.S. 393 (1856).

35. *Plessy*, of course, was decided after the Thirteenth, Fourteenth, and Fifteenth Amendments, and after the Civil Rights Acts of 1866 and 1875. Nonethe-

less, it was the failure of a political commitment to civil rights until the Second World War that marks these cases as pre–civil rights.

36. *Bowers v. Hardwick,* 191 (J. White).

37. The words are Justice Scalia's in dissent in *Romer v. Evans:* "Of course it is our moral heritage that one should not hate any human being or class of human beings. But I had thought that one could consider certain conduct reprehensible—murder, for example, or polygamy, or cruelty to animals—and could exhibit even 'animus' toward such conduct. Surely that is the only sort of 'animus' at issue here: moral disapproval of homosexual conduct, the same sort of moral disapproval that produced the centuries-old criminal laws that we held constitutional in *Bowers* . . . Coloradans are, as I say, *entitled* to be hostile toward homosexual conduct" (644).

38. Among many cases see most recently *Able v. US,* 155 F.3d 628 (2d Cir. 1998); *Thorne v. US,* 1998 U.S. App. Lexis 6904 (4th Cir. 1998), Certiorari Denied, October 19, 1998, 1998 U.S. Lexis 6700.

39. *Nabozny v. Podlesny,* 92 F3d 446 (7th Cir. 1996).

40. *Boutilier v. INS,* 387 U.S. 118 (1967).

41. Consider, for example, how the State of Vermont argued to that state's supreme court that gays deserve no protected class in that state's same-sex marriage case: "While the State concedes that homosexuals have been the subject of discrimination in the past . . . homosexual orientation is not a characteristic that is as readily determinable by third parties as race, gender or alienage. . . . There are conflicting scientific results as to whether sexual orientation is an immutable characteristic, as at least some genetic link, or is behavioral. . . . What is not debatable is the possible fluidity of any class premised upon sexual orientation. What would be the boundaries of such a class? Would having homosexual thoughts make one a homosexual? Would one or two experiences? . . . . Since the outward manifestations of homosexuality are not always apparent and can be hidden, individuals could choose to identify themselves by class status depending upon the situation. Homosexuals simply do not possess the type of clear, immutable traits that limn other suspect classes." State's Appeal Brief, *Baker v. Vermont* (1999). I address this concern with civil rights analogies further in chapter 6.

42. On remand in 1996, a trial court ruled in *Baehr v. Miike* that the state failed to reach that standard and that marriage licenses for same-sex couples should ensue. That ruling was appealed to the Hawai'i Supreme Court, which held in 1999 that the issue of marriage licenses was moot due to the passage of a constitutional amendment lodging jurisdiction for marriages in the legislature. The equal protection holding of the original supreme court decision was not disturbed, but its legal import is not yet clear. The chapters that follow open these legal and political developments to closer scrutiny.

43. As the majority noted in nearly mathematical symmetry with respect to the holding in *Loving,* "Substitution of 'sex' for 'race' and article I, section 5 [of the Hawai'i Constitution] for the fourteenth amendment yields the precise case before us together with the conclusion that we have reached" (*Baehr v. Lewin,* 582).

44. The Alaska legislature in that state's struggle over the wording of an amendment banning same-sex marriage demonstrated that these arguments continue to survive even to 1998: "[A]ll Alaskans retain the right to marry no matter what their gender or their sexual orientation. Homosexuals and lesbians have the same right to marry as other Alaskans; any one man and one woman may marry if they are of appropriate age and familial relation. Conversely, no man is entitled to marry any man and no woman is entitled to marry any woman regardless of their sexual orientation." Supplemental Brief of the Alaska Legislature, *Bess v. Ulmer.*

45. *Singer v. Hara; Jones v. Hallahan.* The argument-by-definition remains a common defense by states against same-sex marriage lawsuits today.

46. *Oncale v. Sundowner,* 523 U.S. 75 (1998).

47. Willi Paul Adams, quoted in plaintiff's brief to the Vermont Supreme Court, *Baker v. Vermont,* 1999.

48. *Brause v. Bureau,* n.p.

49. Gabin (1990, 91) quotes Walter Reuther, former leader of the UAW and the CIO during labor's heyday, who exemplifies labor's rejection of the pluralist strategy thusly: "If there is a special post for Negroes, then in all justice there should be a post at large for the Catholics, the women, the Jews, and the Poles and all the rest. That is not in keeping with democracy or true trade unionism."

50. For arguments skeptical of the strategies and tactics of marriage rights from within the lesbian and gay communities, see Cossman 1994; Ettelbrick 1992; Lehr 1999; Polikoff 1993; Robson 1997, 14ff.; Wolfson 1994, 581ff.

51. Narratives have been argued to be an important aspect of scholarship about lesbian and gay rights (Donovan, Heaphy, and Weeks 1999; Eskridge 1994; Fajer 1994; Plummer 1995; Valdes 1995; see also Abrams 1991; Delgado 1989; Williams 1987). I seek here to expand upon narratives by and about lesbians and gays in order to show the links between civil rights discourse and the politics of exclusion.

Chapter 2

1. This language is drawn from the text of Colorado Amendment 2.

2. Written testimony of Hazel Higa submitted to the House Judiciary Committee, 21 January 1997.

3. Mike Gabbard, president, Alliance for Traditional Marriage, speaking at a public forum on same-sex marriage, 20 October 1998, Honolulu. Transcript by the author.

4. Brief of Take it to the People, *Baker v. Vermont,* 1998.

5. Amendment 2 was initiated by the conservative organization Colorado for Family Values with the slogan, "No Special Rights." It passed on November 3, 1992, with a 53.4 percent majority and was successfully challenged in the state and later federal courts. It was immediately enjoined, and never took effect.

6. State of Colorado Appellant Brief, *Romer v. Evans.*

7. Ibid.

8. Ibid.

9. Written testimony of Peter Brandt submitted to the Hawai'i House Judiciary Committee Hearing on Constitutional Amendment Relating to Marriage, 17 January 1997.

10. Testimony of Debi Hartmann before the Hawai'i House Judiciary Committee Hearing on Constitutional Amendment Relating to Marriage, 21 January 1997.

11. Kealii Watson, letter to the editor, *Honolulu Star Bulletin,* 10 December 1996.

12. Consider the following exchange during oral arguments in an Alaska decision regarding the wording of that state's amendment banning same-sex marriage:

> THE COURT: What if there's a constitutional amendment out there that says no more Judiciary?
>
> MR. CLARKSON: . . . If the Judiciary were to tell the people no, you have to have a Judiciary, I think that would be flipping our Republican form of Government on its head. The people create the Constitution, the Constitution creates the form of government that we have. There may be some form of federal constitutional limitation on that, but within that parameter it's the people's prerogative to create the Constitution.

Official court transcript, oral argument, *Bess v. Ulmer,* 3AN-98–7776, Alaska 3d Cir. (Anchorage), 31 August 1998, 33–34.

13. State of Hawai'i, Commission on Sexual Orientation and the Law, *Report of the Commission on Sexual Orientation and the Law,* 1995, 43 (minority report).

14. State of Hawai'i Defendant's Brief, *Baehr v. Miike,* 10.

15. Written statement of Professor Lynn D. Wardle, entered as testimony in Hawai'i House Hearing on Constitutional Amendment Relating to Marriage, 17 January 1997, 12.

16. State of Vermont Defendant's Brief, *Baker v. Vermont,* 1998.

17. Ibid.

18. State of Colorado Plaintiff's Brief, *Romer v. Evans,* 1995, 13.

19. Ibid.

20. Ibid., at n. 29. See also the discussion of the popularity of this rhetoric of gay power in Keen and Goldberg 1998, 107ff.

21. Brief of "Equal Rights, Not Special Rights, Inc.," *Romer v. Evans,* 1995, at n. 8.

22. Robert Oshiro, letter, *Honolulu Star Bulletin,* 11 December 1996, A10.

23. State of Vermont Defendant's Brief, *Baker v. Vermont,* 1998.

24. Testimony of John Hoag, cochair of Hawai'i's Future Today, Hawai'i House Hearing on Constitutional Amendment Relating to Marriage, 21 January 1997.

25. Testimony before the Commission on Sexual Orientation and the Law in 1995 estimated anywhere from $149 million to $127 million in annual benefit from gays and lesbians traveling to Hawai'i to be married (*Report of the Com-*

mission on Sexual Orientation and the Law, 25). These figures were countered by conservatives who concluded that "it is more likely that Hawai'i's major industry, tourism, will be negatively affected, as the image of Hawai'i deteriorates from the aloha state to the gay honeymoon and wedding destination of the world" (ibid., minority report, 41).

26. State of Hawai'i Post-trial Brief, *Baehr v. Miike,* 8; emphasis added.

27. State of Vermont's Defendant's Brief, quoting *Dandridge v. Williams,* 397 U.S. at 487 (1970), *Baker v. Vermont,* 1998.

28. State of Colorado Plaintiffs Brief, *Romer v. Evans,* 1995, 28–30.

29. Brief of the Oregon Citizens Alliance, *Romer v. Evans,* at n. 3.

30. Ibid.

31. Brief of the Christian Legal Society, *Baker v. Vermont,* 1998. This argument was simultaneously enlarged at the federal level in the proposed Religious Liberty Protection Act, which would have "exempt[ed] religious exercise from [any interfering public] policy." 105 H.R. 4019 (1998). The RLPA was signed into law in 2000 as the Religious Land Use and Institutionalized Persons Act (Public Law 106–274), and now prevents land use regulations that "impose[] a substantial burden on the religious exercise of a person" (section 2 (A) 1).

32. The Mormon Church unsuccessfully sued to intervene in the *Baehr* case because of a concern that religious groups would be forced to sanction same-sex marriages or lose their "licenses" to marry "appropriate" couples. These concerns about church autonomy are also prevalent on the mainland. One petitioner, identified only as "A Child of Christ," wrote, "[M]y biggest concern of all is that [legalized same-sex marriage in Hawai'i] will lead to forcing churches to perform these ceremonies or lose their [tax-exempt] status." Email to Senator Avery Chumbley, 22 March 1997 (in possession of the author).

33. Unofficial transcript of oral arguments, *Evans v. Romer* (Colo. S. Ct.), May 24, 1993.

34. State of Colorado Plaintiffs Brief, *Romer v. Evans,* 1995, 30.

35. State of Hawai'i Post-trial Brief, *Baehr v. Miike,* 1996, 36.

36. Supplemental Brief of the Alaska Legislature, *Bess v. Ulmer,* 17–18.

37. State of Vermont Defendant's Brief, *Baker v. Vermont,* 1998.

38. States represented include Hawai'i, South Carolina, Pennsylvania, Alabama, South Dakota, Illinois, Arizona, Mississippi, Missouri, and Virginia. California withdrew its support for the "Sister States'" brief at the last minute. Utah experienced a fight between the Republican governor, Mike Leavitt, who supported the brief, and Democratic attorney general Jan Graham, who refused to sign on, fearing that this would weaken Utah's argument that the Defense of Marriage Act already nullified the consequences of individual states' decisions in the case of same-sex marriage. *Deseret News* (Salt Lake City) 20 June 1998, B4.

39. Sister States' Brief, *Baker v. Vermont,* 1998.

40. Supplemental Brief of Amici Curiae States of Alabama, California, Colorado, Idaho, Mississippi, Nebraska, South Carolina, South Dakota, and Utah, *Baehr v. Miike,* 1998, 3.

41. Unofficial transcript of oral arguments, *Evans v. Romer,* May 24, 1993.

42. Patricia Williams argues that American slavery was based on the legal idea that blacks lacked will or personality and that they are defined by "irrationality, lack of control, and ugliness" (1988, 11). The destruction of slave law erases some of the legal presumptions inhibiting the metaphysical assumptions of civil rights protection. See also Roediger 1991, 167ff., who argues that the Civil War allowed a new alliance around civil rights especially because slavery no longer was available as an alter against which the identities of white workers were formed.

43. Post-trial Brief, *Baehr v. Miike*, 1996, filed by Representatives Abinsay, Kahikina, Kanoho, Meyer, Stegmaier, Swain, Cachola, Ward, 9.

44. Colorado Appellant's Brief, *Romer v. Evans*, 1996.

45. This advertisement image marked a turning point in the campaign, with internal polls showing a jump from 56 to 61 percent support for the amendment. Author's interviews with Linda Rosehill, publicist and media strategist for Save Traditional Marriage '98, 17 February 1999, Honolulu; Barbara Ankersmit, Public Relations Coordinator for Protect Our Constitution and president of Qmark Research, 9 June 1999, Honolulu. I argue that the effectiveness of this advertisement has much to do with the ways in which children are imagined within the wider discourses of governmentality.

46. Defendant State of Hawai'i's Post-trial Brief, *Baehr v. Miike*, 1996, 31–32.

47. AJA voters make up nearly a third of the electorate and have long been the strongest supporters of the liberal wing of the state Democratic party. Polling and focus groups run by POC had shown that AJA women, in particular, were strongly receptive to the idea of civil rights and the linkage of same-sex marriage to the internment during the Second World War. I address the symbolism of AJA internment further in chapter 6.

48. Polling indicated that by November 1998, 27 percent of the electorate would spontaneously report they opposed the amendment because they did not trust the state legislature (figures obtained from Human Rights Campaign). This figure is comparable to the 29 percent of supporters who spontaneously reported that their religious beliefs would compel their vote.

49. *Honolulu Advertiser*, 25 October 1998, A22.

50. Supplemental Brief of Hawai'i's Future Today, *Baehr v. Miike*, 23 December 1998, 1–2.

51. Advertisement for Save Traditional Marriage, *Honolulu Advertiser*, 11 September 1998, A6.

52. Author's interview with David Smith, communications director for Human Rights Campaign and coordinator of Protect Our Constitution, 12 February 1999, by telephone; Ankersmit, interview.

53. J. S. Keali'iwahamana Hoag, *Honolulu Advertiser*, 10 May 1996, A18.

Chapter 3

1. Hawai'i Revised Statutes, sec. 572C (1997).
2. Hawai'i Revised Statutes, sec. 572C-2 (1997).
3. Ibid.

4. These included inheritance rights and survivorship benefits; health-related rights including hospital visitation, family and funeral leave, private and public employee health insurance, mental health commitment approvals; motor vehicle insurance coverage; jointly held property rights such as tenancy in the entirety and public land leases; legal standing for wrongful death, crime victims rights, and domestic violence family status; and some minor benefits related to the use of state facilities and state properties. Left unavailable, but attainable through marriage, were mutual support, divorce, child custody, and federal and state tax advantages and liabilities associated with marriage, most precluded by the Defense of Marriage Act.

5. Hawai'i Revised Statutes, sec. 572C-6 (1997).

6. See Progress nonprofit organization publication *Domestic Partner Listing*, <http://www.bayscenes.com/np/progress/dpb.htm>, (January 1998), and National Lesbian and Gay Journalists Association publication, *Domestic Partner Benefits*, <http://www.nlgja.org/programs/DP/Dpother.htm> (January 1998).

7. *Tanner v. Oregon Health Sciences University*, 161 Ore. App. 129 (1999). That decision is now under appeal by the state attorney general and was challenged by a referendum in June 1999 that was unsuccessful. The referendum was encouraged by legislators who perceived the court decision to "clear the way" toward same-sex marriages in Oregon. "Anti–Gay Marriage Measure up for First House Hearing," AP News Services, 25 May 1999.

8. Exceptions include Hawai'i (which I discuss later in the chapter); the cities of Austin, Texas, where voters passed an ordinance in 1994 nullifying the extension of benefits to city employees, and Minneapolis, where a court invalidated domestic partner benefits; and the District of Columbia, where Congress has refused to fund a domestic partnership law passed in 1992. In the private sector, only one high-profile company has rolled back benefits: Perot Systems.

9. Ed Vitagliano, "Why Boycott Disney?" *American Family Association Journal* (1997), reprinted <http://www.otherside.net/disnebct.htm> (January 1998).

10. Perot Systems used this rationale this year when it became the first corporation to eliminate benefits for partners of new hires. Its returning CEO and founder, Ross Perot, is quoted as saying, "Do we discriminate against people who are homosexual? No we do not. These organizations are very aggressive in trying to embarrass anybody that doesn't do what they want to do. It has nothing to do with homosexuality. If we made this benefit available to everyone living together in the same apartment the cost would be through the roof." "Perot Nixes Gay Partner Insurance," AP News services, 9 April 1998.

11. "Cardinal O'Connor Denounces Proposal on Domestic Partner Law," AP News Services, 25 May 1998.

12. Written testimony of Tom Humphreys, secretary of Alliance for Equal Rights, submitted to the Hawai'i House Judiciary Committee, 21 January 1997, dated 20 January 1997.

13. In contrast to Coleman (1995), Sunstein (1994a, 1994b), and others, Christensen has argued, "By no fair reckoning could it be said that any alterna-

tive status or combination of legal strategies now available or contemplated in the foreseeable future would bring to gay families the 'image' or 'likeness' of the bundle of rights and obligations that flow from legal marriage. . . . The family options open to gay people, by and large, are a 'sham' or 'pretense' compared to the marriage-centered family's rights" (1998, 1782). Even in his objections to such modernist developmental ideas, Christensen argues for the deep interconnections between contract and status.

14. As one advocate of domestic partnership recalls in a letter submitted for testimony before the Commission on Sexual Orientation and the Law, "Back in the late 1980s, I was one of the vocal advocates within Lambda's [Legal Defense and Education Association] civil rights roundtable for bringing marriage litigation. Now I am much less ardent on this score, since I am convinced that the marriage issue (like, probably, the military issue) can only be resolved in the realm of politics, not adjudication." Testimony of Arthur S. Leonard submitted 29 November 1995.

15. Louisiana Revised Statutes 9:272A (1998).

16. Hughes writes that the same-sex marriage debate as seen through the politics surrounding DOMA conflates the real and imaginary. Accepting this confusion (as does Baudrillard in his concept of the simulacrum) "moves [us] beyond the question of which forms of love are legitimate to a question of how legitimacy is negotiated and how we might affect that negotiation. It prompts simultaneous assessment of the existence of a real beneath the rhetoric and of the power of imagination to effect social change" (1998, 239–40).

17. Fitzpatrick (1995b) makes a similar and illustrative argument in his analysis of nationalism, in which the nation is seen as a universal category and attribute (everyone has a nationality) that is simultaneously dependent upon its particularities, including its differences from other nationalities.

18. Grossberg envisions this connection between family and state in his study of nineteenth-century domestic relations law in the following manner: "Under the sway of republican theory and culture, the home and the polity displayed some striking similarities. These included a deep aversion to unaccountable authority and unchecked governmental activism, the equation of property rights with independence, a commitment to self-government, a belief that individual virtue could prevent the abuse of power, and a tendency to posit human relations in contractual terms that highlighted voluntary consent, reciprocal duties, and the possibility of dissolution. Most important, the American family, like the republican polity, suffered from the uncertainties of sovereignty and from the pressures of democratization and marketplace values unleashed by the Revolution's egalitarian and laissez faire ideology" (1985, 6–7).

19. This organization has been influenced by R. B. J. Walker, whose discussion of sovereignty in the context of a critique of international relations has found similar patterns. Walker observes that "starting with quite diverse literatures and debates, the discussion has kept returning to several key themes: identity and difference, inside and outside, space and time. In this respect, the analysis parodies the binary oppositions that have been so evident in the most

familiar texts of the discipline. . . . [These categories] give some indication of how contemporary political thought and action are governed and disciplined by a specifically modern account of political identity, the account expressed most crucially by the principle of state sovereignty" (1993, 160).

20. See also Fraser 1998, whose debate with Butler nonetheless converges on the point that identity issues have significant bearing on material relations. With less scholarly precision, consider the divergent political conclusions of Jim Gordon, a candidate for South Carolina commissioner of agriculture. "We can't have farming based on Bob and Bob being married and a new definition of marriage. . . . American Christian values have encouraged farming. I see the cultural upheaval we're in right now as an attack against farming. The homosexual movement . . . needs to be reversed." "S.C. Candidate Takes on Gay Farmers," A.P. News Services, 19 May 1998.

21. Author's interview with Diane Kurtz, spokesperson for Save Traditional Marriage '98, March 1998.

22. Author's interview with John Hoag, board member and organizer of Hawai'i's Future Today and Save Traditional Marriage '98, January 1999, Honolulu.

23. Author's interview with Father Marc Alexander, cochair, Hawai'i's Future Today, March 1998.

24. Consider, for example, this expression of the meaning of the marriage case for citizenship made by one gay rights activist: "We now have the first legal decisions establishing that gay people are also protected by the constitution." Testimony of William Woods, executive director of Gay and Lesbian Education and Advocacy, before the Hawai'i House Judiciary Committee, 21 January 1997.

25. Author's interview with Bill Paul, spokesperson for Save Traditional Marriage '98, February 1998.

26. Alexander, interview.

27. This support was strongly Catholic and Mormon. The Mormon Church is strong in Hawai'i, but it was the national church in Utah that contributed most heavily, spending six hundred thousand dollars in the final weeks of the campaign alone. "Mormons Give Big to Fight Same-Sex," *Honolulu Advertiser,* 24 October 1998, A1.

28. Author's interview with Debi Hartmann, cochair, Hawai'i's Future Today, February 1998.

29. Hoag, interview.

30. Rosehill, interview.

31. Alexander, interview.

32. Written testimony of Frederick Rohlfing II before the Commission on Sexual Orientation and the Law, 25 October 1995, 11.

33. Author's interview with Janice Pechauer, chair and spokesperson for Save Traditional Marriage '98, November 1998.

34. Written testimony of Jim Hochberg, minority member of the Commission on Sexual Orientation and the Law, submitted to the Hawai'i House Judiciary Committee, 21 January 1997, dated 19 January 1997.

35. Kurtz, interview.

36. Pechauer, interview.

37. Paul, interview.

38. Alexander, interview.

39. Because the RBA was enacted to cover more than just gay and lesbian relationships, the governor refused to sign the bill, allowing it to become law without his signature. His act also symbolizes the claim that the RBA has leaped beyond its proper bounds.

40. Testimony of Mike Gabbard, chairman, Alliance for Traditional Marriage, before the Hawai'i House Judiciary Committee, 21 January 1997.

41. Kurtz, interview.

42. Alexander, interview.

43. Pechauer, interview.

44. Testimony of Rick Lazor before the Hawai'i House Judiciary Committee, 21 January 1997.

45. Written testimony of Tom Ramsey submitted to the Hawai'i House Judiciary Committee, 21 January 1997, dated 20 January 1997.

46. Written testimony of Owen-Pahl Greene submitted to the Hawai'i House Judiciary Committee, 21 January 1997.

47. Written testimony of Wayne Akana submitted to the Hawai'i House Judiciary Committee, 21 January 1997, dated 20 January 1997.

48. Written Testimony of Tracey Bennett submitted to the Hawai'i House Judiciary Committee, 21 January 1997.

49. Letter from Governor Pete Wilson to California Assembly, 11 September 1994.

50. Alexander, interview.

51. Author's interview with Rev. Bill Stonebraker of Calvary Chapel Honolulu, 21 October 1998, Honolulu.

52. Kurtz, interview.

53. Testimony of Marie Sheldon, member of the dissenting minority on the Commission on Sexual Orientation and the Law, before the Hawai'i House Judiciary Committee, 21 January 1997.

54. Archbishop John Quinn of San Francisco, *San Francisco Catholic*, October 1989, 7.

55. Testimony of Bishop Richard Lipka before the Hawai'i House Judiciary Committee, 21 January 1998.

56. Kurtz, interview.

57. Alexander, interview.

58. Advertisement, *Honolulu Advertiser*, 13 July 1997, A33.

59. Ibid.

60. Ibid. This argument has deep resonance with moral critiques of gay rights, as well. Consider the following quote: "When I listen to the arguments, you know, in favor of same-sex marriage and everything else, it is highly individualistic. Highly, you know, emphasizing the virtue of autonomy, and the notion of the common good doesn't come in. It is the same kind of dynamic I

see when people argue certain economic issues, you know. In terms of private property, you know, 'It is mine, I have a right to mine.'" Alexander, interview.

61. Author's interview with Peter Lewis, comptroller, Hawaiian Electric Company, 9 October 1998, Honolulu.

62. *HEI, Inc. et al. v. Lorraine Akiba (Director, Department of Labor and Industrial Relations, State of Hawai'i) and Reynaldo Graulty, Insurance Commissioner, State of Hawai'i*, Civil Case 97–913 in the United States District Court, District of Hawai'i, Complaint for Injunctive and Declaratory Relief, 11 July 1997, 6, 7.

63. Advisory opinion of the Hawai'i deputy attorney general Frances Lum for Attorney General Margery Bronster, to state senators Avery Chumbley and Matthew Matsunaga, 5 June 1997, 2.

64. This included complaints of vagueness, Fifth Amendment due process issues, and commerce clause challenges.

65. Consolidated Omnibus Budget Reconciliation Act of 1989 (COBRA), 29 U.S.C.S., sec. 1161 and the Employee Retirement Income Security Act of 1974, (ERISA) 29. U.S.C.S., sec. 1144.

66. Family and Medical Leave Act of 1993, 29 U.S.C.S., sec. 2611.

67. Declaration of Patricia Foley, *HEI. v. Akiba*, 4.

68. *California Hosp. Ass'n v. Henning*, 569 F. Supp. 1544, 1546 (1983) quoted in Schuler 1996, 783. The reference is to ERISA, 29. U.S.C.S., sec. 1144 (1974).

69. Broad preemption has been upheld in *Shaw v. Delta Air Lines*, 463 U.S. 85 (1983). However, legal exemptions to preemption have recently included alterations to health benefits by providers (*New York State Conference of Blue Cross & Blue Shield Plans v. Travelers Insurance Co.*, 115 S.Ct. 1671 (1995)). In addition, states (including Hawai'i) have demanded and received exemptions for some domestic relations laws (29 U.S.C.S., sec. 1144(b)(7) (1984)) and the Hawai'i Prepaid Health Care Act (29 U.S.C.S., sec. 1144(b)(5)(a) (1983)). Some commentators have begun to argue on doctrinal terms (Schuler 1996) and normative grounds (Hasencamp 1986) that the broad presumption of preemption has run its course, and that domestic partnership agreements should now be developed at the state and not local level (Berger 1991). Clearly, the Hawai'i RBA raises particularly novel issues, such as the creation of new statewide legal statuses and reliance on constitutional language about equal protection that might permit more exemptions to be drawn. What is most significant in this example is the Hawai'i attorney general's unwillingness to press the issue, and, of course, the legislature's unwillingness to rework the RBA to fit under federal guidelines.

70. State of Hawai'i Post-trial Brief, *Baehr v. Miike*, 1996, 36.

71. Campaign literature of State Representative Calvin Say, July 1997, reproduced in Plaintiffs Motion for Partial Summary Judgment, *HEI v. Akiba*, appendix A.

72. Hawai'i Attorney General Advisory Opinion 97–05, 14 August 1997, 6.

73. Twenty-eight active and twenty-six retired workers signed up for RB health plans, thirty of whom were ordered to repay a total of $14,500 on the basis of this opinion.

74. Consent Order, *HEI v. Akiba*, 26 September 1997, 3.

75. Judge David Ezra, transcript of proceedings, *HEI v. Akiba*, 26 September 1997, 10.

76. Statistics from the Hawai'i Department of Health, private communication with the author.

77. Lewis, interview.

78. "A Quiet Revolution," *Honolulu Star Bulletin*, 8 May 1998, A1.

79. Brochure for Save Traditional Marriage '98, Honolulu, 1998.

80. Author's interview with an unnamed activist with Hawai'i's Future Today, February 1998, Honolulu.

81. Ibid.

82. Focus group research made available to the author by Human Rights Campaign.

83. $3.11 million were spent on the same-sex marriage issue, predominantly by Protect Our Constitution ($1.59 million) and Save Traditional Marriage ($1.31 million). Overall, the campaign accounted for almost 37 percent of "special interest money." "Same-Sex Issue Cost $3.1 million," *Honolulu Star Bulletin*, 24 April 1999, A3.

84. Mike Gabbard, chair of Alliance for Traditional Marriage, Hawai'i, *Honolulu Advertiser*, 30 November 1998, B2.

85. Press Release of Mike Gabbard, chair of Alliance for Traditional Marriage, Hawai'i, 5 November 1998.

86. Mary Polly, letter to the editor, *Honolulu Star Bulletin*, 13 November 98, online edition.

87. Mary Polly, letter to *Honolulu Star Bulletin*, 16 January 1999, B3.

88. Randy Obata, communications director for Governor Benjamin Cayetano, letter to the editor, *Honolulu Star Bulletin*, 18 November 1998, A21.

89. "Unwed Partners Losing Benefits," *Honolulu Advertiser*, 20 June 1999, A1, A8.

Chapter 4

1. See *Honolulu Star Bulletin*, 12–15 October 1998.

2. *Public Access Shoreline Hawai'i v. Hawai'i County Planning Commission*, 79 Haw. 425, 903 P.2d 1246 (1995).

3. *Hawai'i AFL-CIO v. Yoshina*, 84 Haw. 374, 935 P.2d 89 (1997). Ballots marked "yes" totaled 163,869; ballots marked "no" totaled 160,153. More than 45,000 ballots were left blank on the question.

4. *Citizens for a Constitutional Convention v. Yoshina*, 140 F.3d 1218 (1998), cert. denied 119 S. Ct. 868 (1999).

5. Hawai'i Senate Judiciary Committee cochairman Avery Chumbley, quoted in *Honolulu Star Bulletin*, 8 April, 1998.

6. *Report of the Commission on Sexual Orientation and the Law*, 9–17.

7. *Baehr v. Lewin*, 560.

8. Written testimony of Rev. Brian Baker, Church of the Holy Nativity (Episcopal), submitted to the Hawai'i House Judiciary Committee, 26 October 1993.

9. Written testimony of ACCT [no explanation for acronym given] submitted to the Hawai'i House Judiciary Committee, 26 October 1993.

10. Unsigned facsimile of testimony submitted to the Hawai'i House Judiciary Committee, 26 October 1993.

11. Author's interview with Tom Ramsey, November 1998, Honolulu.

12. Refer to the more complete history discussed in chapter 1.

13. The words are those of AFL president Samuel Gompers and were spoken about the Clayton Antitrust Act of 1914, which exempted labor unions from antitrust actions under the Sherman Act. For a discussion of labor's early-twentieth-century attitude toward the law, see Dubofsky 1994 and Orren 1991.

14. Author's interview with David Smith, Communications Director of Human Rights Campaign, March 1999, Washington, D.C.

15. Most union leaders agree that the lack of consensus was the result of several high-profile union leaders who were facing reelection in 1998 and 1999 and who balked at support to avoid possible controversy.

16. Testimony of Debi Hartmann, chair of Hawai'i's Future Today, House Hearing on Constitutional Amendment Relating to Marriage, 21 January 1997.

17. Transmitted testimony of Scott VanInwagen, 19 January 1997, House Hearing on Constitutional Amendment Relating to Marriage, 21 January 1997.

18. Transmitted testimony of Janis Judd, 20 January 1997, House Hearing on Constitutional Amendment Relating to Marriage, 21 January 1997.

19. State's Post-trial Brief, *Baehr v. Miike*, 25 October 1996, 4.

20. Transmitted testimony of Vanessa Chong, coalitions coordinator, Coalition for Equality and Diversity and Clergy Coalition, dated 19 January 1997, House Hearing on Constitutional Amendment Relating to Marriage, 21 January 1997.

21. Transmitted Testimony of the Japanese American Citizens League, dated 20 January 1997, House Hearing on Constitutional Amendment Relating to Marriage, 21 January 1997.

22. Transmitted testimony of Patrick Taomoae, American Civil Liberties Union of Hawai'i, dated 18 January 1997, House Hearing on Constitutional Amendment Relating to Marriage, 21 January 1997, Honolulu.

23. Author's interview with Russell Okata, executive director of Hawai'i Governmental Employees Association, 13 August 1997, Honolulu.

24. Author's interview with Walter Kupau, financial secretary-treasurer, Carpenters and Joiners of America, United Brotherhood of Local 745, 6 August 1997, Honolulu.

25. *Hawai'i Carpenter* (Honolulu), October 1998, 11.

26. Testimony of University of Hawai'i Professional Assembly, House Hearing on Constitutional Amendment Relating to Marriage, 21 January 1997, Honolulu.

27. Author's interview with June Motokawa, president, Hawai'i State Teachers Association, 20 August 1997, Honolulu.

28. Author's interview with Karen Guinoza, president, Hawai'i State Teachers Association, 30 November 1998, Honolulu.

29. Memorandum to HSTA Leadership from Joan Husted, deputy executive director, 1 October 1998; emphasis added.

30. HSTA mailing, October 1998.

31. "Some Teachers Protest HSTA Endorsements," *Honolulu Star Bulletin*, 20 October 1998.

32. Letter of George Poliahu Jr. to *Honolulu Star Bulletin*, 20 October 1998.

33. Robert Blainey, letter to *Honolulu Advertiser*, 12 April 1997, A11.

34. Author's interview with Clyde Hiyashi, president of Hawai'i AFL-CIO, 13 August 1999, Honolulu.

35. Author's interview with James Rothschild, International Brotherhood of Electrical Workers 1260, 12 August 1999, Honolulu.

36. ILWU political advertisement run in *Maui News* and *Hawai'i Tribune Herald*, 28 October 1998.

37. Author's interview with Tom Aitken, former chair of the Youth and Human Civil Rights Committee of the Hawai'i State Teachers Association, 26 September 1997, Kona.

38. "Reporting to Our Members," published remarks of Ben Saguibo, business manager, Laborers' Union, in *Hawai'i Laborer*, September–October 1998, 2.

39. Ibid.

40. "Amending the Constitution—Why Church and Community Leaders Say Vote No," *Teamwork*, October 1998, 5.

41. Letter to the author from Peter Sturgis, editor of *Teamwork*, Hawai'i Teamsters and Allied Workers, Local 996, Honolulu, 10 August 1999.

42. Eighteen unions (out of 118) signed agreements with POC that allowed their names to be used on political advertisements. These included the Hawai'i State Teachers' Association (HSTA), Longshore and Warehouse (ILWU) Local 142, Teamsters Local 996, Machinists Union Local 1998, Machinists and Aerospace Workers Lodge 1979, International Brotherhood of Electrical Workers (IBEW) 1260, American Postal Workers Union, Hawai'i American Postal Workers Union, Musicians Association of Hawai'i Local 677, Theatrical Stage Employees Local 665, Marine Fireman's Union, Sailors' Union of the Pacific, Inlandboatmen's Union, Seafarers International Union of North America, Marine Engineer's Beneficial Association, Food and Commercial Workers International Union 480, National Association of Social Workers–Hawai'i Chapter, and University of Hawai'i Professional Assembly. Of these, only UHPA made a commitment prior to the summer of 1998. Several unions, including the Sailors and Machinists 1979, endorsed without extensive discussion, mistakenly explaining to me that this was the wish of the state AFL-CIO. The Inlandboatmen reported to me that their endorsement was for the constitutional convention only, which POC was also opposing. Only UHPA, HSTA, and ILWU conducted campaigns within the union in furtherance of their endorsements for same-sex marriage, although membership opposition, as in other unions in which official endorsed the campaign, remained significant.

43. See Rayside 1998, chap. 5, esp. 175ff. The CAW won collective bargaining agreements covering same-sex benefits and pensions with General Motors Canada in 1996, and through arbitration of a grievance on behalf of employees

with same-sex partners with Chrysler in 1998. The Canadian Union of Public Employees has also pushed hard for same-sex equality in the public sector.

44. CAW, "Statement on Working with Pride," 1998, <http://www.caw.ca /departmts/workingwithpride.html> (September 1999).

Chapter 5

1. Because Hawaiian is an official language of the state of Hawai'i, I do not italicize Hawaiian words. Italicization and diacritical marks or their lack have been reproduced in quotations in accord with the original authors' intentions.

2. Warner (1999, 82) and author's communication with another leading linguist and historian of Hawai'i, Dr. Noenoe Silva of the University of Hawai'i. This interpretation is not at all esoteric. The *Report of the Commission on Sexual Orientation and the Law* noted, "The Commission also listened to Christian testimony that incorrectly interpreted the State motto, 'Ua Mau Ke Ea, O Ka Aina I Ka Pono,' to apply to the issues at hand. Translations of the motto by these public testimonies implied that the common translation 'The life of the land is perpetuated in righteousness' refers to pious Christian behavior. The Commission disagrees with this translation of the State motto as having any sectarian meaning. . . . The word pono stated in conjunction with the words ea, meaning 'sovereignty,' and 'āina, meaning land, in this context refers to the correct political behavior for protecting the land" (29). For historical and linguistic attempts to recover Hawaiian cultural and political meanings, see the scholarship of Kame'eleihiwa 1992; Osorio 1996; Silva 1999, 1998, 1997.

3. As one Native Hawaiian scholar has remarked, "The irony that a proclamation by a native king (that the sovereignty of the native Hawaiian people is perpetuated through a triumph of justice) was subsequently selected as the motto of the state (an extension of the government that trod upon Hawaiian sovereignty) in order to promote the state's own 'distinctiveness' cannot be understated and stands as an extreme case of cultural and linguistic appropriation" (Warner 1999, 82). I explore these colonial implications for legal meaning later in the chapter.

4. *Griswold v. Connecticut*, 381 U.S. 479, 486 (1965).

5. *Bowers v. Hardwick*, 192 (J. White). White cites Kingdom of Hawaii: Haw. Penal Code, chap. 13, sec. 11 (1869) as the antisodomy statute demonstrating Hawai'i's repudiation of same-sex relationships (at n. 6). Antisodomy laws can be traced back to the 1850 penal code, which mirrored the code of Massachusetts—from which many of the early missionaries originated (Merry 2000).

6. Personal communication between Ku'umeaaloha Gomes of Nā Mamo O Hawai'i and the author, March 1999.

7. Author's interview with Noenoe Silva, member of Nā Mamo O Hawai'i, 12 November 1998. Lesbian and gay equality rights were included in the 1994 Interim Constitution in South Africa, and later in the 1995 Constitution, significantly due to the influence of gay rights activists. See the discussion in Stychin 1998, 74 and 52ff.

8. Silva, interview.

9. Ahupua'a were administrative land divisions, roughly triangular in shape, that most often ran from a given span of the ocean to an apex at the ridgeline of the mountainous interior of the islands. These districts functioned as natural resource systems that included fishing and gathering from the ocean, lowland agriculture, and gathering in the upland forests. For a discussion of how this system was regulated in precontact Hawai'i see Martin et al. 1996, 83ff.

10. Document of Nā Mamo statement at Hilo Pūalu at Puhi Bay, 1996. Obtained from Dr. Noenoe Silva, in possession of the author.

11. *Public Access Shoreline Hawaii*, 447, cert. denied, 134 L.Ed. 2d 660 (1996). See also the supreme court's modifications to this doctrine in *State of Hawai'i v. Alapai Hanapi*, 89 Haw. 177 (1998).

12. HRS at 79–13 (1999) amended 1997.

13. Amicus curiae brief of Nā Mamo o Hawai'i, *Baehr v. Miike*, 1996, at 4.

14. State's Supreme Court Brief, *Baehr v. Miike*, 1996, at 1.

15. Amicus curiae brief of Independent Women's Forum, *Baehr v. Miike*, 1996, at 5.

16. Amicus curiae brief of Nā Mamo O Hawai'i, *Baehr v. Miike*, 1996, at 7. The brief supports and furthers the arguments made by the *Report of the Commission on Sexual Orientation and the Law*, 28. See also Minutes of the Commission, 20 October 1995, 14.

17. Nonetheless, Judge Chang acknowledged the diversity of Hawai'i's families in his ruling against the state, which had argued for the optimality of heterosexual nuclear families as a compelling interest in denying marriage licenses to same-sex couples. "[T]here is diversity in the structure and configuration of families. In Hawaii, and elsewhere, children are being raised by their natural parents, single parents, stepparents, grandparents, adopted parents, hanai parents, foster parents, gay and lesbian parents, and same-sex couples. . . . There are also families in Hawaii and elsewhere, which do not have children as family members. . . . The evidence presented by Plaintiffs and Defendant establishes that the single most important factor in the development of a happy, healthy and well-adjusted child is the nurturing relationship between parent and child." *Baehr v. Miike*, 1996, Judge's Finding of Fact and Conclusions of Law, at pars. 123–25.

18. A. Stephen Brewer, letter to the *Honolulu Advertiser*, 9 October 1998, A19.

19. Advertisement of Save Traditional Marriage '98, "#4 in a series," *Honolulu Advertiser*, 19 October 1998, C6; emphasis in the original.

20. Queer fictions of the past are a postmodern alternative politics that acknowledge the difficulties of an ethnic or identity politics based upon a history of identity that is thoroughly modern. See also the supportive arguments of Deloria (1994), who has shown that non-Indians have borrowed Native American religious practices to ameliorate modernist psychic disturbances felt as a loss of "authenticity," or subaltern studies that have argued that modern modes of speech and meaning do not sufficiently convey sovereign concerns (Otto 1996).

21. Author's interview with Ku'umeaaloha Gomes, activist with Nā Mamo O Hawai'i, 4 November 1998.

22. Written testimony of John Hoag submitted to the Commission on Sexual Orientation and the Law, 6 December 1995. Many similar testimonies were recorded throughout the years of the *Baehr* controversy. Arguments were also voiced by rights supporters about the boon to tourism should Hawai'i decide to be the first state to legalize same-sex marriages, with some studies suggesting as much as $153 million increase in tourist revenues from gay and lesbian couples seeking marriages (J. Brown 1995).

23. Written testimony of Laurie Lawson submitted to the Hawai'i House Hearings on Same Sex Marriage, 27 October 1993.

24. See the various essays in Guha and Spivak 1988 and Spivak 1988; and see Otto 1996.

25. Both the Māori of Aotearoa (their name for New Zealand) and the Kānaka Maoli (Native Hawaiians) identify as Polynesian. Their languages are closely related, and their political exchanges in the past two decades have lent a commensurable shape to their respective struggles for sovereignty.

26. As one telling example of this unease, the base commander of Hickam Air Base on O'ahu was forced to publicly apologize after a military exercise was modeled on the threat from a fictional band of terrorists known as "Hawaiian Sovereignty Group." Hawaiian sovereignty groups have been decidedly non-violent in their methods. See Omandam 1999.

27. Author's interview with Rev. Kaleo Patterson, Kamakapili Church, 21 September 1998, Honolulu.

28. Author's interview with Father Alapaki Kim, St. Rita's Church, 26 August 1998, Nānākuli, Hawai'i.

29. Scores of Hawaiian nationalist groups have formed in the last decade, with goals ranging from the restoration of the monarchy to nation-within-a-nation status similar to that endured by Native Americans. Ka Lāhui is the largest of those groups, with at least twenty thousand members.

30. Author's interview with Keali'i Gora, Ka Lāhui Hawai'i, 1 October 1998, Honolulu.

31. Ka Lāhui Hawai'i Resolution Relating to Protecting the Bill of Rights in the Hawai'i State Constitution, passed 6 September 1998.

32. Gora, interview.

33. See also the arguments of Jon Van Dyke (1998), responding to Stuart Benjamin (1996). Van Dyke argues that the political relationship of Native Hawaiians should be viewed as a "special relationship" akin to a trust relationship, despite a status that differs from that of American Indians, whose nations have been constitutionally recognized and not illegally overthrown. Benjamin has called this status an unconstitutional recognition of race, since there is no compelling reason justifying state discrimination. The Supreme Court in *Rice v. Cayetano* (146 F.3d 1075; 528 U.S. 495) (2000) took a third path, arguing that there is no special relationship, but that the issue of state agencies such as the Office of Hawaiian Affairs violated Fifteenth Amendment proscriptions on race-based voting; the Court did not agree that recognition of Native Hawai-

ians by the State of Hawai'i abrogated the Fourteenth Amendment. See also United States Public Law 103–150, 103d Congress Joint Resolution 19, 23 November 1993, officially apologizing for the illegal overthrow of the Hawaiian monarchy. That resolution acknowledged "the indigenous Hawaiian people never directly relinquished their claims to their inherent sovereignty as a people or over their national lands to the United States, either through their monarchy or through a plebiscite or referendum," but Congress did not act to restore sovereignty.

34. In order to determine whether Native Hawaiian voters took a collective position on the constitutional amendment designed to thwart the same-sex marriage case, all state precincts were analyzed for this statistical study ($N = 536$, which includes separately reported walk-in voters and mail-in absentee ballots by precinct or by precinct group). Fortunately for this investigation, precinct voting reports include the number of voters who participated in the election for directors of the Office of Hawaiian Affairs. To be eligible for the OHA ballot, one must be registered as an individual "whose ancestors were natives of the Hawaiian Islands prior to 1778," thus a self-identifying Hawaiian concerned with Hawaiian affairs. The percentage of OHA ballots therefore provide a proxy for the number of activist Hawaiians who voted in each precinct. From this data, precincts were tabulated as above or below the mean of Hawaiian activist voters as a percentage of all voters in the precinct. Similar dummy statistics were created for precincts based on percentage of vote for the amendment and for the constitutional convention, both of which were targets of campaigns by the Office of Hawaiian Affairs, Ka Lāhui, and other nationalist groups. The null hypothesis tested was that there was no relationship between precincts with higher Hawaiian activist votes and votes for or against the amendment and the constitutional convention.

Results of the tests show that while there is a slight positive direction in the association between higher Hawaiian activist voting and support for the amendment, this is statistically insignificant (Chi-square = 2.4179, $p = 0.1200$, $DF = 1$, $N = 536$). The null hypothesis is not refuted. The near-universal condemnation of the constitutional convention by concerned Hawaiian groups suggests the hypothesis is defeated in this test; however, the direction is otherwise than predicted (Chi-square = 4.6648, $p = 0.03808$ [significant], $df = 1$, $N = 536$). Precincts with above-median Hawaiian activist voters show a significant, though very slight, tendency for increased support for the convention. The explanation for this unanticipated direction is not clear.

The author wishes to thank Larry Nitz of the University of Hawai'i for his technical assistance in these statistical tests. All responsibility for errors is retained by the author.

35. OHA trustee Haunani Apoliona, quoted in Anwar 1998, B2.

36. Campaign brochure of Native Vote '98, October 1998.

37. Unnamed participant in a focus group, May 1998, "Public Attitudes towards Legislative Referendums: Qualitative Study," 21. Study funded by Human Rights Campaign and conducted by QMark Research and Polling, Honolulu. Study in possession of the author.

38. Gomes, interview.

39. This unmediated relationship is captured by the common indigenous sentiment that "abstract Euro-American land titles do not, and cannot, change the reality of Aboriginal Indigenous connection to the land" (Wub-e-ke-niew 1995, 230).

40. Gomes, interview.

41. Author's interview with Lynette Cruz, Ahupua'a Action Alliance, 14 October 1998.

42. Author's personal communication with S. Kaleikoa Ka'eo, 1999.

43. Cruz, interview.

44. Author's interview with Val Kanuha, 10 November 1999.

45. Written testimony of Mike Gabbard, chairman of Alliance for Traditional Marriage, Hawaii, submitted to the Hawai'i House Judiciary Committee, 21 January 1999. The included quotation, attributed to Paula Ettlebrick, former legal director for the Lambda Legal Defense and Education Fund, was widely repeated in public testimony against domestic partnership and in favor of an amendment to derail the *Baehr* case. Ettlebrick was alleged to have written, "Being queer is more than setting up house, sleeping with a person of the same gender, and seeking state approval for doing so. . . . Being queer means pushing the parameters of sex, sexuality, and family, and in the process, transforming the very fabric of society. . . . We must keep our eyes on the goals of providing true alternatives to marriage and of radically reordering society's views of reality."

46. Gora, interview.

47. One popular television commercial developed by Save Traditional Marriage '98 used Charles Toguchi, Hawai'i director of human services, to explain this relationship in the following manner: "Most traditions don't need a legal definition. It used to be that way with marriage. But now certain groups are forcing themselves upon this long and beautiful tradition, and this is not right. We wish these groups no harm. We only wish they would respect our traditions. And that is why we have to define what marriage is in the constitution."

Chapter 6

1. This analogy was explicitly rejected by the Supreme Court in *Bowers v. Hardwick*. Justice White argued that "none of the rights announced in [prior privacy cases] bears any resemblance to the claimed constitutional right of homosexuals to engage in acts of sodomy that is asserted in this case" (190–91). See also the precedents of *Griswold v. Connecticut; Eisenstadt v. Baird,* 405 U.S. 438 (1972); and *Carey v. Population Services,* 431 U.S. 678 (1977).

2. This naturalized racism was the basis of the trial judge's conclusion that the antimiscegenation statutes were valid. He said, "Almighty God created the races white, black, yellow, malay and red, and he placed them on separate continents. And but for the interference with his arrangement there would be no cause for such marriages. The fact that he separated the races shows that he did not intend for the races to mix" (*Loving v. Virginia,* 3).

3. Iglesias and Valdes explain that the *Latina/o* moniker is emblematic of the antisubordination political project. It replaces the postcolonial term *Hispanic* with a regional, hemispheric, and indigenous label more attuned to local experiences. Whereas *Hispanic* connotes "whiteness," *Latina/o* explicitly calls upon color and the hidden, non-Spanish elements of the (North, Central, and South) American experience. In addition, the self-identification *Latina/o* "rejects the gendered inequality that is integral to the structure and elements of Spanish. . . . This usage denotes the practice of anti-subordination principles within LatCrit discourse because it looks to, and attempts to center, the relative 'bottom' of the relevant categories—in this instance, of syntax, gender" (Iglesias and Valdes 1998, 573ff.).

4. Written testimony of Dawn Underwood submitted to the Commission on Sexual Orientation and the Law, 6 December 1995.

5. Issue poll conducted for the Human Rights Campaign by QMark Research and Polling, May 1998. Report provided by HRC and in possession of the author. Consider the following letter written to the *Honolulu Advertiser* following the final supreme court ruling in the *Baehr* case: "Thank you, Supreme Court. Your ruling to not recognize gay marriage is a ruling in favor of civil liberties: the liberties of the rest of us that will not condone the gay/lesbian lifestyle. We all come into the world with choices, and those who choose the gay lifestyle also choose and accept what comes with it. Why should we make concessions to OK a deviant lifestyle? Why is it that gays seem to think they deserve special treatment, i.e., going against the laws of human nature and wanting the world and our courts to condone it? Special treatment is deserved for the handicapped of our society for they are handicapped through no choice of their own making. We make special rules to allow them the dignity of leading as near a normal life as possible. Gays choose to be gay, and when they make that choice they took the 'ground rules' that came with it. We're not dealing with a minority as the gay community would like to be viewed. By definition, we're dealing with a lifestyle that goes against all biological, physiological, philosophical and biblical reasoning." Letter by Ken Spicer, 16 December 1999, A13.

6. The fear of the disruptive consequences of romantic love can best be seen in the debates over gays in the military. However, such fears can even be seen—perhaps comically—in the bureaucratic concerns about space travel. NASA, for example, worries about the effect of sexual love in spacecraft on crew performance and mission success, made more acute by planning for interplanetary travel. Retired astronaut Norman Thagard is quoted as saying about sex: "It's just one more problem that can potentially cause the whole thing to come apart" (Gallagher 2000, 22).

7. Seventy-six percent of respondents rated this argument "very convincing" or "somewhat convincing." High marks were also found for the following statements: "Our constitution should treat everyone equally and fairly. We should not amend it to treat homosexuals any differently than anyone else" (74 percent) and "We should not amend our Constitution's Bill of Rights to suit the agenda of one special interest group. Our basic rights are too precious and need

to be protected" (75 percent). Both became background themes of the campaign, but focus group research found that fairness arguments "backfired" once specific issues of civil rights for lesbians and gays were raised (Ankersmit, interview). By contrast, 55 percent agreed that "The spirit of Aloha is the spirit of fairness, and singling out one group and limiting their rights violates this spirit." Only 35 percent found convincing the argument that "Defeating this referendum would give Hawai'i's economy a boost. Allowing gays and lesbians to get marriage licenses would bring in a billion or more dollars in tourism, as people from all over the country would visit Hawai'i to marry." Issue poll conducted for Human Rights Campaign by QMark Research and Polling, May 1998. Report provided by HRC and in possession of the author.

8. Written testimony of the Japanese American Citizens League submitted to the Hawai'i House Judiciary Committee, 20 January 1997.

9. JACL Post-trial Brief, *Baehr v. Miike*, 1996.

10. The brief noted that 45 percent of children born in Hawai'i during the 1980s had parents with different ethnic backgrounds. Japanese American Citizens' League of Honolulu Post-trial Brief, *Baehr v. Miike*, 2 June 1997, 6.

11. Ibid., 10.

12. Martial law was declared in the Territory of Hawai'i on December 7, 1941. About 2 percent of the AJA population, 1,875 persons, were sent to labor camps. According to Mackey, the myth of racial acceptance was somewhat in play during the war as the loyalty of the AJA community, the largest plurality of ethnic groups in Hawai'i, was debated. Against the hardliners who advocated internment on the mainland, moderates argued that the security risk was diminished because of the special character of ethnic interaction. See Mackey 1995, 165ff.

13. Cooper and Daws write, "From 1960 to 1980, Japanese averaged 50% of the total membership of both houses. From 1955 to 1980, the percentage of Japanese Democrats in the Legislature was twice the percentage of Japanese in Hawaii's population. In 1960, when Japanese were 32% of population, they were 67% of Democratic legislators in both houses. In 1970, with 28% of population, they were 58% of Democratic legislators. In 1980, with 25% of population, they were 60% of Democratic legislators" (1985, 42). See also Kotani 1985.

14. Advertisement, *Honolulu Advertiser*, 3 November 1998, A27. Although Senator Inouye was reported as concerned that the Hawai'i Constitution would have discriminatory language added to it by the amendment, when POC seized upon this as evidence of support, Inouye's press secretary, Michele Konishi, denied the validity of this interpretation two days before the election. "He's not telling people to vote one way or the other. If he was going to do that, you would have heard from our campaign" (quoted in Mike Yuen, "Battle over Same-Sex Unions Takes Last-Minute Twists, Turns," *Star Bulletin*, 3 November 1998, accessed on-line November 1998).

15. Stonebraker, interview.

16. Kanuha, interview.

17. Hawai'i joined Nebraska, South Carolina, Pennsylvania, Alabama, South Dakota, Illinois, Arizona, Mississippi, Missouri, and Virginia in a brief

that identified the intervenors as "co-sovereign member's [*sic*] of the United States of America who perceive a substantial threat to the basic principles of cooperative federalism." Vermont was argued to have a "compelling state interest in not drastically redefining marriage in a way that will undeniably create tremendous confusion, imperil the interjurisdictional recognition of Vermont marriages, and promote divisive, coercive pressures on other States that may severely strain Vermont's relations with its sister States." The cited doctrine of cooperative federalism refers mainly to the relationships of states to the federal government. Replacing an earlier notion of dual federalism in which the sovereignty of states and the federal government were each seen to be supreme within their own spheres of power, cooperative federalism suggests a blurring of sovereignty and a sharing of power. "Cooperative federalism . . . allows the States, within limits established by federal minimum standards, to enact and administer their own regulatory programs, structured to meet their own particular needs." *Hodel v. Virginia Surface Mining*, 452 U.S. 264 (1981) at 289. Deviating from this principle of state action based on state need, the brief controverts the logic of DOMA—a more appropriate exemplar for cooperative federalism, which acknowledges the possibility, if not probability, of states choosing to recognize same-sex marriage.

18. "An Open Letter from Hawai'i's Citizens to Vermont's Citizens," 24 April 1999, signed by Save Traditional Marriage; Alliance for Traditional Marriage Hawai'i; Sen. David M. Matsuura (D); Sen. Jan Yagi Buen (D), Sen. Sam Slom (R); Sen. Norman Sakamoto (D); Sen. Jonathon Chun (D); Rep. Dennis Arakaki (D); Rep. Bob McDermott (R); Rep. Colleen Meyer (R); Rep. Mark Moses (R); Rep. Michael Puamamo Rahikina (D). The mailing was reported by the *Honolulu Advertiser* (24 April 1999, A3) to have cost forty to fifty thousand dollars, a sum paid by a Vermont businessman and cosponsored by Citizens for Community Values of Cincinnati, Ohio.

19. Kanuha, interview.

20. Appellants' Brief, *Baker v. Vermont*, text at n. 44.

21. Appellants' Reply Brief, *Baker v. Vermont*, n. 61.

22. Written testimony of Martin Rice submitted to the House Judiciary Committee, 20 January 1997.

23. Rick Weiss, letter to the *Honolulu Advertiser*, 27 October 1998, A11.

24. Alaska Legislature Supplemental Brief, 15 September 1998, *Brause v. Alaska*, 11.

25. Quoting Dupuis 1995. *Baehr v. Miike*, Hawai'i Post-trial Brief, 25 October 1996, 15.

26. Carl Kawakami, letter to the *Honolulu Advertiser*, 27 October 1998, A11.

27. Plaintiff's Reply Brief, *Baker v. Vermont*, n. 50.

28. *Baker v. Vermont* (1999), Slip at 36.

29. This was not the Reciprocal Beneficiaries Act discussed in chapter 3, which, curiously, was not cited in the opinion. Rather, the Vermont majority cited the comprehensive domestic partnership plan that was endorsed by the Commission on Sexual Orientation and the Law as an alternative to their first

choice of same-sex marriage. The *Baker* opinion makes no mention that marriage was the primary recommendation of the commission.

30. *Baker v. Vermont* (1999), Majority Opinion, Slip at 39.

31. *Baker v. Vermont* (1999), Concurrence and Dissent, Slip at 3.

32. Ibid., 4.

33. *Baker v. Vermont* (1999), Slip at 43. The majority explicitly cites Hawai'i and Alaska in argument with the dissent at this part of the decision.

34. *Report of the Commission on Sexual Orientation and the Law*, 27. Domestic partnership was the alternative policy advocated by the commission after its primary recommendation of legal same-sex marriage.

35. The Danish Registered Partnership Act, 1989, 3 (1). Translation in Sloan 1997, 201.

36. Ibid., 3 (2).

37. For example, "Tourism is very important economically to Hawaii. Should this state turn into another San Francisco and a mecca for homosexual 'marriage,' you will certainly lose the many families who come for vacations from Canada and the Mainland, to say nothing of the families who will move from Hawaii permanently." Written testimony of Janice Judd submitted to the Hawai'i House Judiciary Committee, October 1993 (no day listed).

38. *Rosenberg v. Canada*, Docket No. C22807 (Ont. Ct. of Appeal), 23 April 1998, quoted in Appellant's (Plaintiffs) Reply Brief, *Baker v. Vermont* (1998). First sentence quoted in approval, *Baker v. Vermont* (1999), J. Johnson Concurrence and Dissent, Slip at 14.

39. See *Board of Governors of the University of Saskatchewan v. Saskatchewan Human Rights Commission* (1976), 3 WWR 385 (Sask. QB), holding that sex was purely biological and so complaints of a gay student that he was discriminated against on the ground of sex were without foundation; *Vogel v. Manitoba* (1983) 4 CHRR D/1654 (Man. Bd. Adj.), in which a gay applicant for spousal coverage was denied due to the heterosexual definition of marriage; *Mossop v. Dept. of Sec. State* (1993) 1 SCR 554 (SCC), in which bereavement leave for a death in the family of a same-sex partner was denied because sexual orientation was intentionally not added to the Canadian Human Rights Act at the time.

40. Quebec included sexual orientation in its human rights code in 1977 with little grassroots organizing and little opposition, but because of the sovereigntist nature of the provincial government at the time, little notice was taken outside the province. See Herman 1994, 24, 32ff.; Rayside 1988; 1998, 109.

41. The equality guarantee under section 15 reads, "Every individual is equal before and under the law and has the right to the equal protection and equal benefit of the law without discrimination and, in particular, without discrimination based on race, national or ethnic origin, colour, religion, sex, age or mental or physical ability." The "in particular" phrase has been interpreted to permit, if not encourage, "reading in" other analogous cases of discrimination. See Stychin 1995a for an important political analysis of Canadian analogy law.

42. *Egan v. Canada*, 2 SCR 513 (1995).

43. For a discussion of the case, see Wintemute 1995.

44. *Vriend v. Alberta*, 1 SCR 493 (1998).

45. Canadian judicial review explicitly allows the procedures of reading in or reading out statutory language in order to conform to constitutional interpretation.

46. *M. v. H.*, 171 D.L.R. (4th) 577 (1999).

47. Iacobucci, J., in ibid., at par. 134.

48. Cory, J., *M. v. H.* (1999), at par. 52. However, the lone dissenter, Gonthier, J., argued that marriage was, indeed, at issue. "The spousal support obligation is unquestionably a core feature of the institution of marriage itself. True, that obligation has been extended to unmarried cohabiting opposite-sex couples by legislative action. Yet that should not obscure the fact that the extension was carefully tailored for a specific purpose, and that the nature of the obligation was established in the marriage context before it was ever extended to unmarried cohabiting opposite-sex couples. I thus find Cory J.'s statement that 'this appeal has nothing to do with marriage per se' (par. 52) entirely unconvincing" (at par. 231).

49. In Canada, exclusive legislative jurisdiction concerning marriage and divorce is held by the federal parliament. Provincial governments have exclusive responsibilities for solemnization of marriage, property, and civil rights.

50. *Globe and Mail* survey, 10 June 1999, reported in Casswell 1999, n. 55.

51. Karen Andrews, plaintiff in *Andrews v. O.H.I.P.* (1998), 49 D.L.R. (4th) 584 (Ont. H.C.), quoted in Gavigan 1999, 143.

52. *M. v. H.*, Cory, J., at par. 106. The phrase "public purse" used in this very manner appears more than a dozen times throughout the opinions.

53. Kanuha, interview.

54. *Tanner v. Oregon Health Sciences University*, 971 P.2d 435 (Or. Ct. App.) (1998).

55. Ibid., at 446.

56. Richards has made this argument in his argument for the importance of religious analogy for extending gay and lesbian rights. "The case for gay rights . . . centrally challenges the cultural terms of the unspeakability of homosexuality, the claim of its exclusion from the scope of religious and nonreligious conscience that on grounds of principle, now ostensibly enjoys constitutional protection. It does so in the two ways familiar from the similar protests to racism and sexism: it demands basic human rights of conscience, speech, intimate life, and work; and it challenges, in terms of its own moral powers of rationality and reasonableness, the sectarian terms of the moral orthodoxy that have traditionally condemned homosexuality. . . . Claims of gay and lesbian identity— whether irreligiously, nonreligiously, or religiously grounded—are decidedly among the dissident forms of conscience that should fully enjoy protection under the American tradition of religious liberty" (1999, 90–91).

Chapter 7

1. This included the reported resignation of about a half dozen Vermont town clerks who yielded their jobs before they would issue a license for a civil union. See Susan Smallheer, "Brattleboro Clerk Issues First Civil Union

License," *Rutland Herald,* online edition, <http://rutlandherald.nybor.com /News/Story/9482.html> (July 2000). Cardinal Bernard Law, archbishop of Boston, accused the Vermont legislature of preparing the way "for an attack on the well-being of society itself," setting much of the tone for the opposition: civil union was just a pretense for and possibly a stepping stone to marriage itself. See "Bishops Hit Vt. Civil-Union Law," <http://www.boston.com/ dailyglobe2/162/metro/Bishops_hit_Vt_civil_union_law+.shtml> (June 2000).

2. Author's interview with Tom Humphreys, cofounder of Alliance for Equal Rights and member of Protect Our Constitution, December 1999.

3. Author's interview with Terry Hunt, board member of Human Rights Campaign and spokesperson for Protect Our Constitution, December 1999.

4. Author's interview with Tom Ramsey, board member of Alliance for Equal Rights and Friends of Hawai'i's Equal Rights to Marriage Project, December 1999.

5. Hunt, interview.

6. Ramsey, interview.

Bibliography

Abrams, Kathryn. 1991. "Hearing the Call of Stories." *California Law Review* 79:971.

Aglietta, Michel. 1979. *A Theory of Capitalist Regulation*. London: New Left Books.

Alexander, M. Jacqui. 1994. "Not Just (Any) Body Can Be a Citizen: The Politics of Law, Sexuality, and Postcoloniality in Trinidad and Tobago and the Bahamas." *Feminist Review* 48:5–23.

Amin, Ash, ed. 1994. *Post-Fordism: A Reader*. Oxford: Blackwell.

Anderson, Benedict. 1983. *Imagined Communities: Reflections on the Origin and Spread of Nationalism*. London: Verso Press.

Anwar, Yasmin. 1998. "Office of Hawaiian Affairs Urges 'No' Vote on Con-Con." *Honolulu Advertiser*, 22 September, B2.

Ashley, Richard. 1988. "Untying the Sovereign State: A Double Reading of the Anarchy Problematique." *Millennium* 17 (2): 227–62.

Balbus, Isaac. 1977. "Commodity Form and Legal Form: An Essay on the 'Relative Autonomy' of the Law." *Law and Society Review* 11:571–88.

Balibar, Etienne. 1991. "The Nation Form: History and Ideology." In *Race, Nation, Class*, edited by E. Balibar and I. Wallerstein. London: Verso.

Ball, Carlos. 1997. "Moral Foundations for a Discourse on Same-Sex Marriage: Looking beyond Political Liberalism." *Georgetown Law Journal* 85:1871–1943.

Bauman, Zygmunt. 1996. "Morality in the Age of Contingency." In *Detraditionalization: Critical Reflections on Authority and Identity*, edited by S. L. Paul Heelas and Paul Morris. Oxford: Blackwell.

Bawer, Bruce. 1993. *A Place at the Table: The Gay Individual in American Society*. New York: Poseidon Press.

Beauvoir, Simone de. 1953. *The Second Sex*. New York: Knopf.

Beechert, Edward D. 1985. *Working in Hawaii: A Labor History*. Honolulu: University of Hawaii Press.

Benjamin, Stuart. 1996. "Equal Protection and the Special Relationship: The Case of Native Hawaiians." *Yale Law Journal* 106:537–612.

Bennett, William J. 1993. *The Book of Virtues: A Treasury of Great Moral Stories*. New York: Simon and Schuster.

Berger, Vada. 1991. "Domestic Partner Initiatives." *DePaul Law Review* 40:417–51.

Bergman, Matthew P. 1991. "Status, Contract, and History: A Dialectical View." *Cardozo Law Review* 13 (1): 171.

Berlant, Lauren G. 1997. *The Queen of America Goes to Washington City: Essays on Sex and Citizenship, Series Q.* Durham, N.C.: Duke University Press.

Berlant, Lauren G., and Elizabeth Freeman. 1993. "Queer Nationality." In *Fear of a Queer Planet: Queer Politics and Social Theory,* edited by M. Warner. Minneapolis: University of Minnesota Press.

Bhabha, Homi K. 1994. *The Location of Culture.* London: Routledge.

Blasius, Mark. 1992. "An Ethos of Lesbian and Gay Existence." *Political Theory* 20:642–71.

———. 1994. *Gay and Lesbian Politics: Sexuality and the Emergence of a New Ethic.* Philadelphia: Temple University Press.

Boggs, Carl. 1990. "Economic Conversion as a Radical Strategy: Where Social Movements and Labor Meet." In *Building Bridges: The Emerging Grassroots Coalition of Labor and Community,* edited by J. Brecher and T. Costello. New York: Monthly Review Press.

Bordo, Susan. 1993. *Unbearable Weight: Feminism, Western Culture, and the Body.* Berkeley and Los Angeles: University of California Press.

Boris, Eileen. 1994. *Home to Work: Motherhood and the Politics of Industrial Homework in the United States.* Cambridge: Cambridge University Press.

Bourdieu, Pierre. 1987. "The Force of Law." *Hastings Law Journal* 38:805–53.

Bower, Lisa. 1994. "Queer Acts and the Politics of 'Direct Access': Rethinking Law, Culture, and Community." *Law and Society Review* 28:1009–34.

———. 1997. "Queer Problems/Straight Solutions: The Limits of a Politics of 'Official Recognition.'" In *Playing with Fire: Queer Politics, Queer Theories,* edited by S. Phelan. New York: Routledge.

Boyd, Susan. 1996. "Case Comment: Best Friends or Spouses? Privatization and the Recognition of Lesbian Relationships in M. V. H." *Canadian Journal of Family Law* 13:321–41.

———. 1999. "Family, Law, and Sexuality: Feminist Engagements." *Social and Legal Studies* 8 (3): 369–90.

Brandt, Eric. 1999. *Dangerous Liaisons: Blacks, Gays, and the Struggle for Equality.* New York: New Press.

Bravmann, Scott. 1997. *Queer Fictions of the Past: History, Culture, and Difference.* Cambridge: Cambridge University Press.

Brecher, Jeremy, and Tim Costello. 1990. *Building Bridges: The Emerging Grassroots Coalition of Labor and Community.* New York: Monthly Review Press.

Brenner, Robert. 1998. "Uneven Development and the Long Downturn: The Advanced Capitalist Economies from Boom to Stagnation, 1950–1998." *New Left Review* 229:1–65.

Briggs, Steven. 1994. "Domestic Partners and Family Benefits: An Emerging Trend." *Labor Law Journal* 45:749–61.

Brown, Jennifer. 1995. "Competitive Federalism and the Legislative Incentives to Recognize Same-Sex Marriage." *Southern California Law Review* 68 (4): 745–839.

Brown, Wendy. 1995a. *States of Injury: Power and Freedom in Late Modernity.* Princeton: Princeton University Press.

———. 1995b. "Wounded Attachments: Late Modern Oppositional Political Formations." In *The Identity in Question,* edited by J. Rajchman. New York: Routledge.

———. 1998. "Freedom's Silences." In *Censorship and Silencing: Practices of Cultural Regulation,* edited by R. Post. Los Angeles: Getty Research Institute.

Buck, Elizabeth Bentzel. 1993. *Paradise Remade: The Politics of Culture and History in Hawai'i.* Philadelphia: Temple University Press.

Bumiller, Kristin. 1988. *The Civil Rights Society.* Baltimore: Johns Hopkins University Press.

Burchell, Graham. 1996. "Liberal Government and Techniques of the Self." In *Foucault and Political Reason: Liberalism, Neo-liberalism, and Rationalities of Government,* edited by A. Barry, T. Osborne, and N. Rose. Chicago: University of Chicago Press.

Burstein, Paul, and Kathleen Monaghan. 1986. "Equal Employment Opportunity and the Mobilization of Law." *Law and Society Review* 20:355–88.

Butler, Judith P. 1990. *Gender Trouble: Feminism and the Subversion of Identity.* New York: Routledge.

———. 1996. *Excitable Speech: A Politics of the Performative.* New York: Routledge.

———. 1998. "Merely Cultural." *New Left Review* 227:33–44.

Button, James W., Barbara Ann Rienzo, and Kenneth D. Wald. 1997. *Private Lives, Public Conflicts: Battles over Gay Rights in American Communities.* Washington, D.C.: CQ Press.

Campbell, David. 1992. *Writing Security: United States Foreign Policy and the Politics of Identity.* Minneapolis: University of Minnesota Press.

Casey, Catherine. 1995. *Work, Self, and Society after Industrialism.* London: Routledge.

Casswell, Donald. 1999. "Any Two Persons in Canada's Lotusland, British Columbia." Paper presented to the conference "Legal Recognition of Same-Sex Partnerships," University of London, 1 July.

Chatterjee, Partha. 1993. *The Nation and Its Fragments: Colonial and Postcolonial Histories.* Princeton: Princeton University Press.

Christensen, Craig. 1998. "If Not Marriage? On Securing Gay and Lesbian Family Values by a 'Simulacrum of Marriage.'" *Fordham Law Review* 66:1699–1783.

Coleman, Thomas. 1995. "The Hawaii Legislature Has Compelling Reasons to Adopt a Comprehensive Domestic Partnership Act." *Law and Sexuality* 5:541–81.

Colker, Ruth. 1996. *Hybrid: Bisexuals, Multiracials, and Other Misfits under American Law.* New York: New York University Press.

Connolly, William E. 1991. *Identity/Difference: Democratic Negotiations of Political Paradox.* Ithaca, N.Y.: Cornell University Press.

Constable, Marianne. 1993. "Sovereignty and Governmentality in Modern American Immigration Law." *Studies in Law, Politics, and Society* 13:249–71.

Cook, Alice Hanson, Val R. Lorwin, and Arlene Kaplan Daniels. 1992. *The Most Difficult Revolution: Women and Trade Unions*. Ithaca, N.Y.: Cornell University Press.

Coombe, Rosemary J. 1993. "The Properties of Culture and the Politics of Possessing Identity: Native Claims in the Cultural Appropriation Controversy." *Canadian Journal of Law and Jurisprudence* 6 (2): 249–85.

———. 1998. "Critical Cultural Legal Studies." *Yale Journal of Law and Humanities* 10:463–86.

Cooper, Davina. 1995. *Power in Struggle: Feminism, Sexuality, and the State*. New York: New York University Press.

———. 1998. *Governing out of Order: Space, Law, and the Politics of Belonging*. London: Rivers Oram Press, distributed by New York University Press.

Cooper, George, and Gavan Daws. 1985. *Land and Power in Hawaii: The Democratic Years*. Honolulu: Benchmark Books.

Cossman, Brenda. 1994. "Family Inside/Out." *University of Toronto Law Journal* 44:1–39.

Cox, Barbara J. 1997. "The Lesbian Wife: Same-Sex Mariage as an Expression of Radical and Plural Democracy." *California Western Law Review* 33 (2): 155–67.

Crain, Marion. 1994. "Gender and Union Organizing." *Industrial and Labor Relations Review* 47 (2): 227–48.

Crenshaw, Kimberlé. 1989. "Demarginalizing the Intersection of Race and Sex: A Black Feminist Critique of Antidiscrimination Doctrine, Feminist Theory, and Antiracist Politics." *University of Chicago Legal Forum* 1989:139–67.

———, ed. 1995. *Critical Race Theory: The Key Writings That Formed the Movement*. New York: New Press, distributed by Norton.

Currah, Paisley. 1997. "Politics, Practices, Publics: Identity and Queer Rights." In *Playing with Fire: Queer Politics, Queer Theories*, edited by S. Phelan. New York: Routledge.

Danielsen, Dan, and Karen Engle. 1995. *After Identity: A Reader in Law and Culture*. New York: Routledge.

Darian-Smith, Eve. 1995. "Law in Place: Legal Mediations of National Identity and State Territory in Europe." In *Nationalism, Racism, and the Rule of Law*, edited by P. Fitzpatrick. Aldershot, U.K.: Dartmouth.

———. 1996. "Postcolonialism: A Brief Introduction." *Social and Legal Studies* 5 (3): 291–99.

———. 1999. *Bridging Divides: The Channel Tunnel and English Legal Identity in the New Europe*. Berkeley: University of California Press.

Davis, Mike. 1986. *Prisoners of the American Dream: Politics and Economy in the History of the U.S. Working Class*. London: Verso.

Delgado, Richard. 1989. "Storytelling for Oppositionalists and Others: A Plea for Narrative." *Michigan Law Review* 87:2411–41.

———. 1995. *Critical Race Theory: The Cutting Edge*. Philadelphia: Temple University Press.

Deloria, Vine. 1994. *God Is Red: A Native View of Religion*. Updated ed. Golden, Colo.: Fulcrum.

D'Emilio, John. 1983. Capitalism and Gay Identity. In *Powers of Desire: the Poli-*

tics of Sexuality, edited by A. Snitow, C. Stansell, and S. Thompson. New York: Monthly Review Press.

Desmond, Jane. 1997. "Invoking 'The Native': Body Politics in Contemporary Hawaiian Tourist Shows. *TDR* 41 (4): 83–109.

Dillon, Michael. 1995. "Sovereignty and Governmentality: From the Problematics of the 'New World Order' to the Ethical Problematic of the World Order." *Alternatives* 20:323–68.

Donald, David. 1995. *Lincoln*. New York: Simon and Schuster.

Donovan, Catherine, Brian Heaphy, and Jeffrey Weeks. 1999. "Citizenship and Same Sex Relationships." *Journal of Social Policy* 28 (4): 689–709.

Donzelot, Jacques. 1979. *The Policing of Families*. New York: Pantheon.

Draper, Alan. 1994. *Conflict of Interests: Organized Labor and the Civil Rights Movement in the South, 1954–1968*. Ithaca, N.Y.: ILR Press.

Dubofsky, Melvyn. 1994. *The State and Labor in Modern America*. Chapel Hill: University of North Carolina Press.

Dumm, Thomas. 1994. *United States*. Ithaca: Cornell University Press.

Dupuis, Martin. 1995. "The Impact of Culture, Society, and History on the Legal Process: An Analysis of the Legal Status of Same-Sex Relationships in the United States and Denmark." *International Journal of Law and the Family* 9:86–118.

Eaton, Mary. 1995. "Homosexual Unmodified: Speculations on Law's Discourse, Race, and the Construction of Sexual Identity." In *Legal Inversions*, edited by D. Herman and C. Stychin. Philadelphia: Temple University Press.

Eder, Klaus. 1992. *The New Politics of Class: Social Movements and Cultural Dynamics in Advanced Societies*. London: Sage.

Edsall, Thomas Byrne, and Mary D. Edsall. 1991. *Chain Reaction*. Edited by M. D. Edsall. New York: Norton.

Elshtain, Jean Bethke. 1995. *Women and War*. Chicago: University of Chicago Press.

Ely, John Hart. 1980. *Democracy and Distrust: A Theory of Judicial Review*. Cambridge: Harvard University Press.

Epstein, Richard. 1994. "Caste and the Civil Rights Laws: From Jim Crow to Same-Sex Marriages." *Michigan Law Review* 92:2456–78.

Eskridge, William. 1994. "Gaylegal Narratives." *Stanford Law Review* 46:607–46.

———. 1996. "Outsider-Insiders: The Academy of the Closet." *Chicago-Kent Law Review* 71:977–87.

Esser, John. 1996. "Institutionalizing Industry: The Changing Forms of Contract." *Law and Social Inquiry* 21 (3): 593–629.

Essoyan, Susan. 1997. "Hawaii's Domestic-Partner Law a Bust; Ambiguity Blamed." *Los Angeles Times*, December 23, A5.

Ettelbrick, Paula. 1992. "Since When Is Marriage a Path to Liberation?" In *Lesbian and Gay Marriage: Private Commitments, Public Ceremonies*, edited by S. Sherman. Philadelphia: Temple University Press.

Evans, David. 1993. *Sexual Citizenship: The Material Construction of Sexualities*. London: Routledge.

Ewick, Patricia, and Susan Silbey. 1992. "Conformity, Contestation, and Resistance: An Account of Legal Consciousness." *New England Law Review* 26:731–49.

——. 1998. *The Common Place of Law: Stories from Everyday Life.* Chicago: University of Chicago Press.

Fajer, Marc. 1994. "Authority, Credibility, and Pre-understanding: A Defense of Outsider Narratives in Legal Scholarship." *Georgetown Law Journal* 82:1845–67.

Fantasia, Rick. 1988. *Cultures of Solidarity: Consciousness, Action, and Contemporary American Workers.* Berkeley and Los Angeles: University of California Press.

Feinman, Jay, and Peter Gabel. 1990. "Contract Law as Ideology." In *The Politics of Law: A Progressive Critique,* edited by D. Kairys. New York: Pantheon Books.

Ferguson, Kathy, and Phyllis Turnbull. 1999. *Oh Say Can You See: The Semiotics of the Military in Hawai'i.* Minneapolis: University of Minnesota Press.

Findlay, Barbara. 1997. "All in the Family Values." *Canadian Journal of Family Law* 14:129–96.

Fine, Bob. 1984. *Democracy and the Rule of Law: Liberal Ideals and Marxist Critiques.* London: Pluto Press.

Fitzpatrick, Peter. 1992. *The Mythology of Modern Law.* London: Routledge.

——. 1995a. "'We Know What It Is When You Do Not Ask Us': Nationalism as Racism." In *Nationalism, Racism, and the Rule of Law,* edited by P. Fitzpatrick. Aldershot, U.K.: Dartmouth.

——. 1999. "Law's Pervasion." Paper presented to the Annual Meeting of the Law and Society Association, Chicago.

——, ed. 1995b. *Nationalism, Racism, and the Rule of Law.* Aldershot, U.K.: Dartmouth.

Fortin, A. J. 1995. "AIDS, Surveillance, and Public Policy." *Research in Law and Policy Studies* 4:173.

Foucault, Michel. 1980a. *The History of Sexuality.* Vol. 1: *An Introduction.* New York: Vintage.

——. 1980b. "Two Lectures." In *Power/Knowledge: Selected Interviews and Other Writings 1972–1977,* edited by C. Gordon. New York: Pantheon.

——. 1984. "What is Enlightenment?" In *The Foucault Reader,* edited by P. Rabinow. London: Penguin.

——. 1989. "An Ethics of Pleasure." In *Foucault Live,* edited by S. Lotringer. New York: Semiotext(e).

——. 1991. "Governmentality." In *The Foucault Effect: Studies in Governmentality,* edited by G. Burchell, C. Gordon, and P. Miller. Chicago: University of Chicago Press.

Fraser, Nancy. 1997. *Justice Interruptus: Critical Reflections on the "Postsocialist" Condition.* New York: Routledge.

——. 1998. "Heterosexism, Misrecognition, and Capitalism: A Response to Judith Butler." *New Left Review* 228:140–49.

Freeman, M. D. A. 1999. "Not Such a Queer Idea: Is there a Case for Same Sex Marriages?" *Journal of Applied Philosophy* 16 (1): 1–17.

Gabin, Nancy. 1990. *Feminism in the Labor Movement: Women and the United Auto Workers, 1935–1975.* Ithaca, N.Y.: Cornell University Press.

Galanter, Marc. 1983. "The Radiating Effects of Courts." In *Empirical Theories about Courts,* edited by K. O. Boyer and L. Mather. New York: Longman.

Gallagher, Barbara. 2000. "No Space Sex?" *Scientific American* 282 (1): 22.

Gamble, Barbara. 1997. "Putting Civil Rights to a Popular Vote." *American Journal of Political Science* 41 (1): 245–69.

Gamson, Joshua. 1995. "Must Identity Movements Self-Destruct? A Queer Dilemma." *Social Problems* 42:390–407.

———. 1996. "Must Identity Movements Self-Destruct? A Queer Dilemma." In *Queer Theory/Sociology,* edited by S. Seidman. Cambridge, Mass.: Blackwell.

Gamson, William. 1988. "Political Discourse and Collective Action." In *International Social Movement Research: From Structure to Action,* edited by B. Klandermans, H. Kriesi, and S. Tarrow. Greenwich, Conn.: JAI Press.

Gapasin, Fernando, and Michael Yates. 1997. "Organizing the Unorganized: Will Promises Become Practices?" *Monthly Review* 49 (3): 46–62.

Gavigan, Shelley. 1999. "Legal Forms, Family Forms, Gendered Norms: What Is a Spouse?" *Canadian Journal of Legal Studies* 14:127–57.

Gerstmann, Evan. 1999. *The Constitutional Underclass: Gays, Lesbians, and the Failure of Class-Based Equal Protection.* Chicago: University of Chicago Press.

Giddens, Anthony. 1992. *The Transformation of Intimacy.* Stanford: Stanford University Press.

Gluckman, Amy, and Betsy Reed, eds. 1997. *Homo Economics: Capitalism, Community, and Lesbian and Gay Life.* New York: Routledge.

Goffman, Erving. 1974. *Frame Analysis: An Essay on the Organization of Experience.* New York: Harper and Row.

Goldberg, Suzanne. 1994. "Gay Rights through the Looking Glass: Politics, Morality, and the Trial of Colorado's Amendment 2." *Fordham Urban Law Journal* 21:1057–81.

Goldfield, Michael. 1993. "Race and the CIO: The Possibilities for Racial Egalitarianism during the 1930s and 1940s." *International Labor and Working-Class History* 44:1–32.

———. 1997. "Race and Labor Organization in the United States." *Monthly Review* 49 (3): 80–97.

Gomez, Laura. 1998. "Constructing Latina/o Identities." *Chicano-Latino Law Review* 19:187–91.

Gordon, Colin. 1991. "Governmental Rationality: An Introduction." In *The Foucault Effect: Studies in Governmentality,* edited by G. Burchell, C. Gordon, and P. Miller. Chicago: University of Chicago Press.

Gordon, Linda, ed. 1990. *Women, the State, and Welfare.* Madison: University of Wisconsin Press.

Goss, John. 1993. "Placing the Market and Marketing Place: Tourist Advertising of the Hawaiian Islands, 1972–92." *Environment and Planning D: Society and Space* 11:663–88.

Gramsci, Antonio. 1971. Americanism and Fordism. In *Selections from the Prison Notebooks of Antonio Gramsci.* New York: International.

Grossberg, Michael. 1985. *Governing the Hearth: Law and the Family in Nineteenth-Century America*. Chapel Hill: University of North Carolina Press.

Grossman, Joel B., and Charles Epp. 1991. "The Reality of Rights in an 'Atolerant' Society." *This Constitution* 19:20–28.

Guha, Ranajit, and Gayatri Chakravorty Spivak, eds. 1988. *Selected Subaltern Studies*. New York: Oxford University Press.

Habermas, Jürgen. 1987. *The Theory of Communicative Action*. Vol. 2. Boston: Beacon Press.

———. 1989. *The Structural Transformation of the Public Sphere: An Inquiry into a Category of Bourgeois Society*. Cambridge: MIT Press.

Halley, Janet. 1993. "The Construction of Heterosexuality." In *Fear of a Queer Planet: Queer Politics and Social Theory*, edited by M. Warner. Minneapolis: University of Minnesota Press.

———. 1997. "Romer v. Hardwick." *University of Colorado Law Review* 68:429–52.

Hamilton, Alexander, James Madison, and John Jay. 1961. *The Federalist Papers*. New York: Mentor.

Harris, Angela. 1990. "Race and Essentialism in Feminist Legal Theory." *Stanford Law Review* 42:581–616.

Hasencamp, Laurie. 1986. "ERISA and Preemption of State Fair Employment Laws." *Southern California Law Review* 59:583–601.

Hegel, Georg Wilhelm Friedrich. 1967. *Hegel's Philosophy of Right*. London: Oxford University Press.

Hennessy, Rosemary. 1995. "Queer Visibility in Commodity Culture." In *Social Postmodernism: Beyond Identity Politics*, edited by L. Nicholson and S. Seidman. Cambridge: Cambridge University Press.

Herman, Didi. 1990. "Are We Family? Lesbian Rights and Women's Liberation." *Osgoode Hall Law Journal* 28 (4): 789–815.

———. 1994. *Rights of Passage*. Toronto: University of Toronto Press.

———. 1997. *The Antigay Agenda: Orthodox Vision and the Christian Right*. Chicago: University of Chicago Press.

Hirsch, Susan. 1994. "Kadhi's Courts as Complex Sites of Resistance: The State, Islam, and Gender in Postcolonial Kenya." In *Contested States: Law, Hegemony, and Resistance*, edited by M. Lazarus-Black and S. Hirsch. New York: Routledge.

Hirsch, Susan, and Mindie Lazarus-Black. 1994. "Performance and Paradox: Exploring Law's Role in Hegemony and Resistance." In *Contested States: Law, Hegemony, and Resistance*, edited by S. Hirsch and M. Lazarus-Black. New York: Routledge.

Hobbes, Thomas. 1968. *Leviathan*. Baltimore: Penguin.

Hoffman, John. 1998. *Sovereignty*. Minneapolis: University of Minnesota Press.

Horowitz, Donald. 1977. *The Courts and Social Policy*. Washington, D.C.: Brookings Institution.

Hughes, Heather Lauren. 1998. "Same-Sex Marriage and Simulacra: Exploring Conceptions of Equality." *Harvard Civil Rights–Civil Liberties Law Review* 33:237–52.

Hunt, Alan. 1992. "Foucault's Expulsion of Law: Toward a Retrieval." *Law and Social Inquiry* 17:1–38.

Hunt, Gerald. 1999. "No Longer Outsiders: Labor's Response to Sexual Diversity in Canada." In *Laboring for Rights: Unions and Sexual Diversity across Nations,* edited by G. Hunt. Philadelphia: Temple University Press.

Hutchinson, Darren. 1997. "Out Yet Unseen: A Racial Critique of Gay and Lesbian Legal Theory and Political Discourse." *Connecticut Law Review* 29:561–645.

———. 1999. "Ignoring the Sexualization of Race: Heteronormativity, Critical Race Theory, and Anti-racist Politics." *Buffalo Law Review* 47:1–116.

Iglesias, Elizabeth, and Francisco Valdes. 1998. "Afterward: Religion, Gender, Sexuality, Race, and Class in Coalitional Theory: A Critical and Self-Critical Analysis of LatCrit Social Justice Agendas." *Chicano-Latino Law Review* 19:503–88.

Jacob, Herbert. 1988. *Silent Revolution: The Transformation of Divorce Law in the United States.* Chicago: University of Chicago Press.

Jefferson, Theresa. 1998. "Toward a Black Lesbian Jurisprudence." *Third World Law Journal* 18:263–90.

Johnston, Hank. 1995. "A Methodology for Frame Analysis: From Discourse to Cognitive Schemata." In *Social Movements and Culture,* edited by H. Johnston and B. Klandermans. Minneapolis: University of Minnesota Press.

Kalahele, 'Imaikalani. 1998. "Before Had England." *'oiwi* 1 (1): 33.

Kamahele, Momi. 1992. Hula as Resistance. *Forward Motion* 2 (3): 40–45.

Kame'eleihiwa, Lilikala. 1992. *Native Land and Foreign Desires—Ko Hawai'i 'Aina a me na koi puumake a ka Po'e Haole.* Honolulu: Bishop Museum Press.

Kann, Mark E. 1991. *On the Man Question: Gender and Civic Virtue in America.* Philadelphia: Temple University Press.

Karst, Kenneth. 1995. "Myths of Identity: Individual and Group Portraits of Race and Sexual Orientation." *UCLA Law Review* 43:263–369.

Keen, Lisa, and Suzanne Goldberg. 1998. *Strangers to the Law.* Ann Arbor: University of Michigan Press.

Kelly, John. 1988. *Trade Unions and Socialist Politics.* London: Verso.

Kelsey, Jane. 1995. "Restructuring the Nation: The Decline of the Colonial Nation-State and Competing Nationalisms in Aotearoa/New Zealand." In *Nationalism, Racism, and the Rule of Law,* edited by P. Fitzpatrick. Aldershot, U.K.: Dartmouth.

Kent, Noel. 1983. *Hawaii: Islands under the Influence.* New York: Monthly Review Press.

Kingsolver, Barbara. 1989. *Holding the Line: Women in the Great Arizona Mine Strike of 1983.* Ithaca, N.Y.: ILR Press.

Koppelman, Andrew. 1988. "The Miscegenation Analogy: Sodomy Law as Sex Discrimination." *Yale Law Journal* 98:145–64.

———. 1994. "Why Discrimination against Lesbians and Gay Men Is Sex Discrimination." *New York University Law Review* 69 (2): 197–287.

Kotani, Roland. 1985. *The Japanese in Hawaii: A Century of Struggle.* Honolulu: Hawaii Hochi.

Kropp, Douglas. 1997. "'Categorial' Failure: Canada's Equality Jurisprudence—Changing Notions of Identity and the Legal Subject." *Queen's Law Journal* 23:201–30.

Kua, Crystal. 2000. "Gay Rights Bills Die in House." *Honolulu Star Bulletin,* April 12, 2000, online version.

Kuehls, Thom. 1996. *Beyond Sovereign Territory.* Minneapolis: University of Minnesota Press.

Kuykendall, Ralph S. 1938. *The Hawaiian Kingdom.* Honolulu: University of Hawaii.

Kwan, Peter. 1997. "Intersections of Race, Ethnicity, Class, Gender, and Sexual Orientation: Jeffrey Dahmer and the Cosynthesis of Categories." *Hastings Law Journal* 48:1257–92.

Lal, Brij V., Doug Munro, and Edward D. Beechert. 1993. *Plantation Workers: Resistance and Accommodation.* Honolulu: University of Hawaii Press.

Law, Sylvia. 1988. "Homosexuality and the Social Meaning of Gender." *Wisconsin Law Review* 1988:187–235.

Lehr, Valerie. 1999. *Queer Family Values: Debunking the Myth of the Nuclear Family.* Philadelphia: Temple University Press.

Levin, Daniel Lessard. 1999. *Representing Popular Sovereignty: The Constitution in American Political Culture,* SUNY series, American Constitutionalism. Albany: State University of New York Press.

Levy, Paul. 1985. "The Unidimensional Perspective of the Reagan Labor Board." *Rutgers Law Journal* 16:269–390.

Levy, Peter B. 1994. *The New Left and Labor in the 1960s.* Urbana: University of Illinois Press.

Lind, Andrew. 1943. *The Japanese in Hawaii under Wartime Conditions.* Honolulu: Hawaii Group, American Council Institute of Pacific Relations.

Lipietz, Alain. 1994. "Post-Fordism and Democracy." In *Post-Fordism: A Reader,* edited by A. Amin. Oxford: Blackwell.

Lipset, Seymour. 1986. "Labor Unions in the Public Mind." In *Unions in Transition: Entering the Second Century,* edited by E. Seymour Lipset. San Francisco: ICS.

Locke, John. 1963. *Two Treatises of Government.* Rev. ed. New York: Mentor.

———. 1980. *Second Treatise of Government.* Indianapolis: Hackett.

Luhmann, Niklas. 1986. *Love as Passion: The Codification of Intimacy.* Cambridge: Harvard University Press.

———. 1990. *Political Theory in the Welfare State.* Berlin: Walter de Gruyter.

Luker, Kristin. 1984. *Abortion and the Politics of Motherhood.* Berkeley and Los Angeles: University of California Press.

Mackey, Cindy Kobayashi. 1995. "Out of Rebellion: The Politics of Identity and the Japanese in Hawaii." Ph.D. Diss., Department of Political Science, University of Hawai'i at Mānoa.

MacKinnon, Catharine A. 1987. *Feminism Unmodified: Discourses on Life and Law.* Cambridge: Harvard University Press.

Maine, Henry. 1917. *Ancient Law.* Everyman's Library. London: J. M. Dent and Sons.

Malo, David, and Nathaniel Bright Emerson. 1903. *Hawaiian Antiquities = Moolelo Hawaii.* Honolulu: Hawaiian Gazette.

Marcosson, Samuel. 1995. "The 'Special Rights' Canard in the Debate over Lesbian and Gay Civil Rights." *Notre Dame Journal of Law, Ethics & Public Policy* 9:137.

Marshall, Gordon. 1983. "Some Remarks on the Study of Working-Class Consciousness." *Politics and Society* 12:263.

Martin, Elizabeth, David Martin, David Penn, and Joyce McCarty. 1996. "Cultures in Conflict in Hawai'i: The Law and Politics of Native Hawaiian Water Rights." *University of Hawaii Law Review* 18 (1): 71.

Marx, Karl. 1963. *The Eighteenth Brumaire of Louis Bonaparte.* New York: International Publishers.

———. 1977a. "On the Jewish Question." In *Selected Writings*, edited by D. McLellan. Oxford: Oxford University Press.

———. 1977b. "Preface to a Critique of Political Economy." In *Selected Writings*, edited by D. McLellan. Oxford: Oxford University Press.

———. 1978. "On the Jewish Question." In *The Marx-Engels Reader*, edited by R. Tucker. 2d ed. New York: Norton.

Massaro, Toni M. 1996. "Gay Rights, Thick and Thin." *Stanford Law Review* 49:45–110.

Matthew, Coles. 1997. "The Meaning of *Romer v. Evans.*" *Hastings Law Journal* 48:1343–61.

Maxwell, Nancy, Astrid Mattijseen, and Charlene Smith. 1999. "Legal Protection for all the Children: Dutch-American Comparison of Lesbian and Gay Parent Adoptions." *Electronic Journal of Comparative Law* 3.1. <http://law.kub.nl/ejcl/31/art31-2.html>.

McCann, Michael. 1994. *Rights at Work: Pay Equity Reform and the Politics of Legal Mobilization.* Chicago: University of Chicago Press.

McClintock, Anne. 1992. "The Angel of Progress: Pitfalls of the Term 'Post-Colonialism.'" *Social Text* 31–32:84–98.

———. 1995. *Imperial Leather: Race, Gender, and Sexuality in the Colonial Contest.* New York: Routledge.

McClosky, Herbert, and Alida Brill. 1983. *Dimensions of Tolerance: What Americans Believe about Civil Liberties.* New York: Russell Sage Foundation.

McClure, Kirstie. 1993. "On the Subject of Rights: Pluralism, Plurality, and Political Identity." In *Dimensions of Radical Democracy: Pluralism, Citizenship, Community*, edited by C. Mouffe. New York: Verso Press.

Meiksins, Peter. 1997. "Same as It Ever Was? The Structure of the Working Class." *Monthly Review* 49 (3): 31.

Melucci, Alberto. 1989. *Nomads of the Present.* Philadelphia: Temple University Press.

Merelman, Richard M. 1984. *Making Something of Ourselves: On Culture and Politics in the United States.* Berkeley and Los Angeles: University of California Press.

Merry, Sally. 1990. *Getting Justice and Getting Even.* Chicago: University of Chicago Press.

————. 1991. "Law and Colonialism." *Law and Society Review* 25:889–922.

————. 1998. "Law, Culture, and Cultural Appropriation." *Yale Journal of Law and the Humanities* 10:575–603.

————. 2000. *Colonizing Hawai'i: The Cultural Power of Law*. Princeton: Princeton University Press.

Meyer, Manu. 1998. "Native Hawaiian Epistemology: Sites of Empowerment and Resistance." *Equity and Excellence in Education* 31 (1): 22–28.

Milkman, Ruth. 1997. *Farewell to the Factory: Auto Workers in the Late Twentieth Century*. Berkeley and Los Angeles: University of California Press.

Milner, Neal. 1986. "The Dilemmas of Legal Mobilization: Ideologies and Strategies of Mental Patient Liberation." *Law and Policy* 8:105.

Minow, Martha. 1985. "'Forming Underneath Everything that Grows': Toward a History of Family Law." *Wisconsin Law Review* 1985:819–98.

Montoya, Margaret. 1998. "Religious Rituals and LatCrit Theorizing." *Chicano-Latino Law Review* 19:417–29.

Moody, Kim. 1988. *An Injury to All: The Decline of American Unionism*. London: Verso.

————. 1997a. "American Labor: A Movement Again?" *Monthly Review* 49 (3): 63.

————. 1997b. *Workers in a Lean World*. London: Verso.

Moore, Sally Falk. 1986. *Social Facts and Fabrications: "Customary Law" on Kilimanjaro, 1880–1980*. Cambridge: Cambridge University Press.

Moran, L. J. 1991. "The Uses of Homosexuality: Homosexuality for National Security." *International Journal of the Sociology of Law* 19:149.

Morgan, Edmund Sears. 1988. *Inventing the People: The Rise of Popular Sovereignty in England and America*. New York: Norton.

Morris, Richard, and Mary E. Stuckey. 1997. "'More Rain and Less Thunder': Substitute Vocabularies, Richard Nixon, and the Construction of Political Reality." *Communication Monographs* 64 (2): 140–60.

Morris, Robert. 1996. "Configuring the Bo(u)nds of Marriage: The Implications of Hawaiian Culture and Values for the Debate about Homogamy." *Yale Journal of Law the Humanities* 8:105–59.

Myerson, Allen. 1998. "Perot Ends Benefits for Partners of Newly Hired Gay Workers." *New York Times*, 10 April 1998, online version.

Nicholson, Linda. 1997. "The Myth of the Traditional Family." In *Feminism and Families*, edited by H. Nelson. New York: Routledge.

Nietzsche, Friedrich. 1967. *On the Genealogy of Morals*. New York: Vintage.

Norrie, Alan. 1996. "From Law to Popular Justice: Beyond Antinomialism." *Social and Legal Studies* 5 (3): 383–403.

Offe, Klaus, and Helmut Wiesenthal. 1980. "Two Logics of Collective Action: Theoretical Notes on Social Class and Organizational Form." *Political Power and Social Theory* 1:67–115.

Okin, Susan. 1996. "Sexual Orientation, Gender, and Families: Dichotomizing Differences." *Hypatia* 11 (1): 30–48.

Oliver, Melvin, and Thomas Shapiro. 1995. *Black Wealth/White Wealth: A New Perspective on Racial Inequality*. New York: Routledge.

Olson, Mancur. 1965. *The Logic of Collective Action.* Cambridge: Harvard University Press.

O'Malley, Pat. 1996. "Risk and Responsibility." In *Foucault and Political Reason: Liberalism, Neo-liberalism, and Rationalities of Government,* edited by A. Barry, T. Osborne, and N. Rose. Chicago: University of Chicago Press.

Omandam, Pat. 1999. "Hickam Apologizes for Reference to Hawaiians in Terror Exercise." *Honolulu Star Bulletin,* 24 March 1999, A1.

Orren, Karen. 1991. *Belated Feudalism: Labor, the Law, and Liberal Development in the United States.* Cambridge: Cambridge University Press.

Osborne, Duncan. 1997. "Lavender Labor: A Brief History." In *Homo Economics: Capitalism, Community, and Lesbian and Gay Life,* edited by A. Gluckman and B. Reed. New York: Routledge.

Osorio, Jonathan Kamakawiwoʻole. 1996. "Determining Self: Identity, Nationhood, and Constitutional Government in Hawaiʻi, 1842–1887." Ph.D. diss., Department of History, University of Hawaiʻi at Mānoa.

Otto, Dianne. 1995. "A Question of Law or Politics? Indigenous Claims to Sovereignty in Australia." *Syracuse Journal of International Law and Commerce* 21:65–103.

———. 1996. "Subalternity and International Law: The Problems of Global Community and the Incommensurability of Difference." *Social and Legal Studies* 5 (3): 337–64.

Pashukanis, Evgeni i Bronislavovich, and C. J. Arthur. 1978. *Law and Marxism: A General Theory.* London: Ink Links.

Pateman, Carole. 1988. *The Sexual Contract.* Stanford: Stanford University Press.

Patton, Cindy. 1993. "Tremble, Hetero Swine!" In *Fear of a Queer Planet: Queer Politics and Social Theory,* edited by M. Warner. Minneapolis: University of Minnesota Press.

———. 1995. "Refiguring Social Space." In *Social Postmodernism: Beyond Identity Politics,* edited by L. Nicholson and S. Seidman. Cambridge: Cambridge University Press.

———. 1997. "Queer Space/God's Space: Counting Down to the Apocalypse." *Rethinking Marxism* 9 (2): 1–23.

———. 1998. "'On Me, Not in Me': Locating Affect in Nationalism after AIDS." *Theory, Culture, and Society* 15 (3–4): 355–74.

Perrin, C. 1995. "Approaching Anxiety: The Insistence of the Postcolonial in the Declaration of Human Rights of Indigenous Peoples." *Law and Critique* 6 (1): 55–74.

Peterson, Cynthia. 1999. "Fighting It Out in Canadian Courts." In *Laboring for Rights: Unions and Sexual Diversity across Nations,* edited by G. Hunt. Philadelphia: Temple University Press.

Phelan, Shane. 1995. "The Space of Justice: Lesbians and Democratic Politics." In *Social Postmodernism: Beyond Identity Politics,* edited by L. Nicholson and S. Seidman. Cambridge: Cambridge University Press.

———. 1999. "Bodies, Passions, and Citizenship." *Critical Review of International Social and Political Philosophy* 2 (1): 56–79.

Phillips, Anne. 1997. "From Inequality to Difference: A Severe Case of Displacement." *New Left Review* 224:143–53.

Picciotto, Sol. 1982. "The Theory of the State, Class Struggle, and the Rule of Law." In *Marxism and Law*, edited by P. Beirne and R. Quinney. New York: John Wiley and Sons.

Plummer, Kenneth. 1995. *Telling Sexual Stories: Power, Change, and Social Worlds.* London: Routledge.

Polikoff, Nancy. 1993. "We Will Get What We Ask For: Why Legalizing Gay and Lesbian Marriage Will Not 'Dismantle the Legal Structure of Gender in Every Marriage.'" *Virginia Law Review* 79:1535–50.

Posner, Richard A. 1992. *Sex and Reason.* Cambridge: Harvard University Press.

Pound, Roscoe. 1909. "Liberty of Contract." *Yale Law Journal* 18:454.

Prothro, James, and Charles Grigg. 1960. "Fundamental Principles of Democracy." *Journal of Politics* 22:276.

Puette, William. 1992. *Through Jaundiced Eyes: How the Media View Organized Labor.* Ithaca, N.Y.: ILR Press.

Quadagno, Jill S. 1988. *The Transformation of Old Age Security: Class and Politics in the American Welfare State.* Chicago: University of Chicago Press.

———. 1994. *The Color of Welfare: How Racism Undermined the War on Poverty.* New York: Oxford University Press.

Raffo, Susan, ed. 1996. *Queerly Classed: Gay Men and Lesbians Write about Class.* Boston: South End Press.

Rathke, Wade, and Joel Rogers. 1996. "A Strategy for Labor." *Dissent* 43 (4): 78.

Rayside, David. 1988. "Gay Rights and Family Values: The Passage of Bill 7 in Ontario." *Studies in Political Economy* 26:109–47.

———. 1998. *On the Fringe: Gays and Lesbians in Politics.* Ithaca, N.Y.: Cornell University Press.

Regan, Milton C. 1993. *Family Law and the Pursuit of Intimacy.* New York: New York University Press.

Richards, David A. J. 1998. *Women, Gays, and the Constitution: The Grounds for Feminism and Gay Rights in Culture and Law.* Chicago: University of Chicago Press.

———. 1999. *Identity and the Case for Gay Rights: Race, Gender, Religion as Analogies.* Chicago: University of Chicago Press.

Rifkin, Jeremy. 1995. *The End of Work: The Decline of the Global Labor Force and the Dawn of the Post-market Era.* New York: G. P. Putnam's Sons.

Robson, Ruthann. 1995. "To Market, to Market: Considering Class in the Context of Lesbian Legal Theories and Reforms." *Southern California Review of Law and Women's Studies* 5:173–84.

———. 1997. "The State of Marriage." *Yearbook of New Zealand Jurisprudence* 1 (1): 1–16.

Robson, Ruthann, and S. E. Valentine. 1990. "Lov(H)ers: Lesbians as Intimate Partners and Lesbian Legal Theory." *Temple Law Review* 63:511–41.

Roediger, David R. 1991. *The Wages of Whiteness: Race and the Making of the American Working Class.* London: Verso.

———. 1993. "Race and the Working-Class Past in the United States: Multiple

Identities and the Future of Labor History." *International Review of Social History* 38:127.

Rogers, Joel. 1990. "Divide and Conquer: Further 'Reflections on the Distinctive Character of American Labor Laws.'" *Wisconsin Law Review* 1990:1–147.

———. 1992. "In the Shadow of the Law: Institutional Aspects of Postwar U.S. Union Decline." In *Labor Law in America: Historical and Critical Essays,* edited by C. L. Tomlins and A. J. King. Baltimore: Johns Hopkins University Press.

———. 1995. "A Strategy for Labor." *Industrial Relations* 34 (3): 367–81.

Rohrer, Judy. 1996. "Is It Right to Focus on 'Rights'?" *Harvard Gay and Lesbian Review* 3 (1): 1.

Rose, Nikolas. 1996. "Governing 'Advanced' Liberal Democracies." In *Foucault and Political Reason: Liberalism, Neo-liberalism, and Rationalities of Government,* edited by A. Barry, T. Osborne, and N. Rose. Chicago: University of Chicago Press.

Rose, Nikolas, and Peter Miller. 1992. "Political Power beyond the State: Problematics of Government." *British Journal of Sociology* 43 (2): 173–205.

Ross, Andrew. 1994. *The Chicago Gangster Theory of Life: Nature's Debt to Society.* London: Verso.

Rupert, Mark. 1995. *Producing Hegemony.* Cambridge: Cambridge University Press.

Sahlins, Marshall. 1985. *Islands of History.* Chicago: University of Chicago Press.

Said, Edward W. 1979. *Orientalism.* New York: Vintage.

Sarat, Austin. 1977. "Studying American Legal Culture." *Law and Society Review* 11:427–88.

Schacter, Jane S. 1997a. "*Romer v. Evans* and Democracy's Domain." *Vanderbilt Law Review* 50 (2): 361–410.

———. 1997b. "Skepticism, Culture, and the Gay Civil Rights Debate in a Post-Civil-Rights Era." *Harvard Law Review* 110:684–731.

Scheingold, Stuart. 1974. *The Politics of Rights.* New Haven: Yale University Press.

Schmidt, Alvin J. 1997. *The Menace of Multiculturalism: Trojan Horse in America.* Westport, Conn.: Praeger.

Schram, Sanford. 1995. *Words of Welfare: The Poverty of Social Science and the Social Science of Poverty.* Minneapolis: University of Minnesota Press.

Schuler, Walter. 1996. "The ERISA Pre-exemption Narrows: Analysis of *New York State Conference of Blue Cross and Blue Shield Plans v. Travelers Insurance Company* and Its Impact on State Regulation of Health Care." *Saint Louis University Law Journal* 40:783–831.

Schutz, Alfred. 1970. *On Phenomenology and Social Relations: Selected Writings.* Edited by E. H. Wagner. Chicago: University of Chicago Press.

Scott, Alan. 1990. *Ideology and the New Social Movements.* London: Unwin Hyman.

Sedgwick, Eve Kosofsky. *Between Men: English Literature and Male Homosocial Desire.* New York: Columbia University Press, 1985.

———. 1990. *Epistemology of the Closet.* Berkeley and Los Angeles: University of California Press.

Seidman, Steven. 1993. "Identity Politics in a 'Postmodern' Gay Culture: Some Historical and Conceptual Notes." In *Fear of a Queer Planet*, edited by M. Warner. Minneapolis: University of Minnesota Press.

———. 1997. *Difference Troubles: Queering Social Theory and Sexual Politics*. Cambridge: Cambridge University Press.

Sexton, Patricia Cayo. 1991. *The War on Labor and the Left*. Boulder, Colo.: Westview Press.

Shapiro, Michael J. 1997. *Violent Cartographies: Mapping Cultures of War*. Minneapolis: University of Minnesota Press.

———. 2001. *For Moral Ambiguity: National Culture and the Politics of the Family*. Minneapolis: University of Minnesota Press.

Silva, Noenoe K. 1997. "Ku'e! Hawaiian Women's Resistance to the Annexation." *Social Process in Hawaii* 38:2–16.

———. 1998. "Kanaka Maoli Resistance to Annexation." *'oiwi* 1 (1): 40–80.

———. 1999. "Ke Ku'e Kupa'a Loa Nei Makou: Kanaka maoli Resistance to Colonization." Ph.D. diss., Department of Political Science, University of Hawai'i at Mānoa.

Silverstein, Helena. 1996. *Unleashing Rights: Law, Meaning, and the Animal Rights Movement*. Ann Arbor: University of Michigan Press.

Sinfield, Alan. 1996. "Diaspora and Hybridity: Queer Identities and the Ethnicity Model." *Textual Practice* 10 (2): 271–93.

Skocpol, Theda. 1990. "Targeting within Universalism: Politically Viable Policies to Combat Poverty in the United States." Working paper series no. H-90-2, Malcolm Wiener Center for Social Policy, John F. Kennedy School of Government, Harvard University.

Sloan, Craig. 1997. "A Rose by Any Other Name: Marriage and the Danish Registered Partnership Act." *Cardozo Journal of International and Comparative Law* 5:189–215.

Smith, Rogers M. 1997. *Civic Ideals: Conflicting Visions of Citizenship in U.S. History*. New Haven: Yale University Press.

Snow, David, and Robert Benford. 1988. "Ideology, Frame Resonance, and Participant Mobilization." In *International Social Movement Research: From Structure to Action*, edited by B. Klandermans, H. Kriesi, and S. Tarrow. Greenwich, Conn.: JAI Press.

Snow, David, Burke Rochford Jr., Steven Worden, and Robert Benford. 1986. "Frame Alignment Processes, Micromobilization, and Movement Participation." *American Sociological Review* 51:464–81.

Soguk, Nevzat. 1999. *States and Strangers: Refugees and Displacements of Statecraft*. Minneapolis: University of Minnesota Press.

Sowell, Thomas. 1984. *Civil Rights: Rhetoric or Reality?* New York: W. Morrow.

———. 1998. *Conquests and Cultures: An International History*. New York: Basic Books.

———. 1999. *Barbarians inside the Gates—and Other Controversial Essays*. Stanford, Calif.: Hoover Institution Press.

Spedale, Darren. 1998. "The Sky Hasn't Fallen." *Honolulu Star Bulletin*, 24 October 1998.

Speilman, Sue, and Liz Winfeld. 1996. "Domestic Partner Benefits: A Bottom Line Discussion." In *Sexual Identity on the Job: Issues and Services*, edited by A. Ellis and E. Riggle. New York: Haworth Press.

Spivak, Gayatri Chakravorty. 1988. "Can the Subaltern Speak?" In *Marxism and the Interpretation of Culture*, edited by C. Nelson and L. Grossberg. Urbana: University of Illinois Press.

Stacey, Judith. 1996. *In the Name of the Family: Rethinking Family Values in the Postmodern Age*. Boston: Beacon Press.

Stychin, Carl. 1995a. "Essential Rights and Contested Identities: Sexual Orientation and Equality Rights Jurisprudence in Canada." *Canadian Journal of Law and Jurisprudence* 8:49–66.

———. 1995b. *Law's Desire: Sexuality and the Limits of Justice*. London: Routledge.

———. 1998. *A Nation by Rights: National Cultures, Sexual Identity Politics, and the Discourse of Rights*. Philadelphia: Temple University Press.

———. 1999. "Dis-integrating Sexuality: Citizenship, Space, and the European Union." Paper presented to the Annual Meeting of the Law and Society Association, Chicago.

Sullivan, Andrew. 1996. *Virtually Normal: An Argument about Homosexuality*. New York: Vintage.

———. 2000. State of the Union. *New Republic*, 8 May, 18–23.

Sullivan, John Lawrence, James Piereson, and George E. Marcus. 1982. *Political Tolerance and American Democracy*. Chicago: University of Chicago Press.

Sunstein, Cass R. 1994a. "Homosexuality and the Constitution." *Indiana Law Journal* 70 (1): 1–28.

———. 1994b. "Same-Sex Relations and the Law." *Metaphilosophy* 25 (4): 262.

Takaki, Ronald T. 1983. *Pau Hana: Plantation Life and Labor in Hawaii, 1835–1920*. Honolulu: University of Hawaii Press.

Thompson, E. P. 1975. *Whigs and Hunters: The Origin of the Black Act*. London: Allen Lane.

Trask, Haunani-Kay. 1993. *From a Native Daughter: Colonialism and Sovereignty in Hawai'i*. Monroe, Maine: Common Courage Press.

———. 1999. "Hawaiian Students Deserve Free Tuition at UH." *Honolulu Star Bulletin*, 9 April, A11.

Trubeck, David, and John Esser. 1989. "'Critical Empiricism' in American Legal Studies: Paradox, Program, or Pandora's Box." *Law and Social Inquiry* 14:3–53.

Turner, Bryan. 1984. *The Body and Society: Explorations in Social Theory*. Oxford: Basil Blackwell.

Tymkovich, Timothy, John Dailey, and Paul Farley. 1997. "A Tale of Three Theories: Reason and Prejudice in the Battle over Amendment 2." *University of Colorado Law Review* 68:287–333.

Unger, Roberto Mangabeira. 1987. *False Necessity: Anti-necessitarian Social Theory in the Service of Radical Democracy*. Part 1 of *Politics: A Work in Constructive Social Theory*. Cambridge: Cambridge University Press.

Vaid, Urvashi. 1995. *Virtual Equality: The Mainstreaming of Gay and Lesbian Liberation.* New York: Anchor.

Valdes, Francisco. 1995. "Queers, Sissies, Dykes, and Tomboys: Deconstructing the Conflation of 'Sex,' 'Gender,' and 'Sexual Orientation' in Euro-American Law and Society." *California Law Review* 83:1–377.

———. 1996. "Unpacking Hetero-Patriarchy: Tracing the Conflation of Sex, Gender, and Sexual Orientation to Its Origins." *Yale Journal of Law and the Humanities* 8:161–211.

———. 1997a. "Queer Margins, Queer Ethics: A Call to Account for Race and Ethnicity in the Law, Theory, and Politics of 'Sexual Orientation.'" *Hastings Law Journal* 48:1293–1341.

———. 1997b. "Under Construction: LatCrit Consciousness, Community, and Theory." *California Law Review* 85:1087–1142.

———. 1998. "Afterword: Beyond Sexual Orientation in Queer Legal Theory: Majoritarianism, Multidimensionality, and Responsibility in Social Justice Scholarship, or Legal Scholars as Cultural Warriors." *Denver University Law Review* 75:1409–64.

Van Dyke, Jon. 1998. "The Political Status of the Native Hawaiian People." *Yale Law and Policy Review* 17:95–147.

Viotti, Vicki. 1999. "Crossing Gender Lines More Accepted in Hawaii." *Honolulu Advertiser,* 7 March 1999, E1, E8.

Voos, Paula. 1982. "Labor Union Organizing Programs, 1954–1977." Ph.D. diss., Harvard University.

Waaldijk, Kees. 1999. "What Legal Recognition of Same-Sex Partnership Can Be Expected in EC Law, and When? Lessons from Comparative Law." Paper presented to the conference "Legal Recognition of Same-Sex Partnerships," University of London.

Walker, R. B. J. 1993. *Inside/Outside: International Relations as Political Theory.* Cambridge: Cambridge University Press.

Warner, Michael. 1992. "The Mass Public and the Mass Subject." In *Habermas and the Public Sphere,* edited by C. Calhoun. Cambridge: MIT Press.

———, ed. 1993. *Fear of a Queer Planet.* Minneapolis: University of Minnesota Press.

Warner, Sam No'eau. 1999. "Kuleana: The Right, Responsibility, and Authority of Indigenous Peoples to Speak and Make Decisions for Themselves in Language and Cultural Revitalization." *Anthropology and Education Quarterly* 30 (1): 68–93.

Waterman, Peter. 1993. "Social-Movement Unionism: A New Union Model for a New World Order?" *Review* 16 (3): 245–78.

Weeks, Jeffrey. 1995. *Invented Moralities: Sexual Values in an Age of Uncertainty.* New York: Columbia University Press.

Weir, Margaret, Ann Shola Orloff, Theda Skocpol, and Project on the Federal Social Role (U.S.). 1988. *The Politics of Social Policy in the United States: Studies from the Project on the Federal Social Role.* Princeton: Princeton University Press.

Weldes, Jutta, Mark Laffey, Hugh Gusterson, and Raymond Duvall, eds. 1999.

Cultures of Insecurity: States, Communities, and the Production of Danger. Minneapolis: University of Minnesota Press.

Williams, Patricia. 1987. "Alchemical Notes: Reconstructing Ideals from Deconstructed Rights." *Harvard Civil Rights–Civil Liberties Law Review* 22:401–33.

———. 1988. "On Being the Object of Property." *Signs* 15:5–23.

Williams, Patrick, and Laura Chrisman, eds. 1994. *Colonial Discourse and Postcolonial Theory: A Reader.* New York: Columbia University Press.

Wintemute, Robert. 1995. "Discrimination against Same-Sex Couples: Sections 15(1) and 1 of the Charter: *Egan v. Canada.*" *Canadian Bar Review* 74:682–713.

Wolfe, Alan. 1998. *One Nation, After All: How Middle-Class Americans Really Think About: God, Country, Family, Racism, Welfare, Immigration, Homosexuality, Work, the Right, the Left, and Each Other.* New York: Viking.

Wolfson, Evan. 1994. "Crossing the Threshold: Equal Marriage Rights for Lesbians and Gay Men and the Intra-community Critique." *Review of Law and Social Change* 21:567.

Wub-e-ke-niew. 1995. *We Have the Right to Exist: A Translation of Aboriginal Indigenous Thought.* New York City: Black Thistle Press.

Yang, Alan. 1999. *From Wrongs to Rights: Public Opinion on Gay and Lesbian Americans' Moves toward Equality.* Washington, D.C.: Policy Institute.

Young, Claire. 1997. "Public Taxes, Privatizing Effects, and Gender Inequality." In *Challenging the Public/Private Divide: Feminism, Law, and Public Policy,* edited by S. Boyd. Toronto: University of Toronto Press.

Young, Iris Marion. 1997. "Unruly Categories: A Critique of Nancy Fraser's Dual Systems Theory." *New Left Review* 222:147–60.

Youngdahl, James. 1974. "Preparation, Trial, and Settlement of Employment Discrimination Cases: Perspective of a Union Lawyer." Paper read at Labor Law Developments conference.

Zald, Mayer. 1996. "Culture, Ideology, and Strategic Framing." In *Comparative Perspectives on Social Movements: Political Opportunities, Mobilizing Structures, and Cultural Framings,* edited by D. McAdam, J. McCarthy, and M. Zald. Cambridge: Cambridge University Press.

Zemans, Frances. 1983. "Legal Mobilization: The Neglected Role of the Law in the Political System." *American Political Science Review* 77:690.

Index